Religious Allusion in
the Poetry of
Gwendolyn Brooks

Religious Allusion in the Poetry of Gwendolyn Brooks

MARGOT HARPER BANKS

Vincennes University
Shake Learning Resources Center
Vincennes, In 47591-9986

McFarland & Company, Inc., Publishers
Jefferson, North Carolina, and London

Poetry by Gwendolyn Brooks is reprinted by consent of Brooks Permissions.

LIBRARY OF CONGRESS CATALOGUING-IN-PUBLICATION DATA

Banks, Margot Harper.
　　Religious allusion in the poetry of Gwendolyn Brooks / Margot Harper Banks.
　　　　p.　　cm.
　　Includes bibliographical references and index.

　　ISBN 978-0-7864-4939-2
　　softcover : acid free paper ∞

　　1. Brooks, Gwendolyn, 1917–2000 — Religion.　2. Brooks, Gwendolyn, 1917–2000 — Political and social views. 3. Christianity in literature.　4. Democracy in literature. 5. Sermons in literature.　6. Literature and society — United States — History — 20th century.　7. Brooks, Gwendolyn, 1917–2000.　I. Title.
　　PS3503.R7244Z53　2012
　　811'.54 — dc23　　　　　　　　　　　　　　　　2012023077

BRITISH LIBRARY CATALOGUING DATA ARE AVAILABLE

Front cover images © 2012 Shutterstock

Manufactured in the United States of America

McFarland & Company, Inc., Publishers
　Box 611, Jefferson, North Carolina 28640
　　www.mcfarlandpub.com

To Mom for her example,
to Cecil for his courage,
and to our children for their spiritual and cultural heritage

with appreciation
to Nora Brooks Blakely for her generosity

and to readers Nicole Adams,
Dr. James Conyers,
and Barbara Hallett
for their insights and encouragement

Contents

Preface

While scholarship on Gwendolyn Brooks' body of work is increasing, much is yet to be done. This analysis brings her biblical allusions to the foreground to illuminate their importance to her work. While a few scholars have paid attention to the religious aspect of Brooks' poetry, notably D.H. Melhem and George Kent, the socio-historical and biographical perspectives have dominated Brooksian scholarship; each of the book-length studies has had a different purpose. Henry Shaw's book *Gwendolyn Brooks* (Twayne, 1980) addresses biographical and philosophical elements in Brooks' poetry and prose. It addresses religion in parts but focuses on her themes according to his four-fold matrix: death, fall from glory, the labyrinth and survival. D.H. Melhem's *Gwendolyn Brooks: Poetry and the Heroic Voice* (UP Kentucky, 1987) examines Brooks' poetry using a framework of ideal humanism and heroism/antiheroism. This well documented analysis comments on religious references in some parts but focuses on social and political commentary both in Brooks' poetry and prose. *A Life of Gwendolyn Brooks* (UP Kentucky) by George Kent, primarily a biography, includes commentary on her prose and poetry up to 1978. B.J. Bolden wrote *Urban Rage in Bronzeville: Social Commentary in the Poetry of Gwendolyn Brooks, 1945–1960* (Third World P, 1999) to relate elements in Brooks' poetry to historical and sociological events during the specified period. *Gwendolyn Brooks: Poet from Chicago* (Morgan Reynolds, 2003) is a biography written for high schoolers, and Bloom's *BioCritiques: Gwendolyn Brooks* by Harold Bloom (Chelsea, 2004), like the others in the series, provides a biography with brief critical comments on selected works.

The present work fits with those studies in that it takes a joint formalist and sociological critical approach to the poetry. Similar to Melhem, Bolden and Shaw's works, it examines some poems in the context of social issues. Yet, *Religious Allusion* is quite different from them. This book's analysis of biblical allusion as a vehicle to reveal Brooks' messages is unique.

1

The book presents an intense examination of that one artistic element. It threads that element through her major poems and many of her minor ones to present a comprehensive, critical perspective. Here a key purpose is to reveal philosophical underpinnings that are conveyed by the religious elements of the poems and examine what they reveal about the poet's overarching message. It expands and enlarges criticism on elements only mentioned in previous works. Even articles and essays on Brooks' work have not studied this immensely significant element in her poetry. The scholarship that has been done so far does not speak to the content and issues examined herein. *Religious Allusion* provides fresh new interpretative comment to Brooksian criticism and will illuminate new dimensions of her poetry for students of American poetry.

The present work brings two fields of this author's scholarship together, more than ten years of intensive Bible study through Bible Study Fellowship International and decades of English language and literature study and university teaching, with particular emphasis on poetry. I have studied and taught Brooks' poetry for many years in poetry courses. I conceived of this specific writing project after coordinating a program featuring Gwendolyn Brooks for the university's Contemporary Writers Series in March of 2000, just seven months before her death. I had the privilege of escorting her and having a private talk with her during her visit. I had always been impressed by her poetic genius, but I became just as impressed by her humility and genuine humanity. I traveled to Chicago in 2005 to interview Brooks' daughter, Nora Brooks Blakely, about her mother's views on religion and how they associated with her poetry. (See "Coda: A Conversation with Nora Brooks Blakely.") After that discussion, the project began to take shape and I have been working on the book since then while teaching as a resident professor at a university and leading Bible study. I have meticulously studied Brooks' poetry to understand how and why she incorporated so many religious elements in such diverse ways in her work and I have researched the specific biblical texts that have been referenced. This text is based on extensive library and online research.

This systematic, detailed study of Brooks' work is important to the body of American literary scholarship because of (1) her poetic genius, (2) her stature in American Letters as an African American female writer; and (3) the dearth of comprehensive, non-biographical studies of her work. Brooks' influence on American letters is immense, yet scholarship on her body of work is not commensurate with her stature. This book is a critical resource for students of modern American, African American and feminist poetry.

Prologue

Gwendolyn Brooks (1917–2000) won the Pulitzer Prize for Poetry in 1950. She was the first African American to be so honored. Nineteen fifty was a different era in American culture. The president of the United States was Harry S. Truman; the Korean Conflict was underway; only one-third of American women worked outside the home. And life was extremely difficult for African Americans. That year, 1950, was four years before the Department of Defense Order, which ended segregation in the U.S. Armed Forces. It was four years before the *Brown v. Board of Education* of Topeka, Kansas, decision, which declared that racial segregation in public schools was unconstitutional. It was five years before the lynching of 14-year-old Emmett Till; five years before Rosa Parks refused to give up her seat on a Montgomery, Alabama, bus. It was before America had heard the name the Rev. Dr. Martin Luther King and years before the phrase Affirmative Action had been coined. The year 1950 predated all of those familiar historical moments that awakened the American consciousness to the life experiences and contributions of African Americans to American life and letters. Yet, on May 1, 1950, the announcement was made that 33-year-old Gwendolyn Brooks had been awarded that prestigious literary prize for her second published volume of poetry, *Annie Allen*.

The historical context makes it clear that Gwendolyn Brooks' work was recognized for its merit and against the social odds. From the age of seven her parents had encouraged her dream of becoming a writer. She wrote consistently from childhood until her death. During the early years, her poetry was traditional in form and versification. Her subjects were traditional, but she always incorporated her own African American life experience into her poetry. Over the years her style matured and evolved structurally and conceptually. A master craftsperson, Gwendolyn Brooks wrote all forms of poetry: the mock-epic, the sonnet, montage/collage, ballad, elegy, lyric, sermons, poetic essay and poetic fiction. Her influence on

African American letters and modern American poetry cannot be overstated. Her innovation of the sonnet form alone has influenced generations of poets who have followed her. Her writing career can be characterized by respect for tradition and her ability to embrace new resources for her creativity.

After attending the Second Black Writers' Conference at Fisk University in 1967 and observing the passion and social commitment of young African American poets, Brooks' social and political consciousness was raised. She became more concerned with poetry that communicated more directly with African Americans. Her work gradually incorporated her new vision into the form of her work. She changed the language in her poems; she used more free verse; her themes became more focused on social issues. Her poetry emanated from a spiritual depth with an incomparable clarity of voice and precision of form and style.

This book identifies and exposes religious references, which are woven throughout her poetry. Not only do they reflect her views on religion, but they also reveal how she uses religious allusion as a tool for crafting her poetry. In Brooks' poetry the Christian elements are included in a number of different ways:

> biblical or religious language
> biblical or religious imagery and symbolism
> characterization of God, preachers and biblical figures
> biblical action and events
> sermon genre
> traditional church teaching and Christian doctrine
> Christian doctrine related to social theory

Each of her long poems has been included to show the various ways she integrated religion for her context-specific purposes. It is obvious that much more could be said about every poem discussed in this text, if the analyses were broadened to include other critical perspectives; however, the focus here is limited to the specified approach, except in instances where other comment is necessary for clarity. The selection of shorter poems represents many, but not all of her poems with religious references. Those that have been included here were selected to represent different periods of her work and different artistic strategies.

The book begins with a biographical chapter, "The Life of the Poet," which chronicles the life of Gwendolyn Brooks. Her life experiences frame her ideas and her development as a poet. Chapter two, "Brooks on Religion," follows with a chronological review of Gwendolyn Brooks' comments on religion compiled from a newspaper article she authored, from interviews and from her autobiographies. The clustering of her words on the subject provides insight into her ideas and attitudes toward religion through the years and also provides a conceptual context in which to place the analyses of biblical and Christian allusions in her work. Each of chapters three through seven addresses one of her long poems with an in-depth analysis that focuses on her inclusion of religious references. The sequence is chronological. Each long poem incorporates religion in different ways and the discussion of each poem is organized and informed by Brooks' crafting of that particular poem. "The Anniad" from *Annie Allen*, for example, is allegorical, and the tone and themes of the poem are constructed by the juxtaposing images of heaven and pagan hell. "In the Mecca," which represents the decadence that results from racism and poverty, contains a series of characters who represent various points on a spectrum of religious faith. Other characters operate as prophets inside and outside of the action. "In Emanuel's Nightmare: Another Coming of Christ" utilizes a prophesied biblical event to dramatize humankind's propensity for war.

Chapter six spotlights Brooks' use of the sermon as an oratorical genre in the interlocking trilogies that set forth her "Sermon(s) on the Warpland," which comment on the state of blacks in America at that time. And chapter seven's "In Montgomery" uses biblical quotations and a dramatized church service to chronicle real people and events in a poetic essay about the civil rights movement. Chapters eight, nine and ten use a formalist approach to analyze Brooks' use of religious references as traditional literary elements by taking a critical look at separate elements in selected short poems that are grouped by subject and function: "Depiction of God and Preachers," "Sundays and Church" and "Religion and Contradiction" respectively. All of her poems, whether long or short, show Brooks' range, and her versatility and prowess as a literary artist. Brooks shows her unusually comprehensive knowledge of the bible and Christian doctrine that complements her facility with poetic form and function.

The present work is intended to:

1. show that Christian allusion permeates Brooks' poetry during all periods of her work,
2. show how the content and message of each poem informed Brooks' use of religious elements,
3. show parallels between the messages of the poems and Christian doctrine,
4. show emphasis on contradictions between Christian doctrine and practice in society,
5. expose the expressed relationship between Democracy and Christian ideals,

6. explain Brooks' view of social responsibility, and

7. assert that Brooks was an advocate for the practice of true Christian doctrine.

The book addresses direct biblical references and the degree to which they are tightly integrated into the fabric of Gwendolyn Brooks' poetry. They are essential to her message and structurally integral to the whole. This analysis associates her references with Christianity and the King James Version of the Holy Bible, which is the translation reflected in Brooks' work. At times other translations are included, as well. Also incorporated herein are relevant commentary from other Brooksian scholars to enrich the discussion and includes "Coda: A Conversation with Nora Brooks Blakely" to add a personal, familial view of some of the poems and Gwendolyn Brooks' beliefs.

Ultimately, this text examines how Gwendolyn Brooks, a self-proclaimed nonreligious person, systematically and consistently advocates adherence to Christian ideals by individuals and society-at-large through religious allusions in her poetry.

Chapter One

The Life of the Poet

Very early in life I became fascinated with the wonders language
can achieve. And I began playing with words.
— Gwendolyn Brooks

Life for African Americans in 1917 was difficult. It had been 54 years
since the Emancipation Proclamation had abolished slavery. There were
many living African Americans who had experienced the horrors of slavery
in the United States. Reconstruction had just ended and there was an optimistic spirit among African Americans. But the hope would be short-lived
as it became more and more clear that the legal abolition of slavery and
the promise of equality had not been embraced by the political and social
institutions of the United States, nor had the hearts and minds of white
Americans been changed.

Although there are no statistics for lynching in the United States prior
to 1882, the inhumane treatment of enslaved people is well known. Lynching,
named for maverick Virginia Jurist Charles Lynch (1736–1796) occurred
as punishment for various crimes for some whites and many blacks. In 1882
the *Chicago Tribune* became the first institution to begin keeping an account-
ing of lynching events by year and ethnicity from newspaper accounts. The
paper reported the lynching of 4,743 people between 1882 and 1968. Between
1917 and 1935, the period from Gwendolyn Brooks' birth through her 18th
year, there were 548 newspaper reports of lynching incidents in the *Chicago
Tribune*, often with gruesome photographs (Browner). Not only did such
reports symbolize the racial conflict of the times, but they also provided
a backdrop for African American youth of that era to understand the
difficult social and political setting in which they lived.

There were also signs of social progress for African Americans in the
early 20th century, however. W.E.B. DuBois had published his landmark
treatise, *The Souls of Black Folk*, in 1903, just two years after President

Theodore Roosevelt had caused a furor by inviting Booker T. Washington to dine at the White House. Bethune-Cookman College was founded in 1904. The National Association for the Advancement of Colored People (NAACP) and the National Urban League were organized in 1909 and 1911 respectively. Still, African Americans were on the lowest level of economic and social mobility in the United States. The U.S. census of 1910 reported the population as 93,402,151 and the black population as 9,827, 763 (10.7 percent).

It was into that America that Gwendolyn Elizabeth Brooks was born on June 7, 1917, to David Anderson Brooks and his wife Keziah Corine Wims Brooks. Although she was born in Topeka, Kansas, Gwendolyn lived in Chicago all of her life. Both parents came from gifted families with traditions that would instill strong character traits and generate a community consciousness that would remain with Gwendolyn Brooks throughout her life and become a significant part of her legacy.

Paternal grandfather Lucas Brooks escaped slavery and joined the Union army. Kent reports that Brooks' family oral history maintains that Lucas Brooks threw his master in a hollow stump and ran away to join the Union army. Whether that story is historically accurate or not, it is clear by its retelling that he was highly regarded by his family and that he was seen as strong, brave and resourceful. Lucas Brooks had no formal education, but he had an aptitude for numbers and financial record-keeping skills for which he earned money. Lucas Brooks fought in the Civil War. Later, after satisfying the three-month residency requirement, he filed an Old Soldiers Claim in Oklahoma in an effort to get property and livestock of his own. Although he acquired those things initially, family oral history also reports that his livestock was poisoned by whites, who refused to accept the idea of an ex-slave acquiring such property. He lost them and had to give up his claim. Yet, it demonstrates that he was intelligent, entrepreneurial, ambitious and progressive. His achievements, though thwarted by racism, were extraordinary (G. Brooks, *Report from Part One* 50–51; Kent 2–3).

Lucas Brooks married biracial enslaved housekeeper, Elizabeth, with whom he had 12 children, including David Anderson Brooks, father of Gwendolyn Brooks. The family had a difficult time financially, even living for a time in a tent-covered shack (G. Brooks, *Report from Part One* 51). Some of the children died young from disease and the elements. Sickels reports, "Although food and money were scarce, David's parents often took in boarders and provided free meals to the hungry, an example of the generosity David would later pass on to his own children" (9). Gwendolyn Brooks did not know many of her father's siblings; she knew her Aunt Viola Leath and Uncles Robert and Luther Brooks.

David Brooks was also an extraordinary person. During his childhood, he engaged in outdoor activities such as fishing, playing ball, sledding and ice skating. But, most impressive was David's motivation to learn — to acquire an education. Young David would awaken at five each morning to complete his chores and then walk to school. As they grew, most of his siblings focused on trades and marriage and none of them finished high school. David, on the other hand, graduated from high school. He wanted to become a doctor. He completed one year at Fisk University, but financial responsibility for his siblings after his father died of pneumonia forced him to drop out. In *Report from Part One*, Gwendolyn reported that he never lost his interest in medicine. He used family medical books to research family illnesses and he doctored the family for minor things. David also had a rich baritone voice. As a youngster he was selected, from among his classmates, to present a reading and sing "The Song the Anvil Sings" for Booker T. Washington at a school function. He sang through his adult years in his home. Brooks said, "And it is almost easy to hear him exalting in 'The Song the Anvil Sings' — he, who took such robust pleasure in baritoning, all the years we knew him." She went on to say that his two children saw him as powerful and artistically gifted (G. Brooks, *Report from Part One* 52). His granddaughter, Nora Brooks Blakely, also remembers David Brooks with admiration and respect. In a telephone interview Nora credits him with teaching her kindness and honor and being one of the three most important male figures in her life. She says he taught by his living example.

Gwendolyn Brooks' maternal grandparents, Moses Wims and Luvenia Forte Wims, were also hard working family- and community-minded people. "Moses Wims was one of the most trust-worthy, serious-minded and punctual men in Kansas," Keziah Wims Brooks said of her father. "He could without raising the tone of his voice ... control us [his children] with his eyes" (K. Brooks 98). His morning routine involved getting up very early to read his newspaper and eat a leisurely breakfast before going to work early. Not only did he value order and discipline, but also honesty. She remembered him warmly and commented on how he engaged in lively dinner conversation with his children (98). Keziah Brooks' description of her mother, Luvenia Wims, was more effusive. Luvenia Wims was a busy, productive and community-spirited woman. She raised vegetables in her garden to help with the family's expenses; she did the cooking, baking, sewing, quilting and washing and still found time to help the sick by taking them chicken broth, vegetable broth and fruit juices. But Keziah Brooks indicated, "The church was the source of her greatest pleasure. Her attendance was so regular that when her absence was discovered, her friends assumed one of her children from another city was visiting her and that she was home preparing dinner" (64). Moses and Luvenia's union produced 10 children, three of whom died young, but sons Thomas Wims and William Wims and five daughters, Eppie Wims Small, Gertrude Wims Robinson, Ella Wims Myler, Beulah Wims and Gwendolyn's mother, Keziah Corine Wims Brooks, lived to adulthood. Keziah was named so after the last of biblical Job's three daughters, "who were the best women in the land" (G. Brooks, *Report from Part One* 50). Her name, along with that of their father, points to cross-generational religious values in the family. Keziah was the only sister to have children although her sister Eppie raised adopted children on her 14-acre farm in Kalamazoo, Michigan. Gwendolyn grew up very close to her four aunts, especially her Aunt Beulah, who was a sewing teacher at Booker T. Washington High School in Tulsa, Oklahoma.

Keziah was a modern woman. She sought higher education after high school; she did domestic work and borrowed money from her sister to support herself at Emporia Normal in Kansas. She graduated and became a fifth grade teacher in Topeka. She had aspirations of becoming a concert pianist. She passed her love for playing the piano to daughter Gwendolyn, who also played. Keziah created stories and composed two songs, "Luvenia," in memory of her mother, and a religious song, "I Want to Be Consecrated to Thee" (Kent 2). In 1975 she published *The Voice and Other Short Stories*. Keziah, like David, was a gifted, highly motivated person.

David Brooks met Keziah Wims through a mutual friend and they were married in 1916. She was 28 years old. Both were intelligent, grounded, artistically talented and motivated young people. Kent comments, "Both families stressed order, discipline and usefulness, and provided personnel for the trades." Both families also stressed similar home and religious values (2).

During the African American northern migration of the early 20th century, David and Keziah Brooks moved to Chicago looking for opportunity and the American Dream. They had two children, Gwendolyn Elizabeth and Raymond Melvin, and settled into a traditional lifestyle. After her marriage Keziah stopped teaching and focused on her home and her children. Gwendolyn and Raymond grew up in a two-parent household, attended Sunday school at Carter Temple Church, went with their parents to a weekly movie, and listened to radio shows as a family at home. David worked hard for the McKinley Music Publishing Company, later Targ and Dinner, for more than 30 years. In her memoir Keziah Brooks explained that she and her husband believed that "welfare was only for sick and elderly people" (134), so they had difficult financial times during the depression, but they refused to accept public assistance. Although the Brooks rented the second floor of their home to generate more income, the tenants often could not pay the rent, but the Brooks allowed them to stay. Mother Keziah established a structured daily routine for the household. The work was strenuous beyond the traditional female chores. She lifted coal into the boiler, shoveled snow, mowed the lawn and washed clothes on a washboard since they did not have a washing machine (135).

In their early years Raymond and Gwendolyn wore play clothes in the morning and were allowed free play; then after lunch they were dressed in better clothes and expected to read or draw or perform other activities that were less physical (Kent 3–4). Once they were older, Raymond worked after school and earned enough money to pay for most of his needs even while attending Wilson Junior College. Raymond was a talented artist, whose posters adorned the halls of Wilson in 1939. He began drawing at age 11 and continued through his twenties. Due to the efforts of his art teacher, Raymond received monthly checks for the National Youth Administration* for his work during his college years. One of his drawings of Gwendolyn Brooks is on the cover of *Report from Part Two*. They were very close until his death in 1974 (K. Brooks 57).

Brooks wrote that all holidays and birthdays were celebrated in the traditional way with feast and festivity. Her recollections in *Report from Part One* exude love and warmth.

> Home, however, always warmly awaited me. Welcoming, enveloping. Home meant a quick-walking, careful, Duty-loving mother, who played the piano, made fudge, made cocoa and prune whip and apricot pie, drew tidy cows and trees and expert houses with chimneys and chimney smoke, who helped her children with arithmetic homework and sang a high soprano" (39). "Home meant my father, with kind eyes, songs and tense recitations for my brother and myself. A favorite of his was a wonderful poem about a pie-making lady [52].

Gwendolyn commented further that Keziah "always admired people who read with expression" (G. Brooks *Report from Part One* 52) and she trained a group of children between the ages of 10 and 13 to perform dramatic readings for programs at church. She also rehearsed young Gwendolyn for recitations at Carter Temple Church from the age of four or five. The family had regular family prayer meetings where they also sang (52). During the 1930s Keziah and Gwendolyn attended monthly musical programs at

---

*National Youth Administration (NYA) was a Works Progress Administration (WPA) funded program begun by President Roosevelt in 1936. The purpose was two-fold: to aid public libraries and to provide part-time employment for thousands of unemployed young adults between the ages of 16 and 25 (Sorensen).

Metropolitan Community Church, which featured musicians of various ethnicities and according to Keziah were "highly cultural" (K. Brooks 44). Throughout life Gwendolyn played piano. In a telephone interview Nora Brooks Blakely remembers her mother playing often. Some favorite songs were "But Not for Me," "Mood Indigo" and "Solitude." She also played church and classical pieces, (such as "Just A-Wearyin' for You" and "Chaminade").

The influence both parents had on Gwendolyn Brooks cannot be overstated. The brief narrative above reveals a great deal. Gwendolyn Brooks' Christian humanitarian values, her generosity, her disciplined approach to writing and her gift for combining sounds and rhythms into poetry all relate back to David and Keziah Brooks, who fostered a love for music and poetry in her childhood home. But, her parents' encouragement went beyond passive influence. Her parents proactively supported her development as an intellectual and poet from an early age. Not only did her mother encourage Gwendolyn's writing and reciting of poetry, Keziah also excused Gwendolyn from household chores so she would have more time to devote to her poetry (G. Brooks, *Report from Part One* 49). Not only did Keziah Brooks limit her daughter's work in the home so she could write, but she also discouraged her from working outside the home when she was older, even though the family was experiencing financial problems. In *The Voice and Other Short Stories*, Keziah Brooks states, "Gwendolyn did not work while attending school. She spent her time preparing for her life's work without ever complaining about what we were unable to buy for her" (135). Like her brother, she also made drawings, but poetry was always her primary artistic work. As Gwendolyn's writing improved, her mother asked Gwendolyn to write plays for the other children, which Keziah directed and rehearsed in their home. David Brooks gave Gwendolyn an old desk from McKinley's for her writing materials and books (G. Brooks, *Report from Part One* 56). Brooks said, "My own Book Story begins with my father's wedding gift to my mother. He gave her a bookcase ... it was filled with — *The Harvard Classics!** I shall never forget visiting it as a small girl — over and over selecting this and that dark green, gold-lettered volume for spellbound study" (G. Brooks, *Report from Part Two* 12). Gwendolyn and her parents read and discussed those readings in literature, philosophy, religion and history, as well as their African American books and the NAACP's *Crisis* magazine. Sometimes her father read aloud to the family. In conjunction with those things, her parents made the financial sacrifice

---

**The Harvard Classics* is a 51-volume anthology of classic works from world literature, compiled and edited by Harvard University president Charles W. Eliot in 1910.

of taking both children downtown to buy them personal copies of textbooks that could not leave the school building, so they could study at home and raise their academic performances. Gwendolyn's childhood home life provided a secure foundation of love, religious training and educational enrichment (G. Brooks, *Report from Part Two* 13).

However, when Gwendolyn was enrolled at Forrestville Elementary School at the age of six, she encountered an environment that was not only unfamiliar and cold, but also socially rejecting. Children there valued assets she did not have. Physically, she was dark complexioned with kinky hair in a setting that esteemed light skin and straight hair. She wore lovely dresses made by her Aunt Beulah, but the children saw them as reasons to ostracize her as "stuck up." Socially, she was from a working-class family, instead of the revered professional class. In addition to those things, her "skill set" was different from those of the other children. She played checkers and dominoes, but did not know how to play jacks or ride a bike. Gwendolyn felt that she did not fit in.

But, Gwendolyn most assuredly fit in at home. At seven years old, she wrote a two-line poem for which she was applauded and encouraged by her family; Keziah told her that she would become the lady Paul Lawrence Dunbar. By the time she was 11 years old Brooks had begun to keep her series of poetry notebooks, which are now well known. She wrote her poetry and her annual list of projected writing projects among her personal New Year's resolutions. She made a personal commitment at the age of 11 to write at least one poem a day. That is a telling statement of her dedication and her love for writing! During the preteen years, she wrote about nature, the world around her, religion, even an elegy for her goldfish that had died (Kent 7). She was passionate about writing. By the time she was 13, Brooks had a poem "Eventide" published in *American Childhood* (October 1930). That same year she was introduced to *Writer's Digest* and was delighted to learn that issues she was facing were shared by other writers as well (Newquist 26–27).

Even at that age Gwendolyn Brooks defined herself as a poet. She enjoyed "enchanting" others with products of her mind. She reported that even at 13, she thought, "Of course I would be a poet! Was a poet! Didn't I write a poem every day? Sometimes two poems?" She also related, "When I was busy writing, I preferred not to be disturbed,... One day there was a major fire in the block ... my mother came to tell me.... My answer was 'Yes.' But I continued to write; I did not leave my room" (G. Brooks, *Report from Part One* 50). When she was not writing, Brooks spent significant time reading. She read Emerson, Hume, Locke, Darwin, Wordsworth, Bryant, Longfellow and Keats. She read Paul Lawrence Dunbar, James Weldon Johnson and Langston Hughes. She read anthologies of African American poets, such as *Caroling Dusk* (Cullen, 1927) and *Negro Poets and Their Poems* (Kerlin, 1935). She had a library card and went to the library often (G. Brooks, *Report from Part One* 50; G. Brooks, *Report from Part Two* 12; Kent 17).

During her early teen years Gwendolyn was shy and very quiet. She was still playing with paper dolls at 14 and was not interested in the kissing games in which others engaged at teen parties. Her shyness also reflected her acute awareness of other teens' discrimination based on skin color, although her confidence in herself and her rich brown complexion were strong.

Gwendolyn's high school experiences reminded her yet again that she was different from many of her peers. She attended the predominantly white Hyde Park Branch High School, which had a fine academic reputation but exposed her to racism in a way she had not previously encountered. She then transferred to the Wendell Phillips High School, which was all black, but the separations she had encountered in elementary school were there as well. Her third and final high school, where she had some friends and teachers who encouraged her writing, was Englewood High School. However, she became painfully aware of her position outside the teen social scene when she gave a sweet 16 party and invited many of her school peers; not one of them came. She graduated from Englewood High in 1934.

But, 16 was a year of triumph as well. She sent some of her poems to poet James Weldon Johnson asking for his comments, and he wrote an encouraging response. Johnson suggested that she read T.S. Eliot, Ezra Pound and e.e. cummings. She sent him poems three years later and he published one of them, "Reunion," in *Crisis* magazine (November 1937). His encouragement and constructive comments enhanced her confidence in her writing even though a face-to-face meeting with him later, when Johnson spoke at Carter Temple Church, left her feeling belittled because he did not remember her work. She frequently paired the story of Johnson's "brush off" with that of meeting Langston Hughes at the Metropolitan Community Church in Chicago, who read her poems after his talk and remarked about how talented she was (Lewis 59). His kindness and warm encouragement was much like her own response to young writers later in her life.

After high school Gwendolyn completed a two-year college program at Wilson Junior College. There, like her last high school, she met and became friends with other young people. She also established strong relationships with her teachers. Not surprisingly, her favorite courses were her literature courses. Writing was a consistent part of her life. At Wilson Kent reports that Gwendolyn experienced new ideas and became interested in politics and social issues.

> Gwendolyn published her own mimeographed newspaper — the *News-Review*, priced at 5 cents. A surviving copy, dated October 6, 1937, reports on cultural matters, a speech by Associate Justice of the U.S. Supreme Court Hugo L. Black, and a variety of local happenings. She included an editorial, a short story, a poem, and a cartoon of Justice Black contributed by her brother Raymond. The cartoon shows a black hanging from a tree while a Ku Klux Klansman stands in the foreground, rope in hand. Under the cartoon Justice Black, who had confessed to having been a Klansman, is quoted: "I number among my friends many members of the colored race." The newspaper ran a series of brief biographies of great Negroes.... There are also quotations from Emily Dickinson ... Shakespeare,... and the Rev. Harold Kingsley on the endurance of blacks. Then a quiz on black authors requiring the printed answers James Weldon Johnson, Countee Cullen, Claude McKay, and Langston Hughes [41].

The *News-Review* embodied elements that were constants in Gwendolyn Brooks' life: entrepreneurship, black consciousness, poetry, education and family. The content of the October 6 edition shows her awareness of the major African American issues of the day, her racial pride and her commitment to educating people about African American literature and history.

Brooks' search for employment after college proved frustrating. She attributed her denial of a position as reporter at Chicago's African American Newspaper, the *Chicago Defender*, to her skin color. The editor had been enthusiastic about hiring her based on her recommendations and previous writing until he met her face to face, when he rejected her. But Brooks' continued job search after Abbott's rejection resulted in her attaining a position that inspired significant characters and themes in her seminal human rights poem, "In the Mecca." She was hired as an assistant to E.M. French, who was a spiritual advisor in the decaying Mecca Building. Her job was to sell charms and potions to the residents, allegedly to solve their problems. She found the job distasteful. She was fired after four months for refusing a promotion to "preacher," but the experiences she had with the people of the Mecca Building stayed with her for many years.

During this period Brooks reached out and became active in the community (Kent 57–58). She served as publicity director of the NAACP Youth Council which Kent calls "then a militant organization of young black writers and intellectuals" (43). The members became her lifelong friends. The group included young people who distinguished themselves in different fields of endeavor. Among them were Margaret Taylor Burroughs (1915–2010) artist, poet, educator, curator and cofounder (with husband Charles Burroughs) of Chicago's DuSable Museum, a nationally recognized African American museum and cultural center, and John H. Johnson (1918–2005), founder of Johnson Publishing Company, which has grown to be a black-focused media and cosmetic empire today. It is apparent that the young people had a clear social consciousness and cultural pride. The group participated in protest marches against lynching with other Youth Council members, all of whom wore paper chains symbolizing both the lynching and the enslavement of black people. Gwendolyn Brooks met her future husband Henry Blakely through the NAACP Youth Council. In *Report from Part One* Brooks confessed that when other girls her age had boyfriends, she "wrote, read and reflected." She said she had crushes, but her first love was Henry, whom she met when she was 21 (57).

Henry Blakely, Jr., was the son of Pearl and Henry Blakely, Sr. His childhood had been much different from Gwendolyn's. His father had been intermittently in and out of his life since he was 11 years old when his father left the family in Chicago and moved to Detroit and started another family. On the occasion of his father's funeral Henry wrote a lengthy elegy. In it he drew a picture of man who was smart, engaging, creative and sociable, and who was always on the move. In it Henry referenced grandparents Charlie and Sallie in Atlanta, whom he had never seen, and the absence of financial and fatherly support, which he expressed with some resentment. Yet, it is clear from the poem, "My Daddy," that he loved his father and as an adult, had some understanding of his father's yearning to do more and be more than his situation allowed (H. Blakely 11–18). His mother was the primary parent for Henry and his two brothers. She raised them with heavy-handed discipline. According to Kent, Henry remembered his childhood as a combination of severe whippings and tenderness, which included reading poetry to them (47). With that foundation and an innate creative vision, Henry, like Gwendolyn, had developed a love for poetry at a young age and had begun writing poetry when he was 11 years old. He, too, aspired to be a poet.

The Brooks-Blakely wedding took place in September 1939 after a bit of controversy. After the wedding invitations had gone out, Pearl Blakely had come to Keziah and Gwendolyn Brooks and advised them that she did not believe Henry was ready for marriage. She was opposed to the marriage. She thought him immature, unfocused and financially unprepared for marriage. In spite of her opposition, the marriage took place in her parents' home. Keziah Brooks, not David Brooks, answered the minister's question of who was giving the bride away. Henry was outfitted in a new suit that was a gift from his Aunt Mary Telley (Kent 47).

Gwendolyn Brooks and Henry Blakely were married until his death in 1995.

The early years of their married life involved difficult financial circumstances and a number of moves. In *Report from Part One* (59–64) Brooks speaks of how happy she and Henry were even though they did not have much money. She speaks lovingly of sweet memories of the childhood of each of her children: Henry Blakely III (October 10, 1940) and Nora Brooks Blakely (September 8, 1951). Both Henry and Gwendolyn devoted as much time as possible to writing poetry, however the realities of supporting a family soon took much of Henry's time away from his writing. In a telephone interview, Nora Brooks Blakely remembers her father as a man with a fast wit and a wonderful sense of humor; he appreciated people as individuals. He was the family breadwinner and always supported his wife's career as well as his own. She said that he was always writing. His poetry was published in *Windy Place* and he completed an unpublished novel titled *The Dry Well Papers*. He was also an entrepreneur and wrote a business plan for other business owners and managers.

Gwendolyn Brooks wrote daily. Before the children were in school, she wrote while they slept; later, she wrote while they were at school. After school, she focused her attention on them. The Blakelys enjoyed being parents as well as poets (G. Brooks, *Report from Part One* 204). The children were sometimes the inspiration for poems (Kent 91). Brooks addressed the integration of her poetic and personal lives when she was interviewed for a feature story in the *Chicago Daily News* (September 28, 1963). She said, "I don't think of myself as a poet. I think of myself as the commonest kind of human being there can be — who likes to write poetry. I think it would be terrible and kill your efforts if you were aware of yourself as a "poet.".... Nothing that I do is more important than being a mother, taking care of my husband, and getting a meal together. Living is the most important thing I do, and poetry comes after that" (Kent 152). Brooks enjoyed writing most when she was not thinking of publishing but was writing with the joy of creative expression (G. Brooks, *Report from Part One* 132).

During the 1930s and 1940s, sponsored writers groups were operating in Chicago. In 1935 the Federal Writers Project (FWP), established as part of the New Deal Works Progress Administration (WPA), opened centers in each state, and the Illinois Writers' Project was based in Chicago. Some of the African American writers participated in the FWP and also participated in the South Side Writers Group, which had been started by prominent writer Richard Wright, and met at the South Side Community Art Center. Gwendolyn Brooks joined the South Side Writers Group, although she did not meet Wright himself until later. In 1941 Gwendolyn Brooks attended classes at the center conducted by Inez Cunningham Stark. Stark was a wealthy patron of the arts who wrote and who was interested in cultivating the talent of African American poets. She had requested a list of writers from the NAACP and started a workshop on modern poetry at the center. Gwendolyn and Henry joined the class. Gwendolyn began to focus on the technique of modern poets (Kent 58–61). Participation in the group broadened her writing experience and provided a community of constructive critics to review her poetry. Brooks was an active and open participant in the process. In *Report from Part One* Brooks remembers the benefits of the class as the process of teaching and learning from each other (68). Group members also gave parties at which black and white artists participated in rich discussion of artistic and intellectual issues. Stark encouraged workshop participants to enter competitions for prizes. Here Gwendolyn Brooks truly distinguished herself; she won the Midwest Writer's Conference prize in 1943, 1944 and 1945, yielding attention and interest from publishers.

Around 1943 Brooks sent a collection of poems to Harper and Brothers, publisher of the works of Richard Wright. Editor Elizabeth Lawrence sent Brooks' poems to Wright for his evaluation and provided Brooks with a copy of his comments. Wright was insightful and constructive in his praise for her poetry and suggested that she write a long poem that "carries a good burden of personal feeling" to complete a book of poems. Brooks wrote "The Sundays of Satin-Legs Smith," and with the help of Lawrence, her work was published in *A Street in Bronzeville* (Kent 63). According to Kent, Brooks reached her poetic maturity during World War II (67). By that time she knew the craft and conventions. She was aware of the tension between the traditional and the modern. She created complex forms that reflected the complexities of modern life experiences in her poetry. Some of her most well-known poems were written during that period.

After Gwendolyn Brooks' work was published by Harper and Brothers, she entered a period of professional development and expanding recognition. She and Henry made their first trip to the South where she did poetry readings at Howard University and Atlanta University. She was invited to contribute to a special issue of *Phylon*, a journal based at Atlanta University that addressed the need for universalism in black literature. Brooks' article addressed the creative process and emphasized craft, but did not confront the topic directly. Her poems reflected the black experience, but also had universal application. "Gwendolyn had very early recoiled from the exotic image of blacks ... and had struggled for an art that would present blacks simply as people. This situation provided a range of approach from realistic presentation, with some excursions into the cultural, to exploitation of humanness without identifying tag" (Kent 101).

As Brooks developed her gifts and skills as a poet, she expanded the scope of her work and her exposure. She began writing book reviews. Through the years she wrote reviews for the *Chicago Daily News, Chicago Sun-Times, Chicago Tribune, New York Herald Tribune, Negro Digest* (later *Black World*) and the *New York Times*, among others. She did poetry readings at colleges and universities. She contributed to literary journals. She also wrote editorial essays on topics of social and political significance, such as "They Call It Bronzeville" (*Holiday*, October 1951), which addressed Chicago's housing discrimination as it sought to set boundaries around the area in which African Americans could live.* Gwendolyn Brooks enjoyed growing recognition as a prominent African American artist and she mingled with notable African American public figures of the time at public and cultural events.

During this significant period in her life, Brooks learned she had been awarded the Pulitzer Prize for Poetry for *Annie Allen* on May 1, 1950, having been in competition with Robert Frost's *Complete Poems* and William Carlos Williams' *Patterson III* and the work of many other well-established American poets. *Annie Allen* was her second publication with Harper and Brothers and its critical success was a defining moment in Gwendolyn Brooks' life. She followed *Annie Allen* with the publication of *Maud Martha* in September 1953, a work of fiction with autobiographical elements. While not a best seller, the book generated excellent reviews by white and black reviewers, such as the prestigious *New York Times Book Review*, writer Langston Hughes and novelist Ann Petry (Kent 112). Soon translations of Brooks' work into other languages would broaden her reputation and access international markets. She continued to increase the breadth of her work by writing children's poetry. The juvenile department of Harper and Brothers published Brooks' *Bronzeville Boys and Girls* (1956), and she worked on a novel about Lincoln West, which was later published as a short story in the anthology *Soon, One Morning* (1963) and later as a poem in her book *Family Pictures* (1970).

A burgeoning network of African American artists and intellectuals was engaged in Chicago's cultural scene. They gathered to discuss the political and artistic issues that interested them all and sometimes read first drafts of their work. The Blakelys enjoyed hosting such parties with guests, such as Lorraine Hansberry, Richard Wright, James Baldwin, Carolyn Rodgers, Lerone Bennett, Margaret Burroughs, Haki Madhubuti and

---

*"Between 1940 and 1950, the black population increased from 277,731 to 492,265, yet Chicago and its institutions refused to extend the area to which blacks were, by and large, confined" (Kent 94; Strickland 156–163). Nine major race riots occurred in Chicago between 1945 and 1954 on the issue of housing.

many others. Gwendolyn and Henry prepared the food together. The menu often included red beans and rice, large pans of baked broccoli and cheese, sherry battered shrimp and apricot pie. They always planned enough food to feed everyone at the beginning and again at the end of the evening. They used all the rooms in their modest home to accommodate their many guests. The parties were alive with energetic debates and passionate performance (N. Blakely. Telephone interview). Poet Randson C. Boykin pictured this aspect of Brooks in his poem, "Red Beans and Rice Lady." The last nine lines of the poem read:

> the red beans and rice lady
> sets out a spread
>   of her magic and
> mystical prose; invites us
>   to eat, and drink, and to recite
> our poetry
> we are in this special sanctuary
> of muses, red beans and rice
> and a lady.

Historical events of the 1950s would also impact Gwendolyn Brooks and her art. In 1954 the Supreme Court made history by issuing the *Brown v. Board of Education of Topeka Kansas* decision outlawing school segregation. Surely Brooks, who had been born in Topeka, Kansas, must have related to the Brown family on a personal level. And as an African American she, like millions of others, must have been pleased to see this pivotal step toward equal access to education and the benefits that would flow from it. The very next year, a racist event occurred that shocked the nation and profoundly moved Gwendolyn Brooks. Emmitt Till, a 14-year-old boy from Chicago, went to visit family in Mississippi that summer. He was beaten, castrated and dumped into a river allegedly for whistling at a white woman. Brooks' personal sensitivity to the event was enhanced by the fact that her own son was 14 at the time. In response she wrote two of her most poignant poems, "A Bronzeville Mother Loiters in Mississippi. Meanwhile a Mississippi Mother Burns Bacon" and "The Last Quatrain of the Ballad of Emmitt Till," which specifically reference the incident. The first centers on what the white woman feels as she prepares breakfast for her family the day after her husband has murdered Emmitt Till. Being a mother, she relates to Emmitt Till as a child and sees her husband as a child killer, not a white knight avenging her honor. The second focuses on the feelings of Emmitt Till's mother, Mamie Till, after she lost her only child. Both poems are emotionally heartwrenching; both reveal the personal cost of racist action. Brooks wrote other poems at that time that also referenced the ugliness of racism, such as "The Chicago Defender Sends a Man to Little Rock."

Her New Year's resolutions for 1956 reflect her deep commitment to black people and social justice. "As was her custom Brooks had drawn up among her New Year's resolutions for 1956 several writing projects: a book of poems, *Another Coming of Christ*, and a book of stories, *Bronzeville Men and Women*, and several stories about a whimsical maid, called *Big Bessie*" (Kent 123). It was during this time that she decided to write about her experiences gained from her employment in the Mecca building (Kent 123). Not only do these projects convey her political views but these project beginnings and the works that evolved from them, "In Emanual's Nightmare," "In the Mecca" and the Big Bessie character in the second and third "Sermon[s] on the Warpland," tie her social views to her religious ones — the fused philosophies of democracy and Christianity.

Providing further context for her work during this period was the production of Lorraine Hansberry's play, *A Raisin in the Sun*. Brooks attended the opening night in Chicago in April of 1959. Gwendolyn loved the play for its portrayal of black struggle as well as its literary merit. Brooks was also invigorated by the critical and financial success of the play (Kent 132). Hansberry had addressed the housing issue about which Brooks also cared deeply, and response to the play strengthened Brooks' resolve that literature about black people for black people was not only an artistic, cultural mandate, but was also commercially viable. She also saw that Beat Poets and younger black poets appealed to a broad audience of ordinary African American people.

The Bean Eaters, Brooks' collection of poems from the latter years of the 1950s, was published in 1960 to critical acclaim. It was seen as a culmination of passionate personal reflection on life experience, along with brilliantly executed poetic technique. *The Bean Eaters* included the Emmett Till poems. Kent said, "With its [*The Bean Eaters*] publication she had a body of work that placed her stamp on poetry. One could recognize a Gwendolyn Brooks poem" (152).

In the 1960s Brooks continued working on her piece about life in the Mecca Building while working with her editor, Elizabeth Lawrence, to compile her *Selected Poems* which was published to extraordinary reviews in 1963. Again in the 1960s Brooks expanded her artistic reach. She accepted a position teaching American literature in the Union Leadership Program at the University of Chicago in 1962. This was the beginning of a long and fulfilling association Brooks had with teaching students of literature and young writers in various contexts. In 1960 actress Ruby Dee presented a dramatic reading of several Brooks' poems on CBS in New

York and early in 1961 Brooks herself recorded an hour of her own poems for the Library of Congress. Her exposure in the African American community was expanded further when she was invited to write a poem for *Ebony* magazine's September 1963 special Emancipation Issue. It carried stories of the June 1963 assassination of civil rights leader Medger Evers and the bombing of the Sixteenth Street Baptist Church of Birmingham, Alabama in which four young black girls died weeks after the historic March on Washington had inspired so much hope among African Americans. *Muhammed Speaks*, newspaper of the black Muslims, also published her poem "Negro Hero" about World War II cook-turned-gunnery hero Dorie Miller. All segments of the national African American community knew and recognized the social commitment and the poetry of Gwendolyn Brooks in the early 1960s. The civil rights movement was beginning to yield influence as the Civil Rights Act of 1964 was passed. The law addressed legal issues of race, but could not address the raw racial strife that still permeated American life and consciousness.

The mid–1960s was a rich period of social encounter, experience and change for Gwendolyn Brooks. Her editor and critic, now friend Elizabeth Lawrence, retired from Harper and Row (formerly Harper and Brothers) in June of 1964. After a 20-year professional relationship, Brooks was deeply moved and expressed her feelings in a letter she closed with the words "With real love and respect, with gratitude —" (qtd. in Kent 176). Concurrently, her relationships with other African American writers and thinkers deepened dramatically by the social and artistic activity of the time. Since African American writers were being published more often, speaking more often, and speaking more loudly, more and more conferences of black writers were taking place. Some conference hosts invited writers with a particular perspective, but most invited prominent writers who represented an array of political views. Speakers often included notables like Arna Bontemps, LeRoi Jones (Imamu Amiri Baraka), James Baldwin, Lerone Bennett and John Oliver Killens along with Gwendolyn Brooks. Such conferences had formal literary sessions on craft and the work of prominent writers such as the late Richard Wright, but the cluster of intellectuals — young and old, male and female, conservative and radical, militant and passive, integrationist and separatist, black and white — also generated rich, sometimes fiery, but stimulating social and political discourse in formal and informal sessions.

Kent lists some of the conferences in which Brooks was a participant with quotes from other writers there. It is not difficult to correlate important ideas with Brooks' poems.

American Society of African Culture Conference, March 1965 (187)

African students stated their disillusionment relative to America's lack of democracy for African Americans.	"Another Preachment to Blacks" includes that idea.

The Harlem Writers Guild and New School for Social Research Conference, April 23–25, 1965 (188)

James Baldwin asserted that "the liberation of this country ... depends on whether or not we are able to make a real confrontation with our history."	The Sermon(s) on the Warpland dramatize that confrontation.

The Harlem Writers Guild and New School for Social Research Conference, April 23–25, 1965 (188)

John O Killens asserted that "Black Writers must save America" if it is to be saved.	"Riders to the Blood-Red Wrath" states that very mandate.

Fisk University Conference 1966 (188)

John O. Killens alleged that black literature should have social relevance to the world and especially to black Americans to "de-brainwash" people.	"In Montgomery" is one of many Brooks poems that fulfill that mission.

Asilomar Conference 1966 (189)

Ossie Davis and LeRoi Jones called for a new language and a new image for blacks eschewing the images of Uncle Tom and Honorary White Man.	Brooks poems like "The Wall" reflect that new literary aesthetic.

Together the writers set forth the medley of ideas and philosophies forming and flowing through the African American community in the mid–1960s.

During this period Brooks enjoyed recognition around the country. She was deeply involved in the African American community, seeking to honor fallen civil rights heroes and working to enhance justice in the community. She began receiving awards and honorary degrees, but she also began *giving* awards to encourage aspiring writers, often from her personal funds. She sponsored workshops and poetry contests. She was still working on her poem about the Mecca Building when Malcolm X was assassinated in February 1965. Her elegy, "Malcolm X," became a part of her "After Mecca" section of "In the Mecca." The poem demonstrates her deep respect, and particular admiration for the strength and assertiveness of Malcolm X, who was viewed as politically radical. Brooks did not hesitate to make her philosophy clear and declare her social positions strongly.

In February 1966 Brooks met Dudley Randall, poet and owner of Broadside Press Publishing Company, who became her friend and literary associate. She began contributing individual poems for publication by Broadside. She published an article in *Negro Digest* (later *Black World*) that responded and repudiated an article published about her after an interview by the *San Jose Mercury*. The article had taken a statement she had made out of context and implied that she was not involved in the civil rights movement. She was angered by the implication because she was dedicated to the ideals of the movement (Kent 192–193).

Gwendolyn Brooks identified the Fisk University Writers Conference that took place April 21–23, 1967, as a climactic moment in her philosophical and poetic life. The historians and writers who spoke set forth pivotal issues facing African Americans. Historians Lerone Bennett and John Henrik Clarke spoke about the destruction of the African identity of blacks in the United States. As Clarke put it, "It is singularly the mission of the black writer to tell his people what they have been, in order for them to understand what they are. And from this the people will clearly understand what they still must be." He went on to say, "There is no such thing as a Negro in the true ethnic sense. They gave us a name that referred to a condition, and took away the name that referred to land, history and culture" (Kent 197). He advocated the word "Afro-American." Bennett advocated for a "literature of transformation" (198) which would unite art, literature and a human struggle. There was a call for black writers to come "home" to the black community. According to playwright Ronald Milner, writers should "go home psychically, mentally, aesthetically, and I think physically" (201). The progression culminated with the presentation of LeRoi Jones who eloquently spoke from the perspective of the Black Power — Black Arts Movement and, in response to audience request, read poetry. Brooks was impressed and excited about the black cultural pride and self-love and she was impressed with their determination and resolve to create a new black America (Kent 198–202). The speakers at the Fisk University Writers Conference framed issues and lent new language and form to concepts Brooks had believed and embodied in her poetry for years. Brooks was enthused and invigorated. Like a literary climax, the conference marked a high point in action that had already been building toward the new direction.

When Brooks returned to Chicago, she had a telegram in her mail from producer-singer Oscar Brown, Jr., inviting her to a show created by a street gang, the Blackstone Rangers (Kent 203). At that event Brooks met a Wilson Junior College student, Walter Bradford, who along with Don L. Lee (now Haki R. Madhubuti), was committed to helping gang members get through school (Kent 206). Brooks began a series of writing workshops, which were attended by gang members along with Bradford and Lee. According to Kent, a basic difference between Brooks and the group was Gwendolyn's anchor in clear moral principles and the younger group's view of societal power relationships as espoused by the Black Power movement and evidenced by American history (208–209). The exchange of ideas shaped a new consciousness for all of them. Characterized by heated discussions about poetic structure, philosophy and politics, the workshops became fertile ground for innovation by everyone, including Brooks herself. During this period Brooks expanded her use of free verse and incorporated ideas of the younger, more militant writers into her work. She also read works that Bradford and Lee recommended. Although she was a Pulitzer Prize–winning poet and a generation above them, Brooks was open to learning from them. Brooks told Paul Angle in an interview in 1967 that writers need education in and out of school; she said "no curriculum is complete" (Angle 25; G. Brooks, *Report from Part One* 138). In an interview with Ida Lewis, Brooks explained, "I wasn't reading the books I should have read when I was young. I didn't even hear of W.E.B. DuBois' *Souls of Black Folks* until I was well grown" (60). She said the gaps in her education made her feel ignorant even though she lived "in a tough, raw, down-front city like Chicago" (Kent 225–226). Alternatively, Brooks taught the group about poetry, using works of poetic masters and explaining crafting techniques and poetic voice in the context of poetic tradition. The participants grew as writers. Her mature views tempered their immature ones. Brooks indicated that she had respect for the "vigor" of the young poets and that she felt a great responsibility to work with it without diminishing its passion and power (Kent 227–228). Her poems "Young Heroes I, II and III" and "Speech to the Young. Speech to the Progress — Toward" from the Family Pictures section of *To Disembark* express Brooks' engagement with the workshop participants. She developed a special relationship with Bradford and Lee. In a 1977 interview she said, "He [Walter Bradford] and Haki are equal in my estimation. They are, in a way, sons of mine.... We still think of ourselves as mother and sons" (Hull and Gallagher 99). They became family.

August 27, 1967, highlights this sharing of black aesthetics. On that date the Wall of Respect was dedicated before a street-filled crowd. The wall facing the street was painted with pictures of great black historical figures, such as Malcolm X, Dr. Martin Luther King, W.E.B. DuBois, John Coltraine, Thelonious Monk and Nina Simone, along with the poem "S.O.S." by LeRoi Jones. Gwendolyn Brooks read poetry at the event. Afterward the writers' group took Brooks to a bar called the Playboy Lounge where she and other members of the group read to the patrons who listened and applauded. Brooks recounted the day in subsequent interviews recollecting the warm sense of community that permeated the day. For Brooks that sharing became a mandate for her as a writer. Later, she said the following:

> However, I feel that I was right when in the late sixties, I believed that Blacks should care for each other, nourish each other and communicate with each other. And if that was the right decision, I cannot forget the people who have grown up feeling that they hate poetry; that they would spell the word with a capital P and look upon it with great awe. I feel that there are poems, which these people could enjoy. There are already some and I would like to contribute to this literature which, if they knew it was called literature, they would probably turn away from it [qtd. in Kent 234].

This was a busy time for Gwendolyn Brooks. She was writing, teaching and actively participating in civic and cultural activities. She was a well-known figure in the African American community. In 1968 she was honored at a program called Black History and Culture Come Alive. She spoke out on behalf of African Americans and women. In *Report from Part One* Brooks spoke of her consciousness that "is not against white, but FOR black." She emphasized the need to celebrate "African-ness," acknowledge Kwanzaa and have political unity (G. Brooks 45–46). Regarding the role of black women in the civil rights struggle, Brooks stated, "Black Woman must remember, through all the prattle about walking or not walking three or 12 steps behind or ahead of her male, that her personhood precedes her femalehood; that sweet as sex may be,... She is a person in the world — with wrongs to right, stupidities to outwit, *with her man when possible, on her own when not*" (G. Brooks, *Report from Part One* 204). She was committed to black solidarity, but she had an optimistic, even Christian hope for the ideal of democracy (Kent 208). She continued to emphasize that people are people regardless of gender or ethnicity. She had a full schedule of classes, appearances and readings at colleges and universities. Brooks was named Poet Laureate of Illinois, a singularly distinguished honor. As Poet Laureate of Illinois, Brooks visited hospitals and rehabilitation centers as well as colleges and universities. Magazines featured her work and articles about her. *Ebony* magazine (July

1968) published "Gwendolyn Brooks: Poet Laureate," a feature article by Phyllis Garland.

In 1969 she decided to give up teaching to concentrate fully on writing. She was working on her autobiography at that time. She was also interested in venturing into new genres such as verse plays and short novels in addition to poetry. Brooks also complemented her poetry readings by funding poetry prizes for colleges and the community. Her commitment to developing the talents of young writers continued to be a significant part of her work as a poet.

The year 1970 marked another milestone in the life of the poet. She decided to leave Harper and Row Publishers (formerly Harper and Brothers) and contract with African American publisher Broadside Press, which had been founded by poet and publisher Dudley Randall. At the time Harper and Row was working on a collected works volume tentatively titled *The World of Gwendolyn Brooks*, which would have been a lucrative venture, but Brooks turned away from that possibility to bring her focus and market appeal to an African American publisher. The move was motivated by her belief in black empowerment and her commitment to her role in the African American community. The audience she most sought was a black audience. That year she also hired New York literary agent, Roslyn Targ.

During the 1970s Brooks broadened her cultural imperative with travel to Africa. She made a trip to Dar Es Salaam and Nairobi, Kenya, where Nora was studying in 1971. She noted in her autobiography her pleasure at socializing with other African Americans and Africans in their homes in Dar Es Salaam. She also observed the differences in the affect and self-confidence of the people evidenced in part by the gait of young men there, in contrast with that of young African American males in the United States. She made a point of separating from the official tour to spend time with the people. In 1974 she went to Ghana with Henry and visited Elmina slave Castle and Kumasi, home of the Ashanti people. When she traveled to Africa she noted how ignorant she felt when she realized how little she knew about it. She noted in *Report from Part Two* that she envied African peoples' knowledge of their homeland (G. Brooks, *Report from Part One* 91, 95–96, 122–130, 138; *Report from Part Two* 44).

The 1980s were filled with events that were the culmination of the various sectors of Gwendolyn Brooks' life: community commitment, professional achievement, and engagement of family and friends. Brooks remained active in the African American community while writing, presenting poetry workshops and awards, which she regularly funded from her personal finances. It became a running family joke that she would expand the number of awardees for a particular prize and pay additional prize money out-of-pocket because she was so committed to encouraging aspiring, talented poets. One year all of her poet laureate compensation went to poetry awards (N. Blakely. Telephone interview). She continued to travel, speak and read poetry, often signing books for long lines of admirers. She wrote letters to people she met when she traveled. And of course, she was writing. Her publications during the 1980s reflected her embrace of her African Diasporic community, most apparent in *The Near Johannesburg Boy, and Other Poems* and *In Montgomery and Other Poems*, which included the long, magnificent poem "Song of Winnie" about Winnie Mandela. Brooks started Black Position Press, Brooks Press (now The David Company of Chicago) and published most of her own work, again expanding her vision with entrepreneurship.

On January 3, 1980, she was invited to read poetry at the White House by President and Mrs. James Earl (Jimmy) Carter, Jr., in A Salute to Poetry and American Poets. Then, in 1982 Brooks was invited to participate in a conference of prominent Soviet and American writers in the Soviet Union (G. Brooks, *Report from Part Two* 53) Brooks' international speaking and reading engagements solidified her already stellar literary stature abroad and complemented her reputation in the United States. In 1985 she was named Consultant in Poetry to the Library of Congress. In her 1985–86 tenure she broadened her official consultant duties from inviting and introducing outstanding poets for monthly readings to include inviting students and poets to lunch and to her office to read and discuss poetry. She was presented with more than 75 honorary doctorates. Two parks and five schools have been named after her in Aurora, DeKalb, Harvey, and Chicago, Illinois. The auditorium of the Edward Jenner School is named for Brooks. There is the Gwendolyn Brooks Illinois State Library in Springfield. Western Illinois University in Macomb houses the Gwendolyn Brooks Cultural Center. The main branch of the Chicago Public Library boasts a bust of Gwendolyn Brooks. Chicago State University, which houses the Gwendolyn Brooks Center for Black Literature and Creative Writing, hosts an annual conference, which celebrated its 20-year anniversary in 2010. Gwendolyn Brooks was professor of English at Chicago State University from 1990 until her death. A selection of her numerous honors and awards is cataloged in the Appendix 2.

Throughout her life Gwendolyn Brooks enjoyed a loving circle of family and friends. Although in later years, she had lost her beloved parents and her husband Henry, she had her son, software designer Henry Blakely III and his family with her only grandchild, Nicholas Blakely. Henry III is a writer and graphic artist and Nicholas is a computer game designer in the greater Washington D.C. area. She was especially close to her daughter, Nora Brooks Blakely, founder and artistic director of Chicago's Chocolate Chips Theatre Company. She remained close to surrogate son, author Haki Madhubuti, founder and managing editor of Third World Press, now a DePaul University Ida B. Wells Professor. But the expanse of those who loved and respected her far exceeded her immediate family. Two events exemplify the high esteem in which she was held by many, many others in the United States. Special parties were given in her honor for her 70th and 80th birthdays in 1987 and 1997. Her 70th birthday celebration was marked by a call to a diverse group of prominent poets, writers and artists for submissions to a volume of tributes, *Say the River Turns: The Impact of Gwendolyn Brooks* edited by Haki Madhubuti. The list of contributors consists of major writers, historians and community leaders, all of whom expressed personal messages about and to Gwendolyn Brooks. It was her special surprise at her party. Her 80th birthday festivities were marked with a citywide Gwendolyn Brooks Week in Chicago. Activities were sponsored by the City of Chicago Department of Cultural Affairs and culminated in a special program entitled Eighty Gifts, which was held at the Harold Washington Library Center with two-minute presentations by 80 writers and performers from across the globe. It was a grand celebration honoring a grand Lady of Letters by a diverse community of Americans.

Beyond the American literary giant and beyond the trailblazer was a warm human being who never lost the feeling for the commonplace and never deviated from a simple, genteel lifestyle. In her later years Gwendolyn Brooks would travel, speaking and reading from October to May or June, and then stay in the house during the months of July and August treasuring her quiet time. In her private moments Gwendolyn Brooks was still the young girl who did not interrupt her writing to see the fire down the street. She was still the demure, brown girl who enjoyed her time alone. She did not even go to the market for food, but rather sent Nora with her very imagistic grocery lists. She watched soap operas, she played the piano; she had small dinner parties for longtime friends like Val Gray Ward and Abena Joan Brown, and hosted a traditional Thanksgiving Day dinner every year. When her health prevented her from continuing to prepare meals herself, she would take friends out to dinner. On the Thanksgiving Day that was just days before her death, when she was weak and ill, she was still committed to hosting Thanksgiving Dinner at her home although she needed help (N. Blakely. Telephone interview). Her leaving, like her living, manifested her commitment, generosity, strength, and her grace. Gwendolyn Brooks transitioned from this life on December 3, 2000.

Chapter Two

Brooks on Religion

I rarely go to church. My religion is kindness.
— Gwendolyn Brooks, *Report from Part Two*

To gain a comprehensive view of Gwendolyn Brooks' philosophy on religion in general, and Christianity in particular, one must examine the ideas she expressed directly in her autobiographies, interviews and articles to complement the analysis of her poetry, which is the focus of this study. The subject of religion surfaced again and again in her discourse as she sought to integrate her early training with what she observed and experienced in the society around her — the religious philosophy versus the social reality. This chapter chronicles her journey in her own words.

Gwendolyn Brooks had a strong Christian foundation and the values and messages she espoused reflect Christian doctrine. The roots of her ethical perspective came from her childhood and her family's commitment to church. In an interview Brooks stated:

> When I was a child, my family had a preacher — incidentally, the church was at the corner of the street where I was raised. My parents had deliberately bought a house on a street that had a church at the end of it [Carter Temple Colored Methodist Episcopal (CME)], because they wanted us never to have an excuse not to go to church. If it rained, if it snowed, we could still get there [Howe and Fox 146].

So, Gwendolyn Brooks grew up in a home that viewed going to church as a requirement. Her parents raised the family with strong Christian values. She and her brother attended church with her mother and participated in church functions. They attended Sunday school, where they learned the basics of Christian doctrine. Christmas and Easter, the highest Christian holidays that celebrate the birth and resurrection of Jesus Christ, were celebrated in their home. She made a number of statements that reflected those childhood experiences in her first autobiography published in 1972, *Report from Part One*:

> It was the baking of the fruitcakes that opened our Christmas season. After that, there was the merriest playing of Christmas carols on the piano by my mother and me, with everybody singing. With what excited pleasure my brother and I went to bed,... We went to sleep with radio carols in our ears or to the sweet sound of Mama playing and singing "Silent Night," or "Hark! The Herald Angels Sing," or "O Little Town of Bethlehem." It was for long my own personal tradition to sit behind the tree and read a paper book I still own: *The Cherry Orchard* by Marie Battelle Schiling, and published by the David C. Cook Publishing Company. It had been given me by Kayola Moore, my Sunday school teacher [41–43].
>
> On Easter Sunday.... We — my mother, my brother and I, *never* my father — trotted off to Sunday school. Carter Temple Colored Methodist Episcopal Church was at the northwest corner of our block. After Sunday school we went home, returning in the afternoon to take part in the Easter Program. Before coming back we had found our hidden Easter eggs, and had received our Easter baskets full of chocolate rabbits and cotton rabbits and jelly beans and bright marshmallow eggs and lots of green straw [44].
>
> We attended Sunday school regularly and were participants in the various functions there [47].)
>
> At home we had regular Sunday morning family service. Regular family prayer meetings, at which we all sang and sang. Father, mother, sisters, brothers, aunt, grandmother — we all sang. We sang old gospel songs. Then we would eat. Whatever there was [52–53].

It is evident that Brooks' childhood was steeped in Christian traditions that were reinforced by music, prayer and worship by all generations of the family.

Brooks, who married Henry Blakely, Sr., in 1939 in a traditional Christian ceremony, continued to celebrate Christmas and Easter with her husband and their children, Henry Jr. and Nora. She stated, "Today, my house has not yet escaped the green-tree-fruit-cake-eggnog-gifts-on-Christmasmorning 'esthetic,' even in this our time of black decision and ascent. The human heart delights in celebration" (G. Brooks, *Report from Part One* 43). Note the qualification that her participation is "celebration," a term that can, but may not have religious connotation. Her conflict is evident in the language she chose. Her house "has not yet escaped" the traditional elements of Christmas celebrations, implying that there is movement away, but something is holding her — keeping her attached to the tradition. She still carried the core of the faith with her from her childhood training. And relative to Easter: "At Easter he [Henry Jr.] is a shining little boy in his new navy blue or tan or grayish suit, and his new hat that is almost like a man's. When church-time comes, he takes Mama's arm, helping her through the happenchance of the street. And of all the voices climbing to the high dome of the temple, his is the loudest and the most holy" (60–61). Even the passage about Henry Jr. at Easter has another implicit message. Her tone changed from pride and happiness to reverence once they were inside the church. The phrase "voices climbing to the high dome of the temple" presents an image of humans reaching up musically toward heaven. Finally, it is his innocence that is holy. Brooks was expressing a Christian belief in heaven and the exultation of the innocent.

An article she wrote for the *Chicago American* on February 26, 1958, explains the duality of her feelings at that time, relative to prayer. It was titled, "What Prayer Did for Me." She opened with a discussion of her previous belief, then explained her experience with prayer. A portion of the article appears below.

> [I had believed that] They [people praying] need not wail in the night or day, wanting and hunting some Love that will hold them like babies, and protect them from the stresses of nature, and from the strains imposed on themselves by themselves. I cannot help you by telling you how I began to change, or why. I cannot say it was because I saw, as I grew older, "how the mighty have fallen." I cannot say it was because I saw that good, intelligent people, people I respected, felt differently. These may have been factors, but I cannot say so with decision. Once, when my daughter Nora was 5 months old, I read in a newspaper of another baby 5 months old, certainly dying of some horrible inner abnormality. Looking at my own child, so plump and healthy and glowing, I was overcome with pity and love for the other, and for the first time in decades got on my knees and prayed to God to help that helpless innocent. A year or more later, I only happened to read that the child, "by some miraculous chance," was recovering against the expectations of all. This wonder may have contributed to the direction of my alteration (for I believed that my own prayer, joined with others, was the "miraculous chance!"). But I am not sure. I only know that for some time now, God has seemed a near reality to me…. But for long He has seemed a friend, to "discuss" anything with, tragedy, or wishes for the future, or the loveliness of flowers and blue air!

In 1958 then, the childhood foundations of prayer as a conversation with God, with the accompanying attributes of God as omnipotent, omniscient and omnipresent, are all evident. In addition, Brooks implies that God hears prayers and answers them. Yet, her hesitation is evident. She commented that "for the first time in decades" she got on her knees and prayed to God" Even though she acknowledged the answer to her prayer, she also indicated in the article that she still would not ask God for help with something she could help herself. So, she is expressing the Christian concept of answered prayer, while asserting a level of personal power to make things happen, which is contrary to Christian doctrine of surrendering all things to omnipotent God.

In a 1973 interview with Fuller, Collier, Kent and Randall, Brooks commented again on religion and prayer,

> I haven't sorted out all my feelings about religion yet. There are many things that I don't understand.
>
> I don't understand, for instance, why babies have to suffer the things they do in this world of ours, and yet many of a religious inclination tell me that all this will be explained on the other side and that all I have to do is just wait. That does not seem to be sensible. And other parts of that question I need to do more pondering on. However — well, I'm not flying anymore.... But until I stopped flying in December, I got on planes and loved the experience but found myself saying, always, as soon as I sat down, please God, protect us all [73].

On her first trip to Africa, which included time in Nairobi, Kenya, in 1971 she reported in the "African Fragment" chapter, "A little collection of fast walkers turns down a road. I turn, too. I follow them. They enter a comely church, All Saints Cathedral. I think, 'How happy my mother would be to know that on my first Sunday in Africa, I am going to church'" (G. Brooks, *Report from Part One* 90). She entered the church as a tourist and reported her observations of the congregation, the choir and the minister, but she still associated the experience with her maternal childhood training to attend church on Sundays. The root was still alive; but she expressed her conflict by attending as a spectator, not a participant.

Gwendolyn Brooks also explicitly acknowledged the importance of reading the Holy Bible. In a 1990 interview with Howe and Fox the following exchange occurred.

> H&F: You have talked about reading being influential to you. Was the Bible part of your family reading? Has the Bible influenced you?
>
> B: Yes, my family had a great respect for the Bible. Both my family and my husband's family respected it. You will probably all be shocked to know that I have not read all of the Bible. Has everyone here read every inch of it? [laughter]
>
> H&F: I have. Once I read the whole thing through.
>
> B: Well, I should. I should. The *Holy Bible* is part of education [143].

It is also important to note here that Brooks mentioned her husband's family belief in the Holy Bible that actually reinforced what she had learned from her own family. For writers the Holy Bible informs as doctrine and as artistic resource. Arguably, the Holy Bible is the most influential book in human history. It has been translated into more than 2,100 languages and more copies of it have been distributed than any other book. Genre, topics, themes, and figures of the Bible have provided models and literary conventions for generations of writers, including Gwendolyn Brooks. The preeminent English translation since the middle of the 17th century, and the one referenced in Gwendolyn Brooks' poetry, is the King James Version (KJV) of the Holy Bible.

The conflict for Brooks, then, was not in the essential Christian doctrine, the practice of prayer, the acceptance of God, the recognition of Christ Jesus, the recognition of the church as God's house, or biblical teachings. Rather the disconnect was between (1) the earthly events and relationships that seemed to contradict the positive role Christian teaching asserted that God played in the lives of humans and (2) the incongruities between the institution of the church as a guiding force in society and the behavior of Christian practitioners. She was especially troubled by whites, who declared themselves to be Christians, yet oppressed and abused African Americans. She pondered how theoretical and philosophical Christianity accounted for negative events that unfold in the life of individuals and in society. One catalyst for the evolution and transformation of her belief system was the civil rights struggle.

Gwendolyn Brooks crystallized her thoughts on religion, and from the early 1970s made it clear that her view on religion was bound to the social history of the United States. Her exchange with editor Ida Lewis in a 1971 interview for *Essence* magazine is illustrative.

> LEWIS: During the 1940s and 1950s, how did you view the black world?
>
> BROOKS: I thought that integration was the solution. All we had to do was keep on appealing to the whites to help us, and they would.
>
> LEWIS: Why did you think that?
>
> BROOKS: Because I relied heavily on Christianity. People were really good, I thought; there was some good even in people who seemed to be evil. It's true that I didn't know very much about wicked people or who they were. It was a good world, the best of all possible worlds... [60–61].

She indicated that she *previously* relied on Christianity and her belief that people were good, implying that she had awakened to a different reality that invalidated her previous thinking. Resistance to social equality and racist actions by whites against African Americans were so inconsistent with the Christian doctrine Brooks knew that she separated the practice from the principles. Brooks believed the principles and eschewed the institution that grew from them.

When asked to compare herself to poet Robert Hayden in a 1977 Hull and Gallagher interview, Brooks responded by first addressing Hayden's writing, but then chose to differentiate them by their religious differences, also.

> I don't have any special religion. MY religion is — I guess I'll say something corny — PEOPLE. LIV — ING. I go to church on Mother's Day and Easter Sunday. I will say, however, that when I'm up in a plane and lately when I'm in a car or any other conveyance I say Dear — please protect us all — and then sit back and enjoy the ride [101–102].

In that exchange Brooks disavowed religion, but she did *not* disavow a supreme being to whom she prayed for protection, God.

By the 1990s Gwendolyn Brooks explained her view on religion and spirituality very clearly. In an interview with Howe and Fox for *Literature and Belief*, Brooks expressed her position in the following exchange.

> H&F: Are you aware of the religious and human values that you put into your poetry?
>
> B: I like that phrase "human values." Not everyone in this world of humanity is religious. Or some people might be, but they won't spell it out. I can't speak for the mass-murderers, of course, or the rapists and so forth, but I think that most people have some decency, some values. I like to ask groups of people, "Think about the groups of folks you have met. Weren't most of them decent?" Of course, it just takes one to make things wretched for the rest of us, but generally people have values. That is my optimistic view [141].

Internal to her second autobiography, *Report from Part Two* published in 1996, Gwendolyn Brooks made the belief statement that opens this chapter. She explained further in the following excerpt.

> Having decided that I am not too sinful, that I am allowing myself to be called "American," ... "But! — what about ? Are you not humanitarian?" "Yes." "You call yourself a Black. Doesn't that singularization fight the concept of humanitarianism?"
>
> OF COURSE I am "concerned," tightly, "with human welfare and the reduction of suffering." I cite, star, and esteem all that which is of woman — human and hardly human. And I want people of the world to anticipate ultimate unity, active interest in empathy. I commend a unity of distinct proud pieces. Not a Stew. A unity of distinct proud pieces. Because each entity is lovely-amazing-exhilarating in uniquity and boldness of clear distinction, good design. I hope that in the world, always there will be Black, brown, yellow, white, red (And if Time has some surprises for us let us welcome those too)" [131].

As that excerpt shows, Gwendolyn Brooks spoke and exhibited a belief in a doctrine of universal respect and concern for the welfare of fellow human beings. Her philosophical stance reflects one of the foundational Christian-Judeo tenets, "love your neighbor as yourself," which is expressed in both the Old and New Testaments of the Holy Bible.

In the Old Testament Book of Leviticus, "The Lord said to Moses, speak to the entire assembly of Israel and say to them: Be holy because I, the Lord your God am holy" (*NIV Study Bible*, Lev. 19.1–2). He then gave Moses various laws to communicate to the Israelites. Among them was "Do not seek revenge or bear a grudge against one of your people, but love your neighbor as yourself. I am the Lord" (*NIV Study Bible*, Lev. 19.18). In the New Testament Book of Matthew, Jesus said, "Love the Lord your God with all your heart and with all your soul and with all your mind. This is the first and greatest commandment. And the second is like it: 'Love your neighbor as yourself.' All the Law and the prophets hang on these two commandments" (*NIV Study Bible*, Matt. 22.37–40). The commandment to love your neighbor as yourself, in which "neighbor" has been broadly construed to mean anyone one encounters, was reiterated in the books of Mark (12.31), Luke (10.27), James (2.8) and in two Pauline epistles, Romans (13.9) and Galatians (5.14). The concept is fundamental Christian doctrine and her words on religion show that Gwendolyn Brooks embraced it.

Gwendolyn Brooks' religious philosophy evolved through the years and developed troubling questions in response to social and human issues, but in spite of those questions her comments through the years reveal certain constants:

1. Belief in the fundamental Christian doctrine of Love
2. Belief in human behavior that flows from Christianity as moral behavior
3. Belief that Christian behavior is essential to a Democracy
4. Belief in the existence of God
5. Belief in the efficacy of prayer
6. Belief in the Bible as a holy book

The very fact that she carried the traditions forward in her own home and that she struggled to reconcile the contradictions between the ideology and the practice of Christianity is evidence of the strength of her personal faith. She was a believer in Christian ideology even though she chose to call it "People," "Living" and "Kindness."

Chapter Three

"The Anniad"

Whom the higher gods forgot,
Whom the lower gods berate;
— Gwendolyn Brooks, "The Anniad"

Gwendolyn Brooks Pulitzer Prize–winning volume of poetry, *Annie Allen* is separated into three sections: Notes from the Childhood and the Girlhood (11 poems), The Anniad (43 stanzas plus three appendix poems), and The Womanhood (15 poems). The book chronicles the life journey and experiences of the poor, black, title character and her relationships. In the book she grows from an innocent girl to a worldly woman. The focus of this chapter is the second section, The Anniad. The poem addresses issues of love and war as they impact the lives of a poor black couple.

This complex poem is highly respected among scholars. Henry Taylor speaks to the poetic technique, " 'The Anniad' is a technical tour de force: 301 lines in 43 seven-line stanzas, employing 30 different rhyme schemes, a compelling meter (trochaic tetrameter catalectic) and a diction that is elaborate, dense and compressed" (260). B.J. Bolden comments on the integration of poetic and social patterns:

> The apex of *Annie Allen* is the mock-epic "The Anniad." Brooks makes a mockery of prosodic and linguistic traditions by exploiting poetic form and language to depict the pretentiousness of social conditions for black Americans, especially women. Although the stanzaic pattern of "The Anniad" may be likened to the classical rhyme royal and the "quick rhythms' to ottava rima,... in reality, Brooks' intentional divergences,... suggest her explicit defiance of any semblance of adherence to poetic form and thus signal her intentional deviance from the strictures of classical prosody [*ll*. 62–3].
>
> Additionally the shifting tone of the work, from compassion, mockery, irony sarcasm, ridicule, disdain and finally, to compassion again, suggests the use of satire as a strategy for embedding the strident voice

of social criticism in a work of art that is "uncompromisingly beautiful, yet socially responsible" [95–96].

The title, a homophone for Vergil's *Aeneid*, evokes literary elevation of the poem. The title character, Annie, common nickname for Anne, suggests important associations. While Brooks herself said, "I forget why I changed it [name] to Annie [from Hester]" (Stavros 46), the elegance of the name Anne in contrast with the original name, Hester, is apparent. Interestingly, the Infancy Gospel of James, allegedly written by James, the brother of Jesus, identifies the mother of Mary as Anna. Although it has never been a part of the New Testament, the Infancy Gospel of James has been influential, particularly in Eastern churches (Kirby 1). Melhem also points out that the name Ann originates in the Hebrew name meaning grace. Annie, a diminutive connotes a small or youthful grace (*Gwendolyn Brooks* 56).

Although Brooks made no reference to those specific allusions, she does acknowledge the elevation of the name, Annie. She stated, "Well, the girl's name was Annie, and it was my little pompous pleasure to raise her to a height that she probably did not have (Stavros 46). Since Brooks was creating Annie as a prototype for African American women in economic and social poverty, it was important to identify her nominally as an elevated figure. In addition, Brooks chose to use religious language, imagery and symbolism to raise Annie and her struggle above the natural realm to the philosophical. Annie starts out spiritually elevated and social circumstances bring about her spiritual demise. Brooks uses a sequence of contrasting images of heaven, hell and pagan ritual to symbolize the psychological and social destruction of Annie.

"The Anniad" is allegorical; it has a dual narrative. It is Annie's story and it is the story of innocence meeting experience. The reader understands the plot from Annie's perspective and also from the perspective of an overseeing omniscient figure, who makes editorial comment on Annie's situation and its moral implications. The symbolic elements of the poem function in the foreground and subordinate the literal details to the background. It has elements of social protest and elements of personal tragedy. Among the myriad of complexities of the work, which can be addressed, this discussion focuses specifically on the dualities and contrasts, which are developed through the religious allusions.

The language Brooks uses in "The Anniad," associates with religion. Lines three and four of the first stanza refer to the "higher gods" and the "lower gods," whose lower case and hierarchical context indicate a pantheon of pagan gods, representing authority in the society, and those affecting the life of innocent Annie. "Those [first five] stanzas initially inspire a mythological vision of a young girl who is 'sweet' but whose 'fate' has already been decided by the higher gods of the dominant white society, as well as 'the lower gods' of her own Black cultural community" (Bolden 97). Kent also comments on Brooks' presentation of Annie's social situation:

> Having inherited the love lore of her country and the disabilities imposed upon her black identity, she is, at the beginning, at once the would-be epic heroine of song and story who moves in fairyland and the black woman vulnerable to special experiences fraught with disillusion. Forgotten by the "the higher gods" and berated by the lower ones she must negotiate [85].

She is filled with the romantic fantasies and the unqualified hopefulness of youth.

Annie is oblivious that she has been forgotten and berated by those gods for she is "Fancying on the featherbed / What was never and is not." She is living with a romanticized vision of her lover. Brooks writes, "And the godhead glitters now / Cavalierly on his brow," alluding to Annie's elevated view of him as godlike (7.2–3). Line four of the same stanza enhances that view with Brooks' words "hot theopathy" to describe the feelings Annie is experiencing. The "theo" root word denotes God, while the suffix "pathy" means disease or suffering. Hot theopathy also alerts the reader that Annie's perception of her lover as godlike and her attraction to him are not only unrealistic but a condition from which she suffers. In that way the reality of Annie's life is set in contrast with her innocent fantasy. Whether the characters in the poem marry legally or not is unclear, but it is clear that they marry spiritually and physically.

Brooks presents additional character contrasts with the language used to describe Annie and Tan Man. Tan Man is presented in elevated, non-religious, even pagan images, in sharp contrast with the religious language that permeates descriptions of Annie and her actions. Metaphorically, Brooks is separating religion from the reality of the situation. Tan Man has no name in the poem because he symbolizes all African American men living in poverty. The prewar Tan Man is presented as a worldly man who takes advantage of the naïve Annie's infatuation. Brooks uses a medieval heroic term to identify him as the "paladin" (3.4, 4.1). In those verses Annie is looking for a hero who is pure, handsome with lofty thoughts. She is looking for someone who is "Ruralist and rather bad, / Cosmopolitan and kind" (4.6–7). What she gets is a man of tan who "eats the green by easy stages. / Nibbles at the root beneath / With intimidating teeth" (6.3–5). He devours her innocence easily and erodes some of her sweet spiritual foundation. Those images evoke pre–Christian fertility rites. Stanza eight tells the reader, "How he postures at his height; / Unfamiliar, to be sure, with celestial furniture." He is arrogant and irreverent. He is not religious. He is wicked. Indeed he follows "the path his pocket chooses" and "Leads her to a lowly room" (9.6–7). He is materialistic and he is bringing her down to a lower level. Brooks' medieval language for Tan Man is evident later in the poem after he returns from the war that forever changes him. Stanza 14 states, "Vaunting hands are now devoid" (1). His boastful arrogance was completely gone. And when he returned from war in stanza 15 Brooks uses the words, "Hies him home" (3). Again, she uses a term that hails from the Old English word *h-i-gian,* meaning "to be intent on" to describe his action (Dictionary.com). He is hastening home with purpose. Not only does the characterization of Tan Man omit religious references, but the medieval language associates him with those tumultuous times when the Crusaders fought against Muslims in the name of Christianity and killed thousands, by some estimates a million people. By characterizing Tan Man as a medieval knight without religious references, Brooks is reinforcing Annie's view of him, but she is making it clear that he is aggressive and violent.

Conversely, Annie's character is described, "Like a nun of crimson ruses / She advances, Sovereign / Leaves the heaven she put him in" (9.3–5). Associating Annie with nuns connotes Christianity, humility and virginity. Annie perceived the Tan Man to be supremely powerful, like God. The capitalization of the word "sovereign" emphasizes that point. When Annie engages in sexual intercourse with Tan Man in stanza ten, she has made a "chapel" of the "lowly room" and "genuflects to love" (10.1–2). She was in an inverted kneeling position, showing her spiritual intentions. Even the surroundings were like those of church with "tender candles ray by ray" (10.6). It is the religious references that focus the reader on the inconsistencies between Annie's romanticized spiritual love and that of Tan Man's coarse physicality. Love is defined, denied and defiled in "The Anniad" with contrasting religious and nonreligious language. "Annie's virginal quality is equated with the newness and freshness of 'green' and the 'springtime of her pride,' while the 'man of tan' is likened to an animal who 'Eats' away at Annie's innocence with 'intimidating teeth'" (Bolden 98). Stanza 11 ends the first movement of the poem with Annie having lost her virginity and cool "Silver" images having replaced the warmth of the candles.

The climax of the poem is the war. Subsequent to Annie's loss of virginity in stanza ten, the poem dramatizes the war Tan Man experiences in stanzas 12, 13 and 14. Brooks description of war merges non–Christian pagan imagery with symbols associated with hell. She places the opening auditory imagistic personification of war, "Doomer, though, crescendo-comes / Prophesying hecatombs" soon after Annie's loss of virginity and the cooling emotions that followed, "Silver flowers fill the eves / Of the metamorphosis" (12.1,11.2). Both actions prophesy hecatombs, which were large-scale sacrifices or slaughters in ancient Greece and Rome — another non–Christian reference. Brooks expands the scale of the destruction to a bloody and deadly event. The duality evokes religious sacrifices, framing Annie's sacrifice as a religious ritual, while the sacrifice of life in war pointed to the personal sacrifice. It was slaughter, like the ancient rituals in which 100 or more oxen were sacrificed. Stanza 12 informs the reader that the condemning Doomer "spits upon the silver leaves, / Denigrates the dainty eves" (12.5–6). The war disparages the love and life Annie and Tan Man might have had together. Not only are there two sacrifices, but Brooks' language implies that the second is as important as the first. While the first involves great numbers in a physical sense and the second involves two people in a spiritual sense, the loss of innocence, happiness and psychological well-being make the second equally as devastating as the first. Stanza 13 places him in the war:

> Where he makes the rifles cough,
> Stutter. Where the reveille
> Is staccato majesty.
> Then to marches. Then to know
> The hunched hells across the sea [13.3–7].

The metaphor for war is hell. The reader is made aware of Annie's deep yearning for Tan Man's return. "But idea and body too / Clamor 'Skirmishes can do. / Then he will come back to you' " (14.5–7). The man of tan returns home, however he is not the same.

Stanzas 16 through 22 chronicle Tan Man's feelings and actions after returning home from the war. He has physical manifestations (16.1, 17.2–7) , and he has psychological manifestations (17.1). He also has difficulty facing the racial divide after having spent his time overseas away from it. "And this white and greater chess / Baffles Tan Man" (18.4–5). And further in stanza 19:

> With his helmet's final doff /
> Soldier lifts his power off. /
> Soldier bare and chilly then /
> Wants his power; back again [1–4].

In stanza 20 he "Shudders for his impotence." In his frustration he rejects his life including Annie, and opts for another woman, thus completely separating himself from her spirituality. Tan Man, who had been unenlightened spiritually before going to war, had now metaphorically gone to hell and now back, is *of* it. He rejects the good he had and embraces the evil he now knows.

The narrator describes Tan Man's mistress as snake-like and evil, "With her tongue tucked in her cheek, / Hissing gauzes in her gaze, / Coiling oil upon her ways" (21.5–7). Here is a clear Garden of Eden reference to a serpent-like, sinful woman. In stanza 22 Brooks expands the hellish and antireligious associations by referring to the mistress as a "banshee" and a "bacchanalian lass with a slit-eyed gypsy moan." Since the banshee of Celtic folklore is a female spirit that wails outside a home to signal death, it fits this case in which there is the death of the love and marriage of Annie and Tan Man. A bacchanalian lass, like those of the ancient Roman festival of Bacchus, would engage in drinking, revelry and sex, again evoking pagan rituals in the portrayal of this woman, who is sinful and nonreligious (Dictionary.com).

Stanzas 23 to 40 focus the reader on Annie's attempts to cope with Tan Man's infidelity and the loss of her idealism. The narrator intones:

> Think of sweet and chocolate
> Minus passing-magistrate,
> Minus passing-lofty light,
> Minus passing-stars for night [23.1–4].

At first Annie seeks solace through winter, spring, summer and fall until "all's a falling falling down." She found no solace. So, she starts testing, then participating in behavior associated with the irreverent lifestyle of the street. She "spins and stretches out to friends / Cries, 'I am bedecked with love!' Cries, 'I am philanthropist!' (28.1–3). In stanza 29, "glass begets glass" and in 31 "Meteors encircle her," (31.2). It appears that she begins drinking and becoming free with her sexual favors. The image of meteors, which are fiery, falling stars, reinforce her spiritual fall and her destruction. The scene evokes images of sin and hellfire raining down upon and around Annie (*NIV Study Bible*, Rev. 13.13; 20.9). The narrator speaks of "scenic bacchanal, / preshrunk and droll prodigal!" (35.1–2). During her fall from grace, the man of tan dies. His illness after the war had been introduced earlier in the poem.

> Tan Man twitches: for for long
> Life was little as sand
> Little as an inch of song... (16.1–3)
> Yet there was a drama...
> with blossom in between /
> Retch and wheeling and cold shout,

Suffocation, with a green
Moist sweet breath for mezzanine (17.1, 4–7).

According to Melhem, "The color green, like that of gold, connects his disease (sometimes associated with green-sickness and itself a symbol of the destruction and destructiveness of his illusions) with Annie, her youth and her parallel self-deceptions" (*Gwendolyn Brooks* 66). Tan Man dies in stanza 37. His death is expressed with images of decay; Annie was by his side. "Now she folds his rust and cough / In the pity old and staunch.... / That is dolesome and is dying" (37.2–3,7). The man of tan leaves behind children, his mistress and Annie, "his devotee to bear / Weight of passing by his chair / And his tavern" (40.1–3). Annie is still devoted to him regardless of all that has happened, and she is saddened by his death.

Unlike the first 22 stanzas, 23 through 42 are without religious references except for the words "prodigal," denoting Annie's sinful behavior and "devotee," previously mentioned. This part of the poem narrates the impact the war had on the man of tan and Annie, their relationship and their morality. Here the absence of religious allusions has the impact that their presence had in the first movement of the poem. This part of the poem chronicles Annie's journey in which she first sought solace in nature, without success. Then she succumbed to the lure of physical pleasures. All this is happening during the difficult time when Tan Man, who rejected her and her sweet spirituality, is dying. The dearth of spiritual references places this movement of the poem squarely in the physical realm in which war causes deaths on more than a physical level. Annie's spiritual deterioration culminates in stanza 41 which symbolizes her loveless sexual encounters:

In the indignant dark there ride
Roughnesses and spiny things
on infallible hundred heels
And a bodiless bee stings.
Harried sods dilate, divide,
Suck her sorrowfully inside [41.1–4F, 6–7].

Her innocence and fertility have died. Stanza 42 informs the reader that "all [is] hay-colored that was green" (3).

In the 43rd and final stanza of the poem Brooks gives the reader a vision of Annie. She is "Fingering faint violet, / Hugging old and Sunday sun" (43.4–5). Both lines symbolize Christian messages. In Christian churches, violet is the color of ministerial vestments traditionally worn during the high holy days leading to Easter. The color connotes the suffering of Jesus Christ on the cross; consistently violet is the color of ministerial garments worn for funeral services. The image of Annie fingering faint violet evokes the image of a person fingering violet vestments and experiencing the suffering and death associated with them. She, too, is a victim of society. In the poem Annie is "hugging ... Sunday sun" (i.e., Sunday son, Jesus Christ) implying that she still holds onto the Christianity that is within her even though her life has been destroyed. In despair she finds solace in her spiritual roots.

The overall structure of the poem utilizes images of heaven and hell to chronicle Annie's story. It is a story of the impact of war on the lives of ordinary people. The recurring images of Medieval, pagan / hellish sexual ritual, in contrast with spiritual love, create a powerful motif. The antithetical images create a dissonant tone, which reflects the dissonance of the war, the relationship and the conflicts Annie and Tan Man engage. The images are essential to the fabric of the poem. Brooks uses them to reveal the characters' traits and their behavior. Brooks associates war with hell and illustrates how the war transformed both Tan Man and Annie. She utilizes hellish and pagan imagery to depict the multiple wars of the poem: the war between nations in which Tan Man soldiers; the war between man and woman in which Tan Man and Annie struggle; the inner war in Tan Man caused by the racism he encounters when he returns to the United States from the war; and the moral war within Annie between innocent fantasy and the realities of her life experience. The wars are seamlessly recounted through one central narrative of the social, psychological, physical and spiritual destruction of Annie. Brooks' imagery flows from the heavenly images of the first 10 stanzas through the blood red and deadly images of the war to the dark images of the final three stanzas. Religious references are integral to the design and thematic development of "The Anniad."

Gwendolyn Brooks attached three poems, Appendix to The Anniad: Leaves from a Loose-Leaf War Diary, as the bridge between the second and third sections of *Annie Allen*. In these poems Brooks has a thoughtful Annie address the effects of war on others in different situations. Two of the poems do not have a religious conceptual aspect, but one does use religious allusion to convey its theme. The first poem is entitled *("thousands — killed in action")* and it discusses the coldness — the detachment one must develop — to hear about people killed in action, day after day. The parentheses and lower case letters in the title imply how such information is minimized by the news media and is received by a jaded public. The poem reads, "You need the untranslatable ice to watch" (1). The third poem is called simply, "the sonnet-ballad." It is a beautiful lament of a young woman for her lover who has been killed in the war. It expresses her sadness and her seeking of her mother's wisdom regarding finding happiness in life.

The second poem, which is untitled, expresses the inconsolable grief one encounters when a loved one has been killed in war. It specifically comments on the Christian tenet that believers will meet again in the afterlife. The poem states, "The Certainty we two shall meet by God / In a wide Parlor, underneath a Light / of lights, come Sometime, is no ointment now" (1–3). The word "Certainty" is capitalized for emphasis, so the underlying faith in the doctrine is affirmed, but the poem's message laments that faith does not assuage grief. The poem expresses the need for physical togetherness now instead of spiritual togetherness later.

The poems in the Appendix to "The Anniad" re-emphasize Brooks' antiwar message, the incongruities between Christian doctrine and the harsh impact of war on individuals in society. The poems also introduce the mature Annie who understands life better after her experiences in "The Anniad." The mature Annie comes into full bloom in *The Womanhood*. Kent speaks of the characterization of Annie in the six opening poems of *The Womanhood*. "The imagery and other devices in the sonnets of 'the children of the poor' suggest a person who takes a tough-minded look at the difficulties of life, meets them courageously, and reveals in the process a richly reflective mind. Life is to be fought for and its unchangeable conditions rigorously faced" (86). Annie's spiritual journey in "The Anniad" prepared her for life as a woman in the world of poverty.

Chapter Four

In the Mecca

Mad life heralding the blue heat of God
snickers in a corner of the west windowsill.
"What have I done, and to the world,
and to the love I promised Mother?"
— Gwendolyn Brooks. "In the Mecca"

"In the Mecca" is artistically and philosophically a pivotal work in Gwendolyn Brooks' repertoire. The book contains this title poem and a series of poems entitled "After Mecca," which conclude with "The Sermon on the Warpland" and "The Second Sermon on the Warpland." (See Chapter Six.) The book was Brooks' last collection of poetry to be published by a mainstream press in 1968 and arguably was the first one to reflect the influence of the Black Arts Movement which spanned the period from the mid–1960s to the mid–1970s.

> Both inherently and overtly political in content, the Black Arts movement was the only American literary movement to advance "social engagement" as a sine qua non of its aesthetic. The movement broke from the immediate past of protest and petition (civil rights) literature and dashed forward toward an alternative that initially seemed unthinkable and unobtainable: Black Power [Salaam 1].

"In the Mecca" mirrors ideas of the movement, however it also contains statements advocating social justice that Brooks had been making in earlier poems. Stylistically, she reflected the complexity of the social condition of Black America with complex strategies that interfaced traditional poetic conventions with free verse.

The title poem "In the Mecca" is narrative and is comprised of 57 stanzas of irregular lengths. The plot development is linear, however the development of the catalog of characters and intermittent philosophical digressions give it the impressionistic aspect of a collage. It is Brooks' longest single work with 807 lines. The poem combines some of Brooks' primary social and thematic concerns with a prophetic poetic voice. Among the issues the poem examines are (a) the protection of children, (b) the impact of poverty on individual psychological development and attitudes, (c) the impact of poverty on family life, (d) the attitudes of law enforcement officials toward the urban poor, (e) the role of faith and religion in the lives of the poor, (f) the necessary nexus between African and African American consciousness, and (g) the need for social and legal justice for African Americans. This poem epitomizes the heart and soul of Brooks' poetry by dramatizing the human aspects of racism and poverty, like hopelessness, disillusionment and despair. Kent contends, "During the 1960s the deepest poem to portray the deadened hopelessness of urban blacks which exploded in the city rebellions was (and is) 'In the Mecca' which appeared in the book by that title in 1968" (Kent 66). The poem is political, poetic and prophetic. The poem anticipates much of the political and social unrest of the succeeding years.

The poem narrates the events surrounding a hard working, domestic black mother's search for her missing child, Pepita; it depicts her anguish and her encounters with family, residents of the building and law enforcement. Amid the chaos of the crisis, social, cultural and religious philosophers offer commentary on the greater meaning of the events and the ramifications and reverberations they signal regarding the civil rights movement. In the poem the building takes on a persona that influences the thoughts and actions of the residents. Williams sees the building as a jail-like trap that is confining its residents. "As the search for Pepita continues and the reader is introduced to various characters, one becomes aware that these people are trapped not only by their dreams of urban life, but also by the Mecca itself" (62). "In the Mecca" is dramatic. It is both concrete and abstract. It is social and political. It is spiritual.

The poem is set in an apartment building that was on the south side of Chicago called the Mecca. It was designed by a world renowned architect, Ludwig Mies van der Rohe, who is named in the opening stanza. When it was built in 1891, it was seen as a prototype for luxury apartment buildings in the 20th century. It was a four-story tourist attraction with two atrium courtyards, skylights, fountains, flower gardens and intricate wrought iron balconies (Bluestone 1–2). While it had been designed to be an apartment building for the wealthy, the wealthy population migrated to the north side of Chicago early in the 20th century and the Great Depression followed. Time, the deterioration of the building and the economics of its tenants turned the once elegant building into a slum tenement building. Brooks had personal knowledge of the building because she worked for four months as secretary to a spiritual advisor who was housed in the Mecca after she graduated from Wilson Junior College in 1936. Brooks described her position.

> I was to be a secretary to a Dr. E.N. French, who turned out to be a spiritual advisor. He had a storefront and four secretaries, all of whom were kept busy answering letters, taking the money out of the envelopes, and giving it to him. He would mail the people who sent in money anything they asked for — holy thunderbolts, charms, dusts of different kinds, love potions, heaven knows what all. The secretaries were also expected to help make up some of these charms. He had a regular little bottling operation. Some of his clientele lived or worked in the Mecca Building, and I delivered potions and charms and got to know some of these people. Oh, it was a bleak condition of life [Newquist 28].

So she saw the Mecca and interacted with the residents first hand. Brooks quoted John Bartlow Martin's description of the Mecca building on the back of her title page. In part it states, "A great gray hulk of brick, four stories high, topped by an ungainly smokestack.... The Mecca Building is U-shaped. The dirt courtyard is littered with newspapers and tin cans, milk cartons and broken glass.... Iron fire escapes run up the building's face and ladders reach from them to the roof" (G. Brooks, *Blacks* 404). The discarded trash became a symbol for the discarded people who lived in the Mecca.

The notion that the building and its residents were societal outcasts is also argued by Williams:

> The Mecca became a symbol for the colossal failure of at least one aspect of urban life.... Estimates of the number of people who lived in the building ranged from three to nine thousand. Nobody seemed to know for certain, and no one apparently cared. But the Mecca's great hulk warned a city of its failure to come to terms with change and reminded a group of urban isolates that they had been consigned to the bowels of the city. Razed in 1952, the Mecca remains in memory as a symbol of absolute urban blight [60–61].

Williams' interpretation of the symbolism is shared by other scholars. "This old Mecca, of course, is more than just a run-down apartment house for Negroes; it is a microcosm of the ghettos of all the Northern cities. Its blight, never stated but implied, is the blight that comes from being black and poor" (Davis 101). And Kent states, "The poem is concerned with a universe of misery that extends beyond Chicago, geographically and historically. Its form is essentially that of a series of interrelated vignettes that reveal the pervasiveness of the ills expressed by the central catastrophe" (218).

Although the building was actually named Mecca, it also conjured up political and symbolic implications for African Americans in the 1960s. In 1964 Muslim civil rights Leader Malcolm X made a widely publicized religious pilgrimage to the Holy City of Mecca.* After he interacted with Moslems of all races there, he came to believe in the possibility of racial equality among humankind. His politics changed from one of separatism to one of unity and brotherhood. He returned from Mecca even more committed to social equality because he had seen equality at work among Moslems there. As an African American who had experienced black poverty and who had gone to the Holy City of Mecca, he was the embodiment of hope for social justice for the residents of the Mecca. He was assassinated in 1965. Although Brooks makes no direct reference to Malcolm X in this poem, the time and the message of the poem associate in the name Mecca. His assassination and the death of his hope parallels the hopelessness expressed in the poem "In the Mecca."

While the building was named the Mecca, in fact, Brooks utilizes the spiritual and social symbolism the name evokes to develop the poem. Set against the literary backdrop of Mecca, the Holy City of Islam, the concrete reality of the inhabitants of the Mecca building establishes artistic tension between the concrete and the ethereal — the personal and the universal — the daily journey and the spiritual journey of life. Since Mecca is the destination of a pilgrimage to find spiritual enlightenment, the juxtaposition of the two Meccas is ironic, indeed. Miller also makes the point: "The Chicago Mecca, in this light, becomes ironic when one considers the other Mecca, the holiest city of Islam and birthplace of Mohammed" ("Define ... the Whirlwind" 148). "The name 'Mecca' has acquired the connotation of a special focus or goal. Combining literal and figurative referents, the building achieves its bitter apotheosis as Brooks' central image" (Melhem, "In the Mecca" 168).

The residents, who are also on a life journey, seeking fulfillment, will not reach their goals because of social oppression. Their dreams will not come to fruition just as Mrs. Sallie has no hope of finding her lost Pepita. It can be said, "Her [Mrs. Sallie Smith's] frantic pilgrimage through the Mecca forms the action" of the poem (Melhem, "In the Mecca" 167). And further, "The woman's frantic pilgrimage through the building reveals a failed socioeconomic system, a failed art, a failed religion and their spawn of isolation and rage" (Melhem, "Afterword" 153). Mrs. Smith and all the

---

*Gwendolyn Brooks had great admiration for Malcolm X as evidenced by the elegy to him that she included in the "After Mecca" poems. In it she said, "He opened us — / who was the key, / who was a man." He was assassinated in February 1965.

residents of the Mecca are seeking a socio-economic revival, but Brooks asserts they, and the society at large, need a spiritual one to make the other one happen.

The Christian elements in the poem are introduced even before the poem begins. The epigraph to the title states, "Now the way of the Mecca was on this wise." The epigraph parallels Matthew 1.18 in the King James Version of the Bible, "Now the birth of Jesus Christ was on this wise." "On this wise" is also translated as "was as follows" (New American Standard) or "came about" (New International Version). So, the "way of the Mecca" being "on this wise" signifies that the story of the Mecca was yet to come and that history culminated in the Mecca being the way it was. The tenses corroborate this view, since the epigraph is written in the past tense while the poem, itself, is written in the present tense.

> The religious impulse of "In the Mecca" is cued by the homiletic epigraph set apart on the verso page preceding the poem:... This line was originally the last line of the poem and remained there as late as September 1967 in a revised fragment sent to Harper's The transposition, of course, lends a biblical tone. A parable is forthcoming [Melhem, "In the Mecca" 167].

Religious references are integral to the fabric of the poem. The role of Christianity in the poem can be viewed from various perspectives. Shaw focuses on the role of religion in the survival of African Americans as it is expressed "In the Mecca." "The importance of religion as a device to effect survival through restraint is clearly demonstrated in 'In the Mecca.' While not all the examples of restraint in this poem are directly religious in nature, most of them have religious overtones.... Miss Brooks' treatment of the black man's simultaneous sustaining of physical and spiritual life by maintaining a fine balance between restraint and militance has been demonstrated in ... 'In the Mecca.'" (140, 145).

An explication of religious elements in the poem reveals Brooks' methodology. Gwendolyn Brooks integrates religion "In the Mecca" in two ways. First, the literary elements include religious language, imagery, symbolism, themes and biblical allusions. Second, Christian beliefs are presented in three ways: (1) characters who represent various levels and types of religious beliefs, (2) characters and speakers who are social and religious prophets, and (3) messages of ideal Christian love for humankind. The poem examines the spiritual reality of the world in the Mecca, along with the physical reality of that environment. The analysis here will examine Mecca building residents and the individual and familial issues affecting them. It will analyze social forces that impact the residents such as poverty and law enforcement. In addition it will show how Brooks utilized the religious and political philosophies evident in the Mecca to create a living spirit of the Mecca building, a specter decrying the present circumstance and future results of racial and economic inequality. The discourse will focus on the characters of Mecca, the community of Mecca and the spirit of Mecca.

The first three lines of the poem set the thematic context of falling from grace. The first lines of the poem, "Sit where the light corrupts your face. / Mies Van der Rohe retires from grace. / And the fair fables fall," (1.1–3). They illustrate the Genesis narrative of humankind's fall from grace as a result of human disobedience and the human expulsion from the utopian Garden of Eden that resulted. In this context Brooks draws a parallel between the Mecca, which had been corrupted by society's evil and neglect, and the Garden of Eden, which had also been corrupted by evil. In both cases metaphoric death was the result. The word "light" in the first line of the poem also associates with Jesus Christ. Even the reference to "face" suggests a reference to Jesus Christ, inasmuch as Christians symbolically seek Jesus' face for spiritual guidance on earth and hope to see his face for eternity. Lines two and three end with the words "grace" and "fall" respectively. The theme of the fall permeates the several layers of the poem. The building has fallen into disrepair; the community has stopped caring for one another; the morale and spirit of the community have fallen into hopelessness. It sets the tone for the moral decadence that has resulted in the loss of Pepita and the apathetic attitudes of the residents and the police officers. Gayl Jones contends that

> Brooks' narrator points us toward the Mecca and toward the community, but she uses the imagery and language of the community's more decorative, formal traditions and self-conscious poetic forms, the oratory, the sermon, the spiritual, the proverb. The narrator directs us: "now the way of the Mecca was on this wise." Although the language is elevated, we the readers are still being spoken to; we are addressed and made to not simply observe or read, but to enter and participate in the poem and the upcoming search [Jones 196].

The Characters of Mecca

In the second stanza of the poem Brooks introduces Mrs. Sallie to the reader. Her mailbox reads S. Smith. She is the prototypical single mother coming home from work. It is significant that she is "Mrs." Sallie, informing the reader that she was married at some time in the past. Her name is common and generic to emphasize her typicality. Brooks describes

Mrs. Sallie's mouth as "absurd with the last sourings of the master's Feast" (5). She is returning home, but the capital letter "F" presents an obvious reference to the Holy Sacrament of Communion. Like the reference in line one of the poem, there is a negative aspect to this encounter with Christianity. It is the sour taste Mrs. Sallie retains, not the sweetness of the spiritual food the sacrament represents. It is the antithesis of what she should retain. Even Brooks' use of the word "absurd" adds irony and a tone that mocks the experience and subtly foreshadows the horror Mrs. Sallie will face when she reaches home. Shaw's interpretation of the passage focuses on the spiritual uplift she received. "Miss Brooks, by referring to the 'unrinsed eye' and the remnants from the 'master's Feast' still tasted, makes an allusion to the celebration of the Eucharist and indicates that Mrs. Sallie's perception is still influenced by the religious service" (141). Both perspectives prepare the reader to feel what Mrs. Sallie feels when she learns of Pepita's disappearance. Both connect with the descriptors for her at the end of stanza two. She is referred to metaphorically as a fragrant "district hymn." She is the embodiment of religious music. She is spirit-filled and carries a message of love. However, another important irony must also be noted here. Mrs. Sallie delayed her arrival home to participate in the sacrament. That raises the question of whether her earlier arrival at home might have resulted in Pepita being safe. Again, Brooks is showing how religion may be a hindrance, not a help, in the life of this poor woman.

Stanza nine, which chronicles Mrs. Sallies' entrance into her kitchen, which "is bad, is bad, / her eyes say," quotes her as saying,

> "But all my lights are little!"
> Her denunciation
> slaps savagely not only this sick kitchen but
> her Lord's annulment of the main event.
> "I want to decorate!" [8–12].

Her kitchen is tattered and worn out. She would like to make it better, but she cannot. According to the poem's narrative voice, Jesus "her Lord" has declared her life invalid; her life is void, so she does not have the means to change her circumstance. These three references (the master's Feast, the district hymn and the Lord's annulment of the main event) connect imagistically and symbolically in the kitchen. Mrs. Sallie has little spiritual and physical food to sustain her life. She is practicing her religion, but it is not helping her condition.

Allusions to Jesus appear in other parts of the poem. Stanza 13, which is describing Mrs. Sallie's son Briggs, who has succumbed to the lure of the street gangs, is a good example.

Briggs, how "easy," finally, to accept (after the shriek and / repulsion) /
the unacceptable evil. To proceed with some éclat; some salvation of the
face; awake! To choke the chickens, file their blood" [21–25].

This passage includes references to salvation and blood that has been "filed"
or retained for future use. Both allude to the very heart of Christian doctrine in which Jesus Christ shed his blood and sacrificed his life for the
salvation of all mankind. Briggs is a sacrificial lamb; like Jesus, society has
crucified him. Poverty has claimed him as its victim. Briggs fought the
invitation to go the gang route, as the words "after the shriek and repulsion"
express, but he finally took the path of least resistance and went the designated "evil" route. Stanza 16 queries, "What shall their [thin poor children's] redeemer be?" and answers, "Greens and hock of ham" (7, 9). The
passage expresses the priority of survival needs in the lives of the poor.
"Physical needs must precede spiritual ones. The children are hungry"
(Melhem in Wright 169).

During the first part of the poem, references to Jesus in the language
essentially question what Christian faith is doing for people who are living
in poverty in the Mecca. Later in the poem Brooks incorporates the voice
of Jesus in the quote that opens this chapter. Stanza 47 reads,

> Mad life heralding the blue heat of God
> snickers in a corner of the west windowsill.
> "What have I done, and to the world,
> and to the love I promised Mother?" [35–38].

The sun (i.e., Son) is the heat and life-giving force for the world, and the
blue portion of a flame is the center and hottest part. Yet, here it is snickering, as if a cosmic joke has been played on the world. Still, there is
sadness and regret in the words of Christ to His mother Mary. Here Jesus
is lamenting the lack of love in the world and expressing regret at what
had become of his creation. It mirrors the feeling expressed in *In
Emmanuel's Nightmare* (see Chapter Five). The comment on the lack of
love, which is the core precept of Christianity, is at the center of both
poems' message for society.

At first blush the characters of "In the Mecca" appear to be a mixture
of types and orientations, but a closer look reveals that the development of
major characters in the poem constitute a spectrum of religious beliefs. Each
exemplifies a type of religious attitude. A religious paradigm provides important insights into the poem. There are three major divisions: (a) characters
representing Judeo-Christian beliefs and practices, (b) characters who are
false prophets and worshippers of false gods, and (c) characters who are
true prophets and philosophers. A discussion of each division follows.

Judeo-Christian Believers

Two characters portray Judaism in the poem. During the time dramatized in the poem, the 1940s and 1950s, African Americans often followed Jews into less expensive urban housing. Consequently, a few Jews sometimes remained after the demographic had turned over. Such is the case in the Mecca. The poem has two Jewish characters, Edie Barrow and Loam Norton.

Edie Barrow is a young woman who had a summer romance with a young man, who was "a Gentile boy. / All creamy-and-golden fair" She, on the other hand had "long black eyes. / And he played with my long black hair" (45.2–5). They had sexual encounters and he whispered sweet words to her, however, "Love did not guess in the tight-packed dark / it was flesh of varying kind" (12–13). She loved him without regard for his religious beliefs, however he was using her for sex, while his "gentle Gentile" girlfriend "waited to strap him down" (16–17). Ultimately, he marries the "gentle Gentile" and Edie is left with "a hungry tooth in her breast" (21). The hungry tooth expresses her yearning for him, but it is also a direct reference of the retributive justice she desires. Old Testament scriptures provide for "eye for eye, tooth for tooth" justice (Ex. 21.24, Lev 24.20, Deut. 19.21). Edie is seeking justice for the discrimination she endures as a Jew. But, that discrimination is also against African Americans; it is against women; it is against the poor; it is against other groups who are not in privileged positions in American society.

Some readers interpret Edie as an African American woman, however the specific reference to "Gentile" and "hungry tooth" seem to disqualify that view. On the other hand the discrimination and insensitive treatment that Brooks is portraying is consistent regardless of Edie's ethnicity. Melhem, who sees her as African American, also sees this segment as a reinforcement of the theme of "the fall" previously discussed.

> The ballad of Edie Barrow tells of a "fair" wealthy lover who will marry a "Gentile girl 'come fall, come falling of fall'" while he retains his black mistress. Repetition of "fall" connects with the theme of declining white culture. "Fall" also summons the fall from innocence in the Garden of Eden, Edie's paradisaic innocence (like that of Annie Allen). Her treacherous lover destroys her ingenuous hopes, revealing them as " a fair fable" [Melhem in Wright 168].

Further, Melhem asserts,

> This lyrical interlude [Edie Barrow] poises before the wider hope / despair oscillations in the last third of the poem. It illustrates white perfidy and the exploitation of blacks — and of women generally (the

lover also manipulates his future bride) — by white society. At the same time, it broadens the work to include lyrical expression of a major theme" [Melhem in Wright 178].

The Ballad of Edie Barrow, which is often excerpted and printed as a separate poem, is a significant poetic moment in the Mecca. It symbolizes the hope of the *have-nots* in American society to merge with the *haves* and gain parity. Again, the hopelessness of that dream for those in the Mecca is shown in the abortive ending of the relationship.

Loam Norton is a fascinating character. Like most characters in Mecca, Loam Norton worries more about his own concerns than about Mrs. Sallie's daughter. He remembers Belsen and Dachau, the prison camps of World War II and interjects a searing parody of the 23rd Psalm into the poem. He is also viewed here as a Jewish character because of his references to concentration camps Belsen and Dachau in the opening lines of stanza 28. Is he acknowledging that the Mecca is a ghetto, like the death camps? With reference to the residents of Mecca, Melhem says, "Their fate borders that of the concentration camp inmates of Belsen and Dachau in a deeply moving reflection by Loam Norton. His name denoting earth, he is one of the few caring individuals in the Mecca" (Wright 169). One wonders whether he recognizes the futility in the day-to-day existence of the inhabitants of both. The parallel is reinforced with his line-by-line parody of Psalm 23. It is reprinted here from the King James Version with the parallel lines from stanza 27 of the poem in italics. Loam Norton's concluding comment is, "I am not remote, not unconcerned." That statement makes it clear that he shares the misery of the inhabitants of Mecca because of the history of suffering Jewish people have endured.

[1]The LORD is my shepherd; I shall not want.

The Lord was their Shepherd. / Yet did they want.

[2]He maketh me to lie down in green pastures: he leadeth me beside the still waters.

Joyfully would they have lain in jungles or pastures, / walked beside waters.

[3]He restoreth my soul: he leadeth me in the paths of righteousness for his name's sake.

Their gaunt / souls were not restored, their souls were banished.

[4]Yea, though I walk through the valley of the shadow of death, I will fear no evil: for thou art with me; thy rod and thy staff they comfort me.

They feared the evil, whether with or without God. / They were comforted by no Rod, / no Staff, but flayed by, O besieged by, shot a-plenty.

[5]Thou preparest a table before me in the presence of mine enemies: thou anointest my head with oil; my cup runneth over.

The prepared table was the rot or curd of the day. / Annointings were of lice. Blood was the spillage of cups.

[6]Surely goodness and mercy shall follow me all the days of my life: and I will dwell in the house of the LORD forever.

Goodness and mercy should follow them / all the days of their death. / They should dwell in the house of the Lord forever / and, dwelling, save a place for me [4–18].

The parody underscores Norton's view that faith is futile in circumstances of oppression. He asserts that the faith of the Jews did not help them in the camps. He says, "They should dwell in the house of the Lord forever." There is no certainty that they will, just that they *should*. He does, however, express a glimmer of hope for the faithful in the last phrase, "save a place for me." He is skeptical, but he hopes his faith will get him to heaven. In addition to the religious commentary inherent in the Loam Norton passage, there is the universalizing of the Meccans suffering, even beyond other urban areas of the United States. "Loam Norton broadens the picture of misery, historically and geographically, and clearly connects the Mecca scene with that of all disinherited. His voice gains power through a parody of the 23rd Psalm — a reflection upon a god who has not taken care of business" (Kent 216).

In addition to creating identifiably Jewish characters, Gwendolyn Brooks also created distinctly Christian characters in the Mecca. Mrs. Sallie, who has already been discussed, was described in the first two stanzas in religious terms. Those images paint a picture of a sweet, spiritual woman. Stanza four also says, "She is 'all innocent of saints and signatures, nods [to old St. Julia] and consents, content to endorse the Lord as an incense and a vintage'" (4.2–4). Thus, Mrs. Sallie Smith is shown to be one who does not know a lot about those held to be holy by the church, nor has she studied holy writing, so her knowledge of doctrine is limited. However, she accepts Jesus Christ as Lord and participates in the rituals and traditions of the church. She walks in faith, although she does not reach for deeper understanding.

Like Mrs. Sallie Smith, Old St. Julia Jones is presented as a character with strong Christian faith. The reader first notices that she is designated as old and identified as a saint. She holds a venerated position in the African American community as one who has the wisdom of age and the exceptional holiness or virtue of a saint. Yet, Brooks fixes her firmly in the Mecca community with her common last name, Jones. She is a prototypical religious mother figure. Her name, Julia, has biblical importance. Julia was a Roman Christian woman to whom Paul sent his salutations at the end of his Epistle when he sent greetings to the named, faithful members of the early Roman church (Rom. 16.15). Old St. Julia Jones, like Julia in the Holy Bible, was a true Christian. "We first meet St. Julia Jones, whose sermonic rhythms, biblical strategies in dialogue 'rich with Bible,' perhaps, clue us to (and hark back to) the nature of the beginning of the poem, giving the key to the literary influences of the poet / narrator's own voice" (G. Jones 197). Here Jones is referring to the religious imagery in the opening stanzas, particularly that which relates to Mrs. Sallie, thus is affirming Brooks' religious framework within the poem.

Stanza three opens with Julia rising from "amenable knees." She has submitted to her faith. Further she experiences spiritual joy "Isn't He wonderful wonderful!... Isn't our Lord the greatest to the brim?" (4–5). She goes on to say, "He is the light of my life," reinforcing the earlier light references. Stanza three ends with her statement, "Oh, how I love the Lord." Brooks uses a number of poetic techniques to let the audience know that St. Julia's faith in Jesus reflects the basic element of Christian doctrine. Her view of Jesus' role in her life, her prayer and religious practices are consistent. Yet those ideas are interrupted with lines like, "And I lie late past the still pastures. And meadows" and "He hunts me up the coffee for my cup." The first of those lines is an obvious play on the 23rd Psalm, which is paraphrased later in the poem by Loam Norton, with allusion to the green pastures. These "still" pastures are not fertile; they are unyielding, unfruitful and immovable. That one phrase undercuts some of the hope and optimism of old St. Julia's character. Even the notion of Jesus "hunting me up the coffee" undercuts the accepted portrayal of Jesus whose divinity would preclude the need to hunt up provision for His flock. So, even though old St. Julia is the prototypical Christian character, Brooks clouds the picture of her as a devoted Christian with references to the difficulties poor followers have meeting basic survival needs. Again, Brooks is interjecting conflicting messages about the efficacy of religion in their lives.

Pops Pinkham is mentioned only briefly in the poem, but Brooks grants him significant status by giving him his own stanza, albeit only three lines. The placement of this stanza refers back to submissive, old St. Julia on "amenable knees" in the preceding stanza. Pops Pinkham represents the Christian who doubts the meek behavior encouraged by the Christian faith. He "is somewhat doubtful of a specific right, / to inherit the earth or to partake of it now." It is apparent that he has had Christian teaching, as the language he is citing alludes to the Beatitudes from Jesus' Sermon on the Mount. His words refer specifically to verse five, which states, "Blessed are the meek: for they shall inherit the earth" (Matt. 5.3–12). It was later in the Sermon on the Mount that Jesus specifically rejects the Old Testament response to injustice and replaces it with a Christian response. "You have heard that it was said, 'Eye for eye, and tooth for tooth.' But I tell you, do not resist an evil person. If anyone slaps you on the right cheek, turn to them the other cheek (Matt. 5.38–39). Pops Pinkham, on the other hand, recognizes that their present condition resulted, in part, from a meek reaction to society's circumstances and wonders whether one should "partake" of one's earthly inheritance now. His use of the biblical word "partake" indicates a connection to biblical teaching. But, he is advocating strong action and the immediate *taking* of what is needed. He doubts that it will come after meek behavior later. Brooks is using Pops Pinkham to question whether biblical teaching will provide strategies to attain social justice *now*.

Aunt Dill is a very complex character. She sees herself "at that moment of the Thousand Souls is a Christ-like creature, Doing Good" (37.14–15). She sees herself as being Christian but her comments to Mrs. Sallie are not consistent with Christian beliefs or behavior. The reader meets Aunt Dill in the 37th stanza of the poem. By that time the police have come and gone, so the dramatic tension surrounding Pepita's disappearance and the family's stress is high. The poem states, "Aunt Dill arrives to help them" (37.1), but she begins by telling them about another little girl who had disappeared, who was found dead and disfigured after having been molested. Clearly, those are not comforting words. "She tells a horror story about a 'Little girl got raped and choked to death last week.' Another paradoxical figure, Aunt Dill calls herself 'doing good,' yet even her 'pianissimos and apples' are sinister" (G. Jones 201). She appears again in stanza 54 where the reader is presented with a more comprehensive description of her. She is a widow with no children, who has lovely rich furnishings in her home. We are told, "Dill is woman-in-love-with-God. / Is not / true-child-of-God — for are we ever to / be children? — are we never to mature" (54.14–18). She is the austere Christian who has never grown in faith to have heartfelt love and sensitivity to others. Although Aunt Dill considers herself to be a "woman in love with God," she gives no real assistance to Sallie, whose anxiety (and the reader's) she only intensifies. In addition, she is childless and cannot identify fully with Sallie's feelings. This passage also alludes to her putting on Tabu and that she is trying to forget the hand of God. All of those elements point to disparity within Aunt Dill's religion, which is sterile and a true Christian religion. There is disparity between the behavior she *should* exhibit as a Christian and that which she *does* exhibit. As her name suggests, she is the *sour* unyielding version of Christianity. Brooks, herself, includes Aunt Dill in her poem "family picture": "In the Mecca / Aunt Dill extends / sinister pianissimos and apples" (G. Brooks, *Report from Part Two*, 122, lines 9–10). Aunt Dill is a hypocrite. She is not doing good; she is doing evil in the name of Christian good, yet she does not understand her heresy. The reference to her "extending apples" is arguably a reference to the serpent in the Garden of Eden offering the forbidden fruit (often depicted as an apple) to Eve, which enhances her character as one with a Christian appearance and an evil inner spirit.

False Prophets and Worshippers of Other Gods

There are also characters who worship other gods in the sense that their faith and daily focus is moderated by a belief in something other than traditional religion that informs their behaviors, as well as false prophets who pretend to be religious, but are not.

Way-Out Morgan spends his time "collecting guns" and "Remembering three local-and-legal beatings," "his sister mob-raped in Mississippi" and "mates in the Mississippi River ... with black bodies once majestic" (51.12–13, 22–23). Way-Out Morgan is angry. He is seeking revenge for the racist atrocities African Americans have suffered. He holds to the Old Testament doctrine of retributive justice. Way-Out Morgan has faith in revenge, violence and death. He "fills fearsomely / on visions of Death-to-the-Hordes-of-the-White-Men! Death!" (5–7) and "predicts the Day of Debt — pay shall begin, / the Day of Demon-diamond, / of blood in mouths and body-mouths, / of flesh-rip in the Forum of Justice at last!" (18–21). He is so zealous in his beliefs that he barely eats or has sex with his woman. His primal physical needs are set aside while his spiritual ones are fed by his religion, which is vengeance.

Enrico Jason, the lawyer, who speaks for his client Prophet Williams is described in stanza 46 from different perspectives. He is described physically as dark skinned and rotund. He is described politically as one who "enhances Lawmen." His actions within the community assist the anti-community forces imposed on it by the police. With the negativity surrounding lawmen in this community, and in this situation specifically, Enrico Jason is portrayed as a participant in the neglect of this poor community. He is part of the insensitivity to this poor community; he intensifies it through his work. There is also a spiritual and ethical element to his short description. It is said that he will lie beside "his Prophet in bright blood, a rhythm of stillness above the nuances" (46.45–47). This passage is revealing. First, there is the notion that he and Prophet Williams are bleeding their people, taking their money, preying on their hopes and dreams. It is an inversion of the Christian notion that the shedding of Jesus' blood provided salvation and eternal life for believers; on the contrary this blood from Jason and Williams is draining lives and leading to a spiritual death for those who follow them. Then, there is the image of both he and Prophet Williams lying dead, concretely and symbolically indicating that they are dead spiritually and ethically. Few lines are devoted to Enrico Jason, but he is a prototypical sycophant who cannot be ignored. He is an evil element in the community. He worships Prophet Williams and personal gain.

The most apparent character who worships another "god" is the false prophet, Prophet Williams. While he calls himself a prophet, in fact he is a hustler. When the reader meets him in stanza four, the speaker indicates that Williams knows the Bible, he is full of blemishes and "reeks with lust for his disciple." Both lust as one listed among Christian deadly sins and the word "disciple" show his perversion of the role of spiritual counselor. He is a fraud. In stanza 46 the reader also learns that "his suit is shabby and slick" although "he is not poor" (5). So, he is base on yet another level. His spirit, body and clothing all reflect his damaged and soiled soul. In addition, the reader is told that his deceased wife "died alone" (4.14) in "self-defense" (4.11) so she too had been under attack and suffered death as the outcome of a relationship with him, a fate that others who believe him will also suffer.

Brooks uses images that reference Prophet Williams as "an engine of candid steel hugging combustibles" (4.7–8). He is machine, not human, and his fire, unlike God's holy fire, is manmade. He embodies destructive fire and can set others on fire. Those who wage war against God's people are sometimes depicted in the Bible as machine-like.

> The locusts looked like horses prepared for battle. On their heads they wore something like crowns of gold, and their faces resembled human faces. Their hair was like women's hair, and their teeth were like lions' teeth. They had breastplates like breastplates of iron, and the sound of their wings was like the thundering of many horses and chariots rushing into battle. Their breastplates were fiery red, dark blue, and yellow as sulfur. The heads of the horses resembled the heads of lions, and out of their mouths came fire, smoke and sulfur [Rev. 9.7–9, 17].

In the case of Prophet Williams in the Mecca, he is certainly warring against the people by taking advantage of them. The Bible also foretells a fiery end for false prophets like Prophet Williams. His is the fire that associates with damnation for false prophets.

> But the beast was captured, and with it the false prophet who had performed the signs on its behalf. With these signs he had deluded those who had received the mark of the beast and worshiped its image. The two of them were thrown alive into the fiery lake of burning sulfur [Rev. 19.20].
>
> They will be tormented day and night for ever and ever [Rev. 20.10b].

Yet, Prophet Williams has many followers in the Mecca. He is persuasive: "One visit will convince you" (46.26). He is adept at deceiving people into thinking he can solve their problems.

Although a religious leader would be concerned about Pepita's disappearance on a moral and a human level and would seek to lend comfort, Prophet Williams is unconcerned. The passage in which he is asked whether he has seen Pepita cites his yawn preliminary to his question, "Pepita who?" (46.1). In this stanza the reader learns how he makes his money and what his priorities are. People pay him for various magical remedies for their problems and receive lucky numbers for gambling. He provides "Holy Thunderbolts, and Love Balls too" (46.15) for those with difficulties in love relationships. He provides a magic cloth to wrap around one follower's paralytic leg. Enrico Jason, his lawyer, sums up Prophet Williams' profession as one who will "help you hold your job ... give you trading stamps and kisses,... Lucky days and Lucky Hands. Lifts you from Sorrow and the Shadows. Heals the body" (46.15–29). All of those are contrary to the work of a religious leader. He is the quintessential false prophet — a prophet for profit. There are numerous biblical admonitions against false prophets who promise rewards to others but only deliver rewards to themselves. "And many false prophets shall rise, and shall deceive many" (Matt. 24.11). Prophet Williams is certainly deceiving many and he is supporting himself by deceiving those who seek solutions for their problems. He is an antagonist to Christian principles in the way he presents himself and the way he treats others.

The most inhumane and nonreligious character is the collective set of policemen who are referred to simply as The Law. Brooks capitalization of both words may allude to the Mosaic Law or Ten Commandments, which are referred to biblically as The Law. The phrase is used more than 300 times in the Bible, referring to the Judeo-Christian code of conduct for moral behavior. But Brooks' use of the phrase includes social applications. She sets the stage for the entrance of The Law in stanza 35 with rhetorical questions that ask how they will respond to the situation in which an innocent little black girl is missing. Then, The Law arrives. They are late; they have little motivation to pursue this case aggressively. They take the complaint from the distraught Mrs. Sallie and leave "with likeness of a 'southern' belle" (36.1). They view her as a stereotypical black woman, not an individual. She is a poor black women from the south living in an impoverished environment, not a loving mother whose child is lost. When they return, they set out to question the neighbors, and even in that endeavor, they are insensitive. They "pound" (38.2) a dozen doors in a building that has thousands of inhabitants. Clearly, they were neither conducting a thorough investigation nor making this a high priority case. When we meet the officers again in stanza 50 the narrator charges, "Officers!— / do you nearly wish you had not come into this room?" (1–2). The officers are questioning 60-year-old twin sisters who have not seen Pepita, yet they do not want to enter the apartment. They want to remain apart from the people who live in the Mecca. Their inquiry does not go beyond the surface. The reader's final meeting with The Law occurs in stanza 56 when they question the murderer himself. "The murderer of Pepita / looks at The Law unlovably, Jamaican / Edward denies and thrice-denies a dealing / of any dimension with Mrs. Sallie's daughter" (3–6). So The Law is not just late, unmotivated, insensitive, and unwilling to do the job, they are also ineffective. Ironically, they do interview the murderer and do not identify him as such. For the residents of the Mecca, the law is as false as Prophet Williams. The policemen are pretending to represent the laws of the United States, however, they too are hustling the inhabitants of the Mecca. Here Brooks' allusion creates dramatic irony. The policemen in the poem are the antithesis of the Judeo-Christian tenets set forth by Mosaic Law. In theory they have faith in the secular laws of the United States, which they represent, but in practice they demonstrate that their *faith* does not extend to communities of those who are poor and black like those in the Mecca.

True Prophets and Philosophers

Brooks narrates the story of Pepita's disappearance with a parallel set of commentators who intervene in the action reminiscent of the intervention of the gods and the chorus in classical tragedy. Like the chorus, these commentators represent the community of the drama. They summarize and comment on the action; they sometimes reveal information, but most often they set forth doctrine and ideas that universalize the narrative. George Kent concurs, "Memorable younger men, including the historical Don L. Lee, act as choruses" (216). Brooks' philosophers are Mecca's Alfred, Africa's Leopold Senghor, America's Don Lee and the Bible's Amos.

ALFRED

The most significant commentator, who is internal to the community of the poem, is certainly Alfred. Alfred is a teacher who is charming and attractive to the ladies. Although Alfred is courted by another teacher, he "goes to bed with Telly Bell in 309, or with that golden girl, or [he] thinks, or drinks until the Everything is vaguely a part of the One thing and the One thing delightfully anonymous and undiscoverable" (6.22–27). He drinks himself into oblivion. The narrator describes Alfred as having a "decent enough no-goodness" (6.29). But, Mecca's Alfred also has a god. When Mrs. "Sallie sees Alfred. Ah, his God!— / To create! To create!" (6.2–3) is her comment. His desire was to write creatively, which he worked diligently to do, however, "Alfred is untalented. Knows [it]" (6.12–13). Still, he worships the muse of creative writing. Kent says, "Alfred's is the philosophical voice or perspective in most of the poem — a charming but dissolute teacher, would-be writer, and dreamer of a better world. He is trapped and neutralized within his reveries while articulating the ills of the Mecca" (216).

But Alfred's description is not what makes him so significant to the poem. It is his comments and their placement in the poem that are revealing. It is their religious language and implications. In stanza 17 Alfred laments "the faithless world" that is betraying the "trinities ... a world without charity, offering no meaningful Christianity that will feed its hungry children" (Melhem in Wright 169). At this point in the poem, Mrs. Sallie is just about to discover that Pepita is missing. Alfred is setting the stage for the dramatic scene that follows and he identifies the situation as one that betrays Christian doctrine. He goes on to foretell events at Pepita's molestation and murder. He tells of "the scuffle," "the short pout," "a pressure of clanking and affinities / against / the durable fictions of a Charming Trash" which describes where she is, when no one else knows her whereabouts until it is revealed at the end of the poem (10–14). Alfred is functioning as a true prophet in the sense that he is providing information that he would have no way of knowing, except through divine revelation.

At the beginning of stanza 39 the reader is told parenthetically that Alfred, "(who might have been an architect) and (who might have been a poet-king ... can speak of Mecca" with authority. Alfred, who was not an extraordinary or gifted poet, can and does express the feelings, descriptors and events of Mecca with all the chaos, negativity, unhappiness and positive elements. He was *of* Mecca and knew the character and life-blood of the community. He relates that Mecca is alive. Those lines personify the Mecca building as having "firm arms" around "disorder, bruising ruses, small hells and small semi-heavens" Here Mecca is characterized in religious terms. It has both "small hells" and "semi heavens"— evil and good— all on a less than universal scale. Those arms would hug "barbarous rhetoric" made up of "buzz, coma and petite pell-mells" representing gossip, lack of consciousness and chaos (2–8). The community is a microcosm of the city and it has a living spirit.

Stanza 43 puts forth one of Alfred's most significant statements with a poem within the poem, "To be a red bush." The passage operates on multiple levels. It is a poem about a bush whose leaves have turned red during autumn. The season of autumn, during which growing things are dying, takes the reader back to the opening tercet of the poem, "fair fables fall," which portends the fall of the Mecca, the building and its residents. As the symbolic red bush, Alfred wishes to stand strong and brilliant, yet like the mediocre poet he is, he conceives of a strong vision, but cannot find the exact word to express it. The color of the bush is so rich, contends the poet, that crimson does not describe it, "although [it is] close to what I mean." The passage portrays both his desire for himself as a poet as well as his thought process while writing the poem. The parenthetical last line of the stanza states, "(But the bush does not know it flames.)" (43.9). So the symbolic bush is unaware of its superior beauty or the impact it has on those around it, like Alfred as the philosopher of the Mecca.

On another level the bush represents Pepita. It is a bush, not a tree; it is small. Pepita, who was innocent, who had no knowledge of her beauty, has been murdered. She will not know that her situation, symbolic of societal indifference to a poor, African American child's loss of life, is a flame that will ignite social unrest.

The religious reference is obvious. It represents the burning bush through which God spoke to Moses. Exodus says, "There the angel of the Lord appeared to him in flames of fire from within a bush. Moses saw that the bush did not burn up though it was on fire. When the Lord saw that he had gone over to look, God called to him from within the bush.... The Lord said, 'I have indeed seen the misery of my people in Egypt. I have heard them crying out because of their slave drivers, and I am concerned bout their suffering. So I have come down to rescue them from the hand of the Egyptians and to bring them up out of that land into a good and spacious land, a land flowing with milk and honey'" (3.2; 3.7). Miller also acknowledges the relationship between the passage and the biblical burning bush. "When Alfred dreams of being a red bush 'In the West Virginia autumn,' the image implies the appearance of the Lord to Moses" ("Define ... the Whirlwind" 155). Again, Alfred's poetic vision symbolizes the growing unrest in the African American community and the escalating civil rights movement. Alfred and Pepita, and all those they represent, must see the burning bush and respond. Regardless of what happens with Pepita's case, the flame will not die. The passage also uses the analogy between the plight of disenfranchised African Americans and the children of Israel in Egypt, which has deep roots in African American religious rhetoric, music and literature.

The trilevel symbolism crystallizes the intensity of the situation being portrayed. The fire shows the potential for destruction and purification of the social ills of the Mecca. The red bush signals a new beginning by serving as a signal light to draw attention to socio-political conditions.

The first three lines of stanza 49 inform the reader of Alfred's search for artistic inspiration and social relevance by making specific references to poems and poets of the past. They address Alfred's actual level of influence versus his desired level of influence to impact conditions in the Mecca. The capital letters inform the reader that they refer to specific literary titles, "Alfred's Impression — his Apologie — / his Invocation — and his Ecstasie" (49.1–2). The choice of these works by these poets specifically reflects Mecca's Alfred and his poetry. In the first two lines Brooks chose to name works from poets whose careers reflect Alfred's own. A brief comment on each illuminates the character and purpose of Alfred in the poem.

"Impression" most probably refers to Lord Alfred Douglas for whom Alfred in the poem is named. He was a minor poet of the late 19th and early 20th century, known mostly for his liaison with Oscar Wilde, not for his poetry. His poem "Impression de Nuit — London" describes London at night, analogizing the city to a giant, panting woman, through which men "creep like thoughts" (poemhunter.com/lord-alfred-douglass). The depiction is similar to Alfred's description of Mecca in stanza 39, which has already been discussed. Both Mecca and the London of Douglas' poem are personified and are seeking, but not receiving, fulfillment. "His Apologie" suggests Sir Phillip Sydney's *An Apologie for Poetrie*, published posthumously in 1595. While Sidney's *Apologie* is a discussion of the role of poetry, it also advocates a type of humanism that emphasizes education and action. Sir Phillip Sydney was also known as a soldier and a scholar (poemhunter.com/sir-phillip-sidney). Alfred the teacher is an advocate for education, and Alfred the poet is an advocate of action to change conditions in the Mecca. Alfred hoped to write poetry that would impact others. There is also the subliminal notion that Alfred is apologizing for his inability to use his poetry to effect change.

"His Invocation" would refer to 19th century romantic poet Percy Bysshe Shelley's famous lament *Invocation,* in which Shelley asks why poetic inspiration has left him. As a literary convention, invocation involves calling upon external forces (e.g., the Muses, inspiration) for help with the composition of a piece. Shelley's speaker sets forth his sadness at the loss of inspiration; he concludes the poem with the lines, "But above all other things, / Spirit, I love thee — / Thou art love and life! O come! / Make once more my heart thy home" (Shelley, lines 45–48 in wordpress. com). But, there is a parallel religious aspect to the title. An invocation is a religious convention, as well as a literary one. In religious gatherings the invocation invites the spirit and presence of God into the gathering. Alfred is seeking poetic inspiration for his poetry, and also God's spiritual help for his people.

And Brooks' last associative descriptor for Alfred, "Ecstasie," may refer to the 1822 *Errors of Ecstasie* by poet George Darley. Darley called himself a failure as a poet when he wrote about his work. Most scholars agree. Darley lived an isolated life and failed to distinguish himself among the poets of his time, such as Byron (poemhunter.com/george-darley). Darley's plight mirrors that of Alfred. He continues to reach for success as a poet in the Mecca. The implication from all descriptors of Alfred's talent is that he is a minor, untalented poet who will know little success as a poet. Loneliness and melancholy will be his companions. While he will see the circumstances and comment on them, he will neither receive the inspiration nor the words to write the poetry of the revolutionary movement that is gaining strength around him. Yet, he feels the situation deeply and understands it thoroughly.

Alfred's thoughts are expressed further in his second poem internal to stanza 49. It begins with the words, "Not Baudelaire, Bob Browning, not Neruda" (3). He recognizes that he will not follow the paths of these three he posits as literary giants. Alfred will not begin a literary movement or portray the nobility of the commonplace like Charles Baudelaire. Baudelaire, who introduced many of the themes of modernism in the 19th century, stressed the need to represent the contemporary and the heroism of everyday life. Alfred will not hold to high artistic principles, even in the face of public opposition like Robert Browning. Browning, who combined intellectual self-confidence with curiosity about mankind's external relationships, was unwilling to subordinate his artistic vision to please his readers (online-literature.com/robert-browning). Alfred will not be the voice of protest for his people like Neruda. Pablo Neruda, twentieth century poet and political activist, protested against fascism and oppression of the people of Chile (nobelprize.org). Alfred will not meet that standard; instead, he will look to his circumstance in the Mecca and write poetry that expresses important truths that will not be read.

Even if Alfred's poetry about the experience of Mecca were read, that would not be enough to right the wrongs inherent in the circumstance. Toward that point Brooks has Alfred continue with lines stating, "Giants over Steeples" are wanted — something more powerful than the church — something bigger and stronger than great poets, something bigger and stronger than religion. It implies that God (in three persons) is needed. Alfred goes on to say, "We part from all we thought we know of love [the church] and of dismay-with-flags-on [the country] because there is 'confusion and conclusion' (4–9). Brooks' Alfred alleges that neither church nor state will help—that poor black people must separate from them and seek higher moral strength to right the conditions. Ultimately Alfred says, "Farewell, and Hail! Until Farewell Again" (13). Alfred is vocalizing his disillusionment and his search for something new that will change the conditions of the residents of Mecca and all disenfranchised black people.

> His impotent intellectualism, lined in stanzas 4 and 38, undergoes modification with the insights of 48, where he turns away from Baudelaire, "Bob Browning," and Neruda, foreign white poets dealing with foreign matters, to the need for native "Giants over Steeples." The giants are empowered, super- (as opposed to supra-) human beings who will rise above the very edifices of religion [Melhem in Wright 173].

Alfred says, "Even the hardest parting [departure from black people's previous approaches to social problems] is a contribution" to a new day for African Americans (11). Alfred will do what he can, no matter how small, to suggest change. That fiftieth stanza opens with the one word line "Officers!" which serves as ending punctuation for Alfred's commentary and a salutation addressing Mecca's antagonist in the struggle for social justice. In addition, it particularizes the opposing force and presents a concrete, dramatic scenario around this abduction case.

In stanza 55 Alfred responds to Pops Pinkham's doubt of God's beneficence in granting the earth to the meek and to Aunt Dill, who is cynical of her religion and "tries to forget the hand of God." Neither the Bible nor faith is providing what they need. Alfred, who is leaning on his balcony, says "I hate it." The pronoun "it" refers to the decadence of Mecca. One wonders if he is viewing the debris in the courtyard below. He hates it, but he stays on. Even his profession as a teacher would imply that Alfred *could* move from the Mecca, but he chooses to stay because "something in Mecca" is calling him. Alfred is called spiritually, like a minister is called. Brooks reduplicates the word for emphasis, "something, something in Mecca continues to call!" (4). To say it continues is to say it began in the past and persists to the present. It is "substanceless" and eternal as mountains, rivers, oceans, trees and the wind. It is something "black and electric ... that is Construction" Alfred has been called by his blackness; he has become conscious of his cultural connection to the community in Mecca on a cosmic, religious level. It builds to "reportage and redemption" (8–9). Alfred's redemption—his salvation—will come from the spirit of black people. The balcony scene, which is just two stanzas from the end of the poem, is an epiphany for Alfred and an emotional crescendo toward the end of the poem, which trumpets the revelation of Pepita's whereabouts.

Regardless of Alfred's lack of success as a poet, Brooks gives him a prominent position in the poem as a philosopher-seer. He understands the Mecca as an entity. Melhem says, "Alfred's development critically supports the theme of possible redemption reminding that his Anglo-Saxon name, originally 'elf-in-council' means 'good counselor'" (Melhem in Wright 174). The role of good counselor is an elevated, spiritual one as it is another name for Jesus Christ spoken by the prophet Isaiah. "For unto us a child is born, unto us a son is given: and the government shall be upon his shoulder: and his name shall be called Wonderful, Counsellor, The mighty God, The everlasting Father, The Prince of Peace" (*KJV* Is. 9.6).

LEOPOLD SENGHOR

In stanza 39 the reader is told that Alfred is not a "poet-king" (39.8) himself, but he can speak about poet-king Leopold Senghor. Senghor was the first president of Senegal, West Africa; he was a poet-philosopher and one of three writers credited with founding the Negritude literary, political movement. The others were Aime Cesaire and Leon Damas (Carlberg 1). Brooks devotes 28 lines of the poem to an exposition of Senghor's philosophy and the African aesthetic of the Negritude movement through the voice of Alfred. Leopold Senghor functions as a spirit who is external to the Mecca, yet inherent in it — the African connection.

La Negritude (first named in 1935 by Aime Cesaire) developed primarily among poets of African descent in Africa and the Caribbean who were rebelling against European colonial political, social and cultural imperialism. They sought to express a true African identity — an African aesthetic comprised of a renewal of innate rhythms, styles and world-view throughout the African Diaspora. The movement is deeply cultural, political and spiritual.

Culturally the movement does not ascribe to the traditional images of the western literary canon, such as "fairy story gold, thrones, feasts, the three princesses, summer sailboats"; instead Negritude writers believe in the validity of beauty that has a black "filter" or perspective — a true African aesthetic (18–19). And yet, the evil antithesis of the black aesthetic rears up and tries to negate its nobility and validity. Brooks cites "Klansmen" and "Old cobra / coughs and curdles in his lungs, / spits spite, spits exquisite spite, and cries, 'Ignoble!'" (25–27). So, the necessity for the rebellious attitude expressed by writers in the Negritude movement is necessitated by the strong opposition to it. Senghor is celebrated for his ability to promote cultural positivism in his work while surrounded by European literature and culture.

Brooks demonstrates the political relationship by drawing analogies between the activities of the people of Mecca and their African ancestors.

The people of Mecca are engaged in "royal rage" in recognition that some of their ancestors were African royalty, yet they are in the throes of poverty, social inequality and "conditional pardon" that is freedom granted on the condition of passivity (13). Then she cites "the line of Leopold" refusing to protect store, "outmoded love" in "mothballs"—because "Senghor will not shred love" (14–16). They will not hold to the past, distorted definitions of love nor wait on kind treatment and justice. Again, Brooks uses love to make a point about the lack of Christian love afforded black people. Senghor's vision, Alfred contends, is one of true brotherhood and love, which are the essential truths of Christ's commandment to love one another as oneself (John 13.34, Rom. 13.8). Brooks contends that the descendents of Leopold are dense with "Scriptural drops and rises," whose capitalization and related love clearly associate with values of the Bible (11).

Alfred affirms that he "needs negritude" like Senghor who, "negritude needing, speaks for others" (31–32). Like Senghor, Alfred "listens to the rich pound in and beneath the black feet of Africa" (36–37). He is *hearing* the beat of his African ancestors and expressing it. The heritage of Africa is a spiritual, religious entity in the Mecca.

DON LEE

Brooks devoted a stanza of the poem to another social philosopher who is outside the narrative, Don Lee (Haki Madhubuti), who has been author, poet and black activist since the 1960s. Like Senghor he represents a strong pro–civil rights persona. He is one of Brooks' chorus of social philosophers. Lee's philosophy is presented outside the stated religious context, but the images of light are reflective of traditional religious symbolism. The passage asserts that the nation should be a "light that waxes ... he [Lee] ... is not candlelit / but stand out in the auspices of fire / and rock and jungle-flail" (42.5, 10–12). Brooks presents Lee as one who wants a nation of equality for all—one who illuminates progressively larger areas, like a light of the world—a traditional Jesus reference. Lee does not want to be exorcized, adjoining and revered; he does not want his *African-ness* to be driven out. Brooks borrows religious words "revered," to explain the perceived racial hierarchy he rejects, and "exorcism," to show the negativity associated with denying or eliminating ones' African cultural aspects. He does not want to have an American embellishment. He does not want an "impish" (42.9) obligation to be American.

For Brooks, Lee is not a candle, which has a small light, but instead stands out in the bright aura of a fire that shows the way to many from a long distance and "rock and jungle-flail." He is to wave and swing his stick as an African American. He promotes the African aesthetic, Senghor's

Negritude, in a loud attention-getting way — "a new music screaming in the sun" — and perhaps in the face of the Son (15). "The Don Lee stanza, about two-thirds into the poem, together with stanza 54 near the end, forms the pivot of hope countering Pepita's fate as the pivot of despair" (Melhem, "In the Mecca" 171). Lee's flame establishes the fire symbol that is enhanced in Alfred's red bush poem in the stanza that follows. The social philosophy presented in the Lee passage also reinforces ideas of the Negritude movement. The passage is narrated in the third person by an unnamed voice; it is the outside philosophical voice of the Mecca.

AMOS

The reader is told in stanza 44 that "Amos (not Alfred) is speaking." Amos' comments come from an overarching spirit that is bringing the Old Testament message of the Judean prophet Amos to the Mecca. Amos earned his living from shepherding and tending a sycamore-fig grove; he was not a professional prophet who earned his living from his religious prophecy (Amos 7.14–15). Amos wrote his prophecies in what is now the thirtieth book of the Holy Bible; it may be the first prophetical book to have been written (circa 760 B.C.). Amos had learned the laws and traditions that had been handed down from Moses. He traveled to the cities of Samaria and Bethel and observed social conditions there. Amos, herdsman-prophet, set forth the notion that learning the commandments was not enough — that people must apply them to everyday life in practical ways. He opined that the spirit of God / Holy Spirit must be a part of the social order in the form of social justice. He discussed the relation of the individual to society in the sight of God. He spoke of the perversion of religion in practice. He prophesied that Israel would fall in the hands of a pagan people for their transgressions.

> The dominant theme is clearly stated in 5.24, which calls for social justice as the indispensable expression of true piety.... Amos declared that God was going to judge his unfaithful, disobedient, covenant-breaking people.... Amos condemns all who make themselves powerful or rich at the expense of others.... Even so, if they would repent, there was hope that "the Lord God Almighty [would] have mercy on the remnant" (5.15, 5.4–6.14).... In fact, the Lord had a glorious future for his people [Barker 1337–1338].

So, the book of Amos reminded people of God's retributive justice to call them to repentance. It reveals Amos' five visions of judgment on the Israelites and ends with hope for the rebuilding, repairing and restoration of Israel (Amos 9.8–15). Brooks brought Amos into the circumstances of the poem because the philosophy of his ministry echoes the concerns and issues she was exploring in the Mecca poem.

The 44th stanza of the poem begins with an exchange between "the gradualist," who indicates that it "Takes time," and Amos inquiring, "Starting from when?" Not only does the Amos of "In the Mecca" disagree with the gradualist who is willing to wait for *gradual* equality, he raises a series of rhetorical questions: "Shall we sit on ourselves; shall we wait behind roses and veils for monsters to maul us,... shall we ... point air-powered hands at our wounds, reflect on the aim of our bulls?" (4–9). Amos is asking the oppressed black people whether waiting for social justice, whether protecting themselves with fragile, thin shields will stem the onslaught of injustice, whether pointing to atrocities inflicted upon them and whether thinking about the next unjust action will make a difference in their condition.

In this Amos passage Brooks compares mainstream America to the unfaithful Israelites. In the next movement of the passage Amos describes an Old Testament ritual, the sacrament of atonement. He prays for America and calls for a blood sacrifice. "Bathe her in her beautiful blood. / A long blood bath will wash her pure" (11–12). The ritual sacrifice will purify her from her sins. The third movement of the passage describes God's wrath, "good rage" being visited upon America in harsh actions such as "Slap[ing] the sweetness from her face, / Great-nailed boots / must kick her prostrate, heel-grind that soft breast" (15–18). Brooks uses violent, harsh actions to portray an overpowered America who has nothing to do but think about her historical "flogging her dark one with her own hand," signifying that repentance is possible (25). Ultimately, the passage says, "Then shall she rise, recover / Never to forget." There is hope; she will "recover" (27–28).

The progression of the stanza follows that of the three parts described in the five visions of judgment and prophecy in the Book of Amos. The first two visions set forth the destruction of the people of Israel, the third one sets forth god's judgment against Israel, the fourth foreshadows the approaching end of Israel, and the fifth shows God destroying the temple and the Israelites themselves. After the five visions, Amos makes declarations about the restoration of Israel. So, the book ends on an optimistic note.

Here Brooks makes her exceptional knowledge of the Bible apparent once again with references to the content and structure of the Book of Amos. The parallels between modern day social oppression with the concerns of Amos are very strong. Social inequality and oppression by the wealthy and powerful resulted in the deplorable conditions in the Mecca. In the poem Amos, who spoke and represented the merging of religious law with secular law, alerts the reader to a higher moral judgment that is weighing the circumstances of the Mecca. Further, if the ungodly treatment of the poor is not remedied, according to Amos, it will bring about God's vengeance. Yet, there is hope for redemption if the needs of the poor population are met by society.

A fascinating post-script to the analysis of Amos as philosopher in the Mecca comes from Melhem, who sets up an interesting triad of Amos, Way-Out Morgan and Don Lee as philosophers.

> This rage, the extreme of and alternate to apathy / coolness; surges variously at three critical points: the descriptions of Amos, Way-Out Morgan and Don Lee. Amos, namesake of a prophet of a vengeful God demands a blood bath, a "good rage" to wash America pure.... It relates to the Don Lee stanza (41) which calls for "a new music screaming at the sun"—and to the Way-Out Morgan stanza (50) summoning a terrible vengeance as he collects guns in his fourth floor room.... The three represent phases of rage: prophecy, destruction, and construction. "In the Mecca moves from expression to interpretation; from questions to possibilities for action" [Melhem in Wright, 170–171].

To Melhem all three seek to wretch social justice from the powerful, but with different means and philosophies. However, Alfred and Senghor must also be included in the paradigm of righteous rage, if it is to be applied fully. Both of them recognize the social deconstruction that has taken place and they both seek to construct new cultural imperatives to restore and build a new social order. Brooks presents a coherent and cohesive message across a broad range of philosophers.

The Community of Mecca

Through "In the Mecca" Brooks created a picture of life in an African American low-income neighborhood. She characterized the environment, discussed the residents' values and the role of their faith. In the end she brings all the strands of her message together through the character of Pepita and her chosen prophets and philosophers.

Brooks uses images and symbols to express how different everything in the life of poor African Americans is from the lives of the rest of society. Brooks likens their environment to living in hell. "In the Mecca" has many references to fires, flames, burning and blazes, which evoke the most common biblical images of hell as fire and damnation. Brooks uses fires in two ways. First, to imply a growing unrest — a smoldering — that will erupt if discrimination is not eliminated. In the poem the fires metaphorically grow. The flame of Don Lee is not a candle but stands in the auspices of fire (42.10–11). Alfred's poetic dream to be a red bush that flames early in the poem correlates with a later stanza in which insane Sophie sees fire in the halls of Mecca. "The fires run up. Things slant. / The pillow's wet. / The fires run down and flatten." The red bush signals and teaches, but the hall fires consume and destroy. Brooks threads "blue heat," "a hot estrangement," and other images of fire through the poem to build the message of the increasing anger and frustration at unfair treatment and the potential conflagration to come.

Brooks also used images of blood and violence to associate the living conditions with hell. Those references are used to describe the treatment and living conditions of the residents of Mecca as hellish. The passages are sometimes reminiscent of the images of hell and damnation in Dante's *Inferno** in which images of fire and blood are threaded through the descending circles of hell. Amos' statement is a good example. While lines 11 and 12 of stanza 44 suggest a blood sacrifice as atonement for her sins, other lines in the stanza show America being punished for her wrongs against black people.

> Let her lie there, panting and wild, her pain
> red, running roughly through the illustrious ruin —
> with nothing to do but think think
> of how she was so long grand,
> flogging her dark one with her own hand
> watching in meek amusement while he bled [21–25].

Even the opening portion of the stanza suggests that for victims, waiting for injustice is a hellish experience: "Shall we sit on ourselves; shall we wait behind roses and veils / for monsters to maul us, / for bulls to come butt us forever and ever, / shall we scratch in our blood (44.4–7). The Way-Out Morgan passage is another example. He predicts "the Day of Demon-diamond, / of blood in mouths and body mouths, / of flesh-rip in the Forum of Justice at last!" (51.18–21). The images are those of Judgment Day in which those who perpetrated racist acts will receive their punishment. There were other references to blood and hell as well, like the phrase, "In the midst of hells" (15.1–2). Blood is spilled from the cup in the parody of the 23rd Psalm. The evil Enrico Jason, would "lie beside his Prophet in bright blood" (46.45). It is clear from those references, and others that have not been mentioned here, that Brooks associated life for poor blacks with hell as part of the religious system of thought integral to the poem.

Brooks' "Mecca" poem emphasizes the absence of a sense of commu-

---

*First section of *The Divine Comedy*, classical epic poem by Dante Alighieri, written circa 1310–14.

nity. Brooks speaks little about the material deprivation of the families in the Mecca; instead she focuses on the lack of humanitarian values and the loss of empathy and concern for human life. Brooks encompasses the institutions of the greater society also by using The Law as synecdoche in the poem. As representatives of the greater society, the officers do not respond to the residents of the Mecca building as members of their own community. They distort the values of law and order and equal protection under the law, and the higher spiritual law to love one another. But, the residents of the Mecca building are not a true community either. They are a large group of people living closely together. They share a common experience, but they have lost the sense of caring for one another in the day-to-day struggle to survive. Brooks explicitly expresses the hope for such a communal society in the poem and then dismisses it.

> She
> comes soon alone.
> Comes soon alone or will be brought by neighbor.
> Kind neighbor (31.13–16)
> "Kind neighbor." They consider.
> Suddenly
> Everyone in the World is Mean [32.1–3].

Even Brooks' association of the Mecca with a ghetto, through the Loam Norton comparison of the Mecca to the Jewish ghettos during World War II, reinforces the point that personal survival is paramount. Although the residents of Mecca knew Pepita, they show neither empathy for Mrs. Sallie nor concern for her lost little girl. No one joins the search. Brooks provides a long list of building residents, all of whom are concerned about themselves. Brooks' method of characterizing many individual residents of the building is a very effective means of showing the reader the diverse group of people living there and the density of the population. The individual descriptions of the activities and emphases make the residents *real* for the reader. Indeed, Prophet Williams and Enrico Jason represent the antithesis of the concept of community.

In this poem Brooks also expresses the view that, no matter how important religious faith is to poor black people, faith does not meet their needs. She hints that it is complicit in their oppression. From Loam Norton, old St. Julia and Mrs. Sallie to Prophet Williams, the residents of the Mecca have faith in something. They want some higher power to change their lives. Neither prayers nor potions work. Their prayers have not been answered. The explicit prayer in the poem is for the return of Pepita unharmed. Mrs. Sallie's screamed prayer for Pepita's return, "The mother ... wants her baby. Wants her baby, / and wants her baby wants her baby"

(35.4–5) remains unanswered. In fact, Pepita is not just murdered; she is cast away "in dust with roaches" (56.8). At the end of the poem the reader does not know if Pepita's body is ever returned to her mother. The implicit prayer in the poem is for a change in the social conditions that precipitate the attitudes and actions of the characters in the poem. While there is no definitive answer to that prayer, there is hope expressed through the prophets and philosophers and through the characterization of Pepita.

By commenting that neither the police, as representative of society, nor the self-absorbed members of the Mecca are concerned about the loss of this little innocent girl, Brooks is defining the sociology of deprivation, but she is also suggesting a psychology of deprivation that creates self-centeredness and insensitivity to the needs of others. The inclusion of Wezlyn, the wandering woman, and Insane Sophie support this view. The poet also cataloged other characters, who present with psychological aberrations, as well. Of course, the character who most distorts the values of community and exhibits pathological behavior is Jamaican Edward who raped and murdered Pepita.

In the Mecca poem Brooks uses the death of Pepita and her stolen future life to exemplify the small, bleak futures of poor African American youth. Hyena bursts forth "to the tune of hate" (5.4). Briggs joined the street gangs after having resisted and finding them repulsive (13.21–23). Thomas Earl who tries to spread seeds of hope like "Johnny Appleseed" is "in the midst of hells and gruels" and "the ground springs up; / hits you with gnarls and rust, / derangement and fever, or blare and clerical treasons" (15.2, 7–9). His hope was being devoured. "Emmett and Cap and Casey / are skin wiped over bones" (16.1–2) because they only get a little food to eat. And there are others. Brooks makes it clear that whatever the youngsters' potential might be, their circumstance prevents them from positive development and the opportunity to prosper. They are trapped in the Mecca.

The strongest statement showing the lack of a future for black youth is the physical death of Pepita. Her death is universalized in the poem by the reported murder in stanza 37 of the other little girl in Langley who was raped and murdered and had her gingham, which had been green (symbolizing fertility), was now red with blood and tied around her neck. The children are victims of society. Like the numerous other red images in the poem, the other girl's gingham symbolizes the notion that the community is literally and figuratively bleeding to death and the youth are the innocents being sacrificed. It is not just Pepita's life that has no value to the greater society; it is any young black. It is the black community itself.

Although Brooks' messages evolve from the events surrounding the missing Pepita, she is characterized in only a few places in the poem. Pepita, which is a Spanish name with a Hebrew origin, is a diminutive of the female form of the name Joseph. It means "may Jehovah add and give increase" (meaning-of-name.com). It is a name of hope, in a situation of despair. Her death in the poem symbolizes the death of hope for the residents, yet it carries a glimmer of light. Her mother says, "Pepita's smart" (30.7). She is referred to in the poem as "Pepita the puny — the halted, glad-sad child?" (31.3). The narrator describes her in stanza 34 as the "wee brown-black chime, wee brown-black chastity?" (4). At the end of the poem Pepita is described thusly:

> a little woman lies in dust with roaches.
> She never went to kindergarten.
> She never learned that black is not beloved.
> Was royalty when poised,
> sly, at the A and P's fly-open door,
> Will be royalty no more.
> "I touch"— she said once —"petals of a rose.
> A silky feeling through me goes!"
> Her mother will try for roses [56.8–16]
> She whose little stomach fought the world had
> wriggled, like a robin!
> Odd were the little wrigglings
> and the chopped chirpings oddly rising [57.1–4].

Pepita has become a "woman" in the most heinous way before she ever went to kindergarten. She was too young and innocent to understand racism or even to recognize that getting the supermarket doors to open before her was not done in her power. She was like a robin, a harbinger of spring, that was killed before spring could arrive. She is sensitive and responsive to fragile flower petals. To Miller, "Pepita, on the contrary, is a true poet, just as Alfred is a false one. Despite her youth, she responded to life with sincerity and sensitivity: 'I touch — she once said — petals of a rose. / A silky feeling through me goes!'" (Miller, "Define ... the Whirl- wind" 153). She was an innocent victim of a cruel community and society that do not recognize her worth.

In this poem Pepita symbolizes Jesus in that both were victimized by societies that did not recognize the opportunity for redemption and salvation they represented. Jamaican Edwards' three-fold denial also makes the connection with Jesus. Brooks' Jamaican Edward "thrice denies a deal- ing of any dimension with Mrs. Sallie's daughter" (56.5–6) when he is questioned by the police. His three-time denial mirrors that of the biblical Peter who, after Jesus' arrest, denied knowing Jesus three times even though he was a disciple (Matt. 26.4). The words "thrice denies" invoke the biblical reference and in so doing associates Pepita with Jesus. Both were pure, sacrifices; both were victims of unjust and violent societies. "Jamaican Edward 'thrice denies any involvement with Pepita,' just as the Peter of the New Testament (Matt 26.4) refuses to acknowledge Christ. The girl lies beneath Edward's cot in the dust. Despite differences in sex and age, she resembles Jesus" (Miller, "Define ... the Whirlwind" 155). Pepita is martyred like Jesus was martyred. And like the crucifixion of Jesus provided the means for life. Pepita's death also embodies a hope for redemption and a new life.

Further, Jamaican Edward's denial also fools the police. He is a killer and an evil deceiver living in the Mecca who has victimized the symbol of innocence in the community. He broke Mosaic Law to neither kill nor bear false witness. He is both an antireligious figure and an antisocial one, epitomizing the values antithetical to community.

Brooks advances her advocacy for a humanitarian community through her social and spiritual philosophers and prophets. All of the prophets and philosophers in the poem lend specific ideas integral to Brooks' portrayal of the deleterious impact poverty and racism have on the individual, the community and societal institutions. The philosophers also set forth Brooks' underlying premise that equality and social justice are fundamental rights, whether viewed in secular or religious terms. They espouse a just and equal society in which every person is loved and protected. Alfred laments the lack of charity in the world, and advocates art and education as vehicles for change. Senghor's Negritude advances a positivist view of Africans throughout the Diaspora and a confidence in overcoming adversity. Lee states the need for equality directly and expresses hope for a pure African aesthetic that is heard by society. Amos connects the social issue to religious principles and warns America about God's retributive justice for social injustice, unless change generates redemption. All of them advocate love and brotherhood; all of them posit solutions to address the social conditions exposed in the poem. Through them Brooks defines true community

The Spirit of Mecca

The poem also has an unnamed omniscient voice that intervenes from time to time throughout the poem as a universal omniscient presence. Brooks weaves this narrative voice seamlessly through the poem to lend perspective to the characters and to interpret the action in real time. Like the philosophers, this voice is part of the chorus. It is external to the action, but sees and interprets everything. While the Spirit narrator conjures up the specter of God's presence, it is best understood as the living Spirit of Mecca. This construct is imperative if the reader is to understand the poem; Mecca must have a heart and live and breathe. It is also important if the reader is to understand the spirituality that Brooks is asserting elevates the poor black residents beyond their living conditions.

The Spirit opens the poem by telling the audience that the Mecca apartment building has fallen from grace — that it is now hellish. This sets the religious conflict between moral law and secular law, between society at large and the community in the Mecca. It sets the tone for everything that follows and foreshadows the sad and sinful ending. The Spirit has a socio-spiritual view of the action and exhibits piety as defined by Amos.

In the last lines of stanza 17 in which Mrs. Sallie contemplates the contrast between the toys her employer's daughter has and the toys her children have, Mrs. Sallie fantasizes about exchanging places with them "And that would be my baby be my baby.... / And I would be my lady I my lady" (26–27). Immediately after those lines the Spirit narrator queries in the single-line 18th stanza, "What else is there to say but everything?" The response of the Spirit implies that children's toys just symbolize the complete inequity that exists between those inside the Mecca and those outside it, such as their employers. Everything is completely different on socio-economic and human planes. That question dramatically increases the narrative tension for the reader at that point in the poem. It also foreshadows the emotional and social context for the next two-line stanza in which Mrs. Sallie misses Pepita, "WHERE PEPITA BE?"

Those questions serve as dramatic questions for the different levels of the narrative. "What else is there to say but everything?" raises the *philosophical* question, and "WHERE PEPITA BE?" raises the *literal* question that will be answered by the narrative. The narrative illustrates that answers to both questions are related: (1) her uneducated, working mother, who does not have the financial wherewithal to hire a baby sitter for her children, (2) the unconcerned response of neighbors, and (3) the lackadaisical attitude of the police who investigate and search, which is only eclipsed by their inability to recognize the perpetrator when they see him face to face. Everything in a life of poverty and socio-economic deprivation impacts the search for the little black girl, Pepita.

The first part of stanza 20 is in the first person and is spoken by Mrs. Sallie who is questioning her other children about Pepita's whereabouts. At the end of stanza 20 she says, "My heart begins to race. / I fear the end of Peace" speaking again in first person. The second part of the stanza shifts to the third person and a description of Mrs. Sallie by the Spirit of Mecca.

our Woman with her terrible eye.
with iron and feathers in her feet,
with all her songs so lemon-sweet,
with lightening and a candle too
and junk and jewels too? [5–9].

Here the narrator is giving insight into this woman. She can be tough and angry, yet she is soft and sweet as well. She is mother. The final two lines of the stanza shift back to first person and Mrs. Sallie herself who is intensely anxious and afraid. The loss of Pepita signals the "end of Peace" (20.11) for her and for Mecca, reinforcing the idea that Pepita epitomizes the Meccans' hope for the future. By alternating the first and third persons Brooks effectively merges Mrs. Sallie with the Spirit of Mecca at this point in the poem. Brooks is demonstrating for the reader that the living Spirit comes from the residents themselves and Mrs. Sallie's racing heart becomes the heart of Mecca, again personifying the Spirit of Mecca.

After Mrs. Sallie's children's response to the question of Pepita's whereabouts, "*Ain seen er I ain seen er I ain seen er* / Ain seen er I ain seen er I ain seen er" (21.1–2), the Spirit narrator, like the Coryphaeus of a Greek chorus, interrupts the action, comments on the children of Mecca and metaphorically speaks about the children of the poor. The audience is told,

And they are constrained. All are constrained.
    And there is no thinking of grapes or gold
    or of any wicked sweetness and they ride
    upon fright and remorse and their stomachs
    are rags or grit,
In twos!
In threes! Knock-knocking down the martyred halls
at doors behind whose yelling oak or pine
        many flowers start, choke, reach up,
        want help, get it, do not get it,
        rally, bloom, or die on the wasting vine [25.1–11].

The family is frightened and filled with dread as they knock on doors looking for Pepita. The latter portion of the passage lets the reader know that the children of Mecca, like all poor children, start out beautiful and fragile, and they have aspirations, but they have a difficult time trying to rise up and "bloom" in society. The loss of Pepita symbolizes the loss of their hope and their lives.

After the family questions the neighbors, they call the police. Again, the Spirit narrator sets the tone for the arrival of The Law in a separate stanza. The Spirit narrator informs the audience that the police are taking their time answering the call and then raises the question of how they will respond since the victim is a small African American child, "How shall the Law enchief the chapters of wee brown-black chime, wee brown-black chastity?" (34.3–4). That question is central to the poem, which makes it clear to the reader that they are not responding appropriately. The narrator is foreshadowing events to come. Having understood that question even before "the Law arrives" in stanza 36, the audience has no hope that the police will find the Pepita. The police question Mrs. Sallie, and then leave. The Spirit prophesies again at the opening of stanza 41. The Spirit of Mecca states, "Death is easy. / It may come quickly. / It may come when nobody is ready. / Death may come at any time" (1–4). Although the investigation is still going on, the audience knows that Pepita is dead. And that death to the young is ever-present in communities like the Mecca.

As The Law half-heartedly questions residents, they show little concern for Pepita's disappearance. The Spirit asks, "How many care, Pepita?" at the beginning of stanza 47. The stanza has three sections. Part one catalogs residents focused on their own sinful behaviors, none of whom, have seen Pepita. It ends with references to "Wezlyn, the wandering woman, the woman who wanders / the halls of the Mecca at night, in search / of Lawrence and Love" (26–28) and to "Not Insane Sophie" with the notation that "If you scream, you're marked 'insane.' / But silence is a place in which to scream! / Hush" (30–32). In living circumstances such as those in the Mecca there is little outlet and little treatment for mental aberrations. But added significance is that "the wandering woman" is looking for love and that Sophie has withdrawn into a silent self within the chaos. Again, Brooks emphasizes the search for love in an unloving world by the residents of Mecca and the need to escape the situation. If one cannot get *out*, one goes *in* like Sophie.

Part two invokes the voice of Jesus, and the words that open this chapter. In context those lines are introduced by then followed by the line, "an agitation in occluded trees" (39) and fires. Occluded trees have grown together and closed. They allow no way in or out, as there is no open passage out of poverty and the Mecca. Again, Brooks implies through the words she assigns to Jesus that Christian love will not provide a way out of the condition of poverty. The agitation referenced in the passage is the symbolic unrest of those who need and want a way out of the poverty.

Part three cycles back to the insanity reference and explains that once you are "marked 'insane'" you are different from others even though "like the others you want love." The section ends with a doll becoming the substitute love object. All three parts of the stanza address the lack of love and the people's yearning for love. At the center of the stanza is Jesus' lament, "What have I done, and to the world, / and to the love I promised

Mother?" (37–38). The residents of Mecca do not care about Pepita, because they do not receive love — Christian or human — and have none to give. The answer to *who cares* at this point in the poem is Mrs. Sallie and her other children. Again in the opening line of stanza 48 "the Spirit asks, How many care, Pepita?" More residents are listed who are only concerned about their own lives: "These little care, Pepita, what befalls a / nullified saint or forfeiture (or child)" (18–19). Brooks' reiteration of the question by the Spirit narrator is significant. It underscores the absence of humanitarian concern for Pepita and her family.

In the final two stanzas the Spirit of Mecca reveals the murderer to the reader. In the Mecca building the Spirit narrator also knows what others do not. The voice informs the reader of the location of Pepita's body under Jamaican Edward's cot and expresses her hopeful innocence.

The two rhetorical questions posed by the Spirit narrator, (1) "What else is there to say but everything [is different]?" and (2) "How many care, Pepita?," raise the issues the poem addresses and set the stage for Brooks' commentary. To Brooks, American society must listen to the Spirit voice and stop "everything" from being different for the poor; communities must begin to "care." Miller said:

> For twenty-three years, Gwendolyn Brooks had sought this balance of vision ... but the folk religion lingered. It manifested itself at the end of Annie Allen ... only to reappear more intensely in Mecca. By then Brooks had practiced ironic detachment and varying distance of narration. Drawing upon Christian myth and different strains of Anglo-American poetry helped her to enrich an epic in which the narrator is heroine ["Define ... the Whirlwind" 158].

That narrator/hero is the Spirit of Mecca, suggestive of the Holy Spirit and serving as the conscience of the residents and society. The Spirit provides the context for the action, empathizes with the poor, establishes moral imperatives, prophesies the future and advocates for the Christian philosophy of love for one another. The presence of the Spirit of Mecca in the poem, along with the prophets and philosophers, is Brooks' statement that spiritual truth is present and needs to be heard.

Even though Pepita dies in the poem, Brooks leaves the possibility for America's redemption open, if social change takes place. She insinuates hope into the dismal picture she paints of the lives of the African American poor. This paradox is central to understanding the poem and to recognizing the elements Brooks dramatizes in the poem. "In the Mecca" is an extraordinary jazz piece in which Brooks uses religious and social instruments to create an intricate montage portraying the complex condition of the urban poor — and to witness for hope.

Chapter Five

"In Emanuel's Nightmare: Another Coming of Christ"

> God's Son went home. Among us it is whispered
> He cried the tears of men.
> — Gwendolyn Brooks, *In Emanuel's Nightmare*

Jesus is the central figure in Brooks' narrative poem "In Emanuel's Nightmare: Another Coming of Christ, speaks, among spirit questioners, of marvelous spirit affairs" ("Emanuel's Nightmare"). The poem illustrates Brooks' superb integration of religious literary elements with social commentary. The language of "Emanuel's Nightmare" reflects Christian doctrine. The poem alludes to Judgment Day (stanzas 3–4), the virgin birth of Jesus (4), the spiritual cleansing of the earth (5), power that did not fail (6), religious creed (6), and God's son (9), among others. The poem is a dramatic monologue that is an exposé on man's propensity for war in the face of religious teaching that extols the virtue of peace. Brooks weaves Christian biblical prophecy of the second coming of Jesus Christ into an analysis of humankind's contentious nature.

Brooks makes a direct reference to Jesus with the name Emanuel in the title of the poem. Emanuel, an alternative spelling of the biblical Immanuel, is used three times in the Holy Bible to refer to Jesus: the Matthew verse defines it. "The virgin will be with child and will give birth to a son and they will call him Immanuel — which means, "God with us" (*NIV Study Bible*, Is. 7.8, Matt. 1.23). The title also informs the reader that what Jesus Christ finds will be a "nightmare" to him; in addition, Brooks uses the appellation Christ to refer to Jesus, which means *Messiah* (Hebrew) and/or *Anointed One* (Greek) to emphasize His spirituality and reinforce the title reference to His having coming to earth in human form.

Brooks also includes a parenthetical subtitle, "speaks, among spirit questioners, of marvelous spirit affairs," which describes the discourse that follows. The poem's parenthetical subtext sets up the distinction between spiritual heavenly affairs and earthly ones, which is the philosophical conflict explored by the poem. The conflicts in the poem are multitiered:

a. Jesus' desire for humankind's peace v. humankind's earthly desire for war
b. Jesus' power to stop war v. His granting humankind's desire for war
c. Human v. human conflicts
d. Peace (spiritual value) v. War (physical value)

The subtitle also makes clear the intention of Jesus to communicate to those on earth who seek to understand spiritual issues and to be in their midst.

The second coming of Christ is prophesied as the time Christ will return to mete out justice and collect His people. The Holy Bible says it is the time when believers will be separated from nonbelievers for all eternity. Although Brooks did not specify the Christian *second* coming, she clearly analogizes it, not only with the words "another coming" but also with references to war that parallel the scriptural presentation of Christ's return at the second coming; they serve Brooks' poetic pairing of spiritual conflict with human conflict. It is not the second coming or Judgment Day, as the people in the poem fear; it is *another* coming before Judgment Day. It implies that the situation on earth has become so dire that Christ is making an interim visit to analyze humankind's situation firsthand.

Brooks uses the genre of dramatic monologue to narrate the story of Christ's horrified reaction if he were to return to earth before his appointed time. An irony of the poem is that the human propensity for war on earth is simultaneously a spiritual war against the principles for which Jesus and Christian doctrine stand. According to scripture, Jesus Christ will return as Messiah-Warrior-King for peace, love and goodness. He will carry a sword of justice. The following verses present a brief portion of relevant text:

> I saw heaven standing open and there before me was a white horse, whose rider is called Faithful and True. With justice he judges and makes war. His eyes are like blazing fire, and on his head are many crowns. He has a name written on him that no one knows but he himself. He is dressed in a robe dipped in blood, and his name is the Word of God. The armies of heaven were following him, riding on white horses and dressed in fine linen, white and clean [*The NIV Study Bible*, Rev. 19.11–14].

Brooks' narration of events is consistent with Revelation. The people in *Emanuel's Nightmare* are figuratively waging war against Jesus Christ by fighting against his doctrine. Like the people in Revelation "their armies [are] gathered together to make war against the rider on the horse and his army" (*The NIV Study Bible*, Rev. 19.19).

Brooks opens the poem with a peaceful afternoon shattered by a noise that cannot be identified by the honored speaker in the poem who has "won the Great War-Naming Contest" (2.2). The reader immediately learns that people enjoy war so much that they have created a contest, the winner of which enjoyed prestige and honor among them. Amid the running and screaming that followed, Jesus Christ "was born out of the heaven, in truth." That depiction relates directly to verse 11 above in which He is called "Faithful and True." In *Emanuel's Nightmare*, "He [Jesus] had come down, He said, to clean the earth of the dirtiness of war" (7). His heavenly armies in verse 14 are "dressed in fine linen, white and clean." So, there is a direct association in the word "clean," as well. However, He found that humans have such a thirst for war and violence that they celebrate it. Brooks' poem ends with Jesus going home in tears, leaving war and chaos behind.

Brooks utilizes religious elements in the construction of *Emanuel's Nightmare*. The tone of the poem is controlled by religious references. The exposition of the narrative in stanza one sets the serene tone with "sleepy sun," arguably a play on Son, whose mystical "sleep" allowed war to overtake peace on earth. Stanza two introduces the honor and celebration surrounding war. It foreshadows the coming conflict with the "heat." At this point stanzas three through seven introduce the religious event that is at hand and the spiritual framework underlying the narrative. The fear of women and children and the futility of escape are the dominant emotions in stanza three, developed by the use of "Judgment Day." The virgin birth and the coming of Christ establish an awe-inspiring and inspirational tone in stanza four. Stanza six exclaims the beauty and love of Jesus and the transforming influence of his presence.

> How He was tall and strong!
> How He was cold-browed! How He mildly smiled
> How the voice played on the heavy hope of the air
> And loved our hearts out!
> Why it was such a voice as gave me eyes
> to see my Fellow Man of all the world" [6].

Stanza eight sets up the conflict between Jesus' desire for mankind and human thirst for violence and conflict. "He found how much the people wanted war. / How much it was their creed, and their good joy" (8.3–5). There is a dissonant, unsettled feeling to the passage. In this stanza a chaotic tone is created with clipped sounds and multiple plosives.

The poem fully characterizes Jesus. He is described in physical terms as "a most beautiful man" (4). with a cold brow. His cold brow reflects a cerebral, rational aspect. He is described in spiritual terms as "born out of heaven, in truth" (4). His voice floats through the air and enables the hearer to truly see the world (5). He is powerful enough to stop war, but loving enough as a parent to allow his children to use their God-given free will. Brooks taps into the Godly power of Christ to grant mankind's wish (i.e., prayer) for war while showing the human aspect of Christ who went home and "cried the tears of men," showing the divine/human duality embodied in Jesus Christ. Jesus, the Prince of Peace, was the antithesis of war. Kent expresses the conflict between Christ's power and his empathy in the poem as Christ's failure in His creation. "Thus Christ failed in his mission, not because he lacked the power to accomplish it, but because He 'had not the heart'" (146).

The poem fully characterizes humankind, as well, albeit unflatteringly. Pride, violence and fear are the predominant characteristics of the people portrayed in the poem. Brooks characterizes an individual who personifies war, and a society that celebrates it. In the second stanza the audience learns that the narrator "won the Great War-Naming Contest!" He displays pride and humankind's competitive nature in having "beat / Them all." The pejorative nature of the individual and his victory is shown in stanza 10, which describes him further in a parenthetical comment. He is a self-proclaimed, "snag-toothed fool." This phrase alerts the reader that he is as old as human history.

> (In me, in your snag-toothed fool /
> Who won the Great War-Naming Contest and
> all the years since has bragged how he did Beat
> His Fellow Man) [2–5].

Brooks uses capital letters to emphasize and satirize the nature of the contest. It is clearly not "great," and he "beat" his fellow man not by winning the contest but by glorifying the physical violence of war. By using the image of him as a "snag-toothed fool" Brooks symbolizes humankind's glorification of war as ages old and, of course, foolish.

Brooks' description of society is equally unflattering. In stanza four she shows the people screaming and knocking each other down when they think it is Judgment Day. They were knocking each other down looking for an impossible way out. They also "thought they had but to beat their Fellow Man / To get to and get out of one [door] again" (7–8). After explaining the reason for Jesus' unannounced visit, Brooks described the human thirst for the violence and conflict of war: "He found how much the people wanted war" and refers to war as "their chief sweet delectation" in stanza eight. Indeed, instead of people finding religion and spiritual joy, they have made war "their creed, and their good joy"— in essence their religion. Brooks continues in *Emanuel's Nightmare* with the societal constructs that reflect how deeply war, competition and violence are engrained in human psychology and culture.

Brooks also uses biblical references in stanzas three through seven to build the narrative tension of a conventional plot. Stanza four introduces the notion of Judgment Day, stanza five sets forth the virgin birth, stanza six describes Jesus, and stanza seven implies Jesus' power to "clean the earth" as an expression of his love for mankind. The narrative climaxes in the tenth stanza, which states in part:

> The people wanted war. War's in their hearts.
> ....It is the human aim.
> Without, there would be no hate. No Diplomats.
> And households would be fresh and frictionless" [1.5–7].

Here Brooks makes clear that the propensity for war begins in the foundational unit of society — the home. The human inclination toward conflict exists between individuals and between nations, as well. Diplomats, among others, symbolize the economic aspect of war. The language of the last four lines releases the narrative tension culminating in a denouement that poignantly expresses Jesus' sadness:

> God's Son went home. Among us it is whispered
> He cried the tears of men [11.1–2].
> Feeling, in fact,
> We have no need of peace [12.1–2].

As the foregoing discussion demonstrates, the religious events interspersed through the narration, control the pace and rhythm of the poem.

The message of the poem is stated by the title in the words "Emanuel's Nightmare." Commenting on *Emanuel's Nightmare* Brooksian scholar B.J. Bolden says, " Religion is the vehicle and peace is the message. Brooks' speaker artfully weaves religious subterfuge to suggest that humans really do not advocate harmony at all" (138). Humankind's perennial history of wars could not be expressed more eloquently or more poignantly than Brooks' poetic contrast between God's wish for man — peace (which man continually extols) and man's wish for himself— war (which man continually wages). Peace and love, symbolized by Jesus coming face-to-face with war, symbolized by the snag-toothed fool, create a compelling emotional moment. The portrayal of Jesus weeping, again victimized by humankind's penchant for violence, is profoundly moving. *Emanuel's Nightmare* is a compelling, reflective allegorical poem.

Chapter Six

Sermons on the Warpland

Build with lithe love. With love like lion-eyes.
With love like morningrise.
With love like black, our black —
— Gwendolyn Brooks, *The Sermon on the Warpland*

Like James Weldon Johnson before her, Brooks chose the African American sermon as a literary vehicle to address the black community with philosophical and political statements on the times. She had utilized the sermon genre earlier in poems like "Maxie Allen" and "Another Preachment to Blacks," however she demonstrated her mastery of the form in a beautiful trilogy of poetic sermons for black people that expresses her social philosophy about equality and social justice for black people. The sermons fulfill Brooks stated mission: "There were things to be said to black brothers and sisters, and these things, annunciatory, curative, inspiriting, were to be said forthwith, without frill and without fear of a white presence" (G. Brooks, *Of Flowers* 1).

The trilogy comprises "The Sermon on the Warpland (First Sermon)," "The Second Sermon on the Warpland," and "The Third Sermon on the Warpland." The first two were published together in the volume "In the Mecca" in 1968, among the "After Mecca" poems. The third one was written in 1969 and published in 1981 in *To Disembark* as part of the opening section called Riot. The poem is the centerpiece of a three-poem sequence: "Riot," "The Third Sermon on the Warpland" and "An Aspect of Love, Alive in the Ice and Fire." The religious intent of the sermons on the Warpland is obvious from Brooks' selection of the sermon genre. Although Brooks published the third sermon with another set of poems, the parallel title and structure clearly connect the third sermon to the other two, and those with which she frames it.

All three poems are sermons by appellation, purpose, structure and message. "A sermon is an oration by a prophet or member of the clergy. Sermons address a Biblical, theological, religious, or moral topic, usually expounding on a type of belief, law or behavior within both past and present contexts" (http://en.wikipedia.org/wiki/Sermon). Brooks' first two sermons utilize direct address (imperative mood) and the third alternates between third person narrative and direct address, using oratorical mode. In the afterword to *Report from Part Two*, D.H. Melhem commented, "The two Sermon(s) on the Warpland proclaim her 'grand heroic' style, as distinguished from the 'plain heroic' of some later works, and adapt the sermon, particularly in the changed genre, as an art form. As a stylistic term, 'grand heroic' indicates use of imperatives, parallel constructions, redundant phrasing, metaphor and metonymy and biblical modes" (G. Brooks, *Report from Part Two* 154). The sermon genre presents a message from God, rooted in religious philosophy, that presents a moral or lesson. It is a discourse exhorting others to duty or it is a formal reproof for past behavior. In "Heralding the Clear Obscure" Wheeler states, "In the first sermon she encloses her preaching in quotation marks, in the second she pronounces without mediation, and in the third she steps back from sermonizing directly, although her attitudes about the rioting she depicts remain implicit" (3). The sermon is an especially effective genre for the African American audiences Brooks sought to reach. Many were accustomed to listening and learning from sermons, which traditionally use a three-point sermon pattern to connect theology, philosophy and sociology in the development of its message. The concepts of hope and future triumph for a suffering people, as illustrated by the Israelites in the Holy Bible, were and remain familiar to an African American audience. The African American sermon is characterized by a central metaphor, parallel structure, repetition of words and phases, and call and response including multiple people. Brooks utilizes all of those elements in the poems. "Preaching is dialogue rather than monologue, and the mixture in terms of call and response makes for an experience that is more orchestral than antiphonal" (W. Jones 7).

The phrasing of the title also parallels that of the biblical passage commonly called the Sermon on the Mount (Matt. 5.3–7.27, Luke 6.20–46), at which Jesus presented a sermon outlining a code of ethics to thousands of ordinary people. The Sermon on the Mount includes the Beatitudes, which Brooks references in "In the Mecca," and presents characteristics for godly living. The Beatitudes explain the rewards in the kingdom of heaven for the humble and spiritually in-tune, and the woes for the immoral, insensitive rich and powerful. The Sermon on the Mount continues with discussion of loving one's enemies, judging others, having a good heart and building a life on a godly foundation. The sermon includes the admonition, "Do to others as you would have them do to you" (Luke 6.31), which is also stated, "So in everything, do to others what you would have them do to you, for this sums up the Law and the Prophets" (Matthew 7.12). The underlying premise is that the sacrificial spiritual life carries a promise of God's faithful justice and that a moral decision is required of everyone. Brooks' sermons are also seeking justice for poor and the oppressed. The parallels are clear and the sermon format is a suitable vehicle for expressions of divine justice for oppressors. The biblical Sermon on the Mount and Brooksian Sermon(s) on the Warpland connect social and political-economic issues to religious doctrine and tell African American people how to live.

An explication of the word "Warpland" in the poem's titles reveals Brooks' vision of the United States at that time. In these poems the speaker addresses people in a land that is warped, in a planned war, on a war plan, and in a war plane — people in the United States. The word brilliantly portrays the unevenness of economic and social opportunity and the struggle of black people for justice. Even a graphic rendering of the five poems is like a plane with the first two sermons horizontally presented and the three parts of "Riot" attached vertically at the end with the third sermon as the nexus. A central metaphor ties the three poems together: the notion of society being out of kilter and uneven. Brooks would not have used the parallel titles for the poems if she did not plan their connectedness around that metaphor. It is significant that they are sermons on the Warpland. They are about the Warpland and on top of it; they are not in it; they are not a part of it." It is the land she introduced in her poem 'The Leaders' in which she said 'their country is a Nation on no map.' In these Warpland poems Brooks presents a fully defined vision of the metaphoric country. Along with the warped aspect of the land, Brooks also presents love as the redemptive force of hope. Shaw's sees the hope as a harvest theme in the poems.

> The subtheme of harvest as a metaphor for Rebirth is not uncommon in Miss Brooks's later poetry. "The Sermon on the Warpland" represents a continuation of the harvest subtheme,... The title itself is suggestive of the whole planting-harvest cycle. Warpland refers to the residual effects of the black experience, which create a fertile soil for the seeds of revolution and promise of a bountiful harvest of freedom [Shaw 159].

In "First Sermon" there are three movements. The first establishes the awakening of black consciousness and the spirit that will deliver the sermon, expounding on the rejection of the status quo. After recognizing that rejection with "saying No" (2.1), the speaker gives the prime directive, which is that African Americans must change the flow and course of events in America. "My people, black and black, revile the River. Say that the River turns, and turn the River" (2.2–3). Then the speaker acknowledges the dual "seeds" (3.2) that exist at that historical moment in the black experience, which has elements that can evolve into war and a Dante-esque "hell" that will precipitate a healthy America. Shaw believes, "The poem is an exhortation to black people to prepare to wage a bruising conflict for freedom:... The double pod refers to destruction and construction together" (Shaw 159). Brooks' doublepod embodies the conflict and dual prospects for the country at that time.

The second movement describes the coming war as "the coming hell" with terrible atmosphere, beasts and "pains; / the bruising." The images mirror those in Revelation during the final judgment. Revelation, chapter 16, which speaks of the seven bowls of God's wrath on earth, contains references to "ugly and painful sores" and "rivers and springs of water, and they became blood" (2–4). Brooks' poem goes on to discuss "brash and terrible weather," suggesting Revelation 16, verses 8 and 12: "The sun was given power to scorch people with fire" and "The sixth angel poured out his bowl on the great river Euphrates, and its water was dried up." In later chapters the woman and the beast are defeated and Satan has been imprisoned for a thousand years. Then Christ Jesus passes judgment and the Holy City comes down from heaven. Brooks makes a direct reference to that event in "First Sermon," which has the line, "The collapse of bestials, idols" (3.6). The final chapter of Revelation focuses on the river of life. It is the complement to the river in the Garden of Eden. This war for justice will bring humankind back to the God-intended state of spirituality like that originally intended for Adam and Eve. "Then the angel showed me the river of the water of life, as clear as crystal, flowing from the throne of God and of the Lamb down the middle of the great street of the city (Rev. 22.1). The allusions to Armageddon are so clear; the allusions to turning the bloody, dried-up river into the healthy River of Life is also parallel. Brooks capitalizes the word "River" to emphasize its importance and relate it to the biblical river. Indeed the events of Armageddon are the "clear obscure" (3.9). It will be "the heralding" (3.9) (i.e., harbinger) of the "clear obscure" or the illuminating of those who are currently hard to see in the society. That is the new order, which will bring poor African Americans to the forefront of society. The "clear obscure" oxymoron also reinforces the doublepod symbol for the duality in the African American experience.

The third and final movement commands black people to "Build now

your Church, my brothers, sisters.... / Build with lithe love" (4.1,3). This
new and different church is built with love, black love, which will empower
black people to change the flow of history. It must be "black —/ luminously
indiscreet; / complete; continuous" (4.6). Brooks is using "church" to symbolize both spirituality and ethics. She instructs African American people
to bring America back to ethical behavior, consistent with Christian values.
The church, as she defines it, is central to a new, moral America.

In the poem Brooks tells people what to say, how to prepare for the
war, what the war will be like, and then describes the reward for winning
the war, which will be a nonphysical church that is shining, full of promise
and eternal. This message echoes Christian theology and biblical prophecy.
Wheeler summarizes the progression of the poem. "The future, the sermon
declares, geminates in 'doublepod,' containing seeds for the coming hell
and health together." Progress becomes organic, the word "hell" breaking
out of its pod, swelling or maturing into "health," the fullgrown flower.
This blossoming out of stasis requires the building of a new church,"
(Wheeler, 4). It invokes the new heaven and new earth promised in Revelation.

"The Second Sermon on the Warpland" also has three movements:
the first, in numbered sections one and two, give the prime directive, which
is that African Americans must live life fully in spite of the antagonistic
social circumstances surrounding them. Brooks explained her whirlwind
symbol in an interview.

> There is a whirlwind. The world is a whirlwind. The social world is a
> whirlwind. And what do we do? Do we tell ourselves that we'll wait
> until it's all over and everything will be peaceful and loving? We might
> be waiting in vain. We don't know when things are going to quote "get
> better"— and we don't seem inclined to force them to be better. So we
> see to it that we bloom, that we attend to our growth in spite of the
> awful things that are happening" [Hull and Gallagher 102].

The poem contends, "This is the urgency: Live! And have your blooming
in the noise of the whirlwind" (1.1–2). The whirlwind image is a biblical
one from Hosea 8.7, which Brooks references again in "In Montgomery."
The whirlwind metaphor, which will be discussed in detail in chapter
seven, presents the world in which African Americans live as chaotic and
filled with destructive forces, which are always swirling around in the
atmosphere surrounding the community. Brooks provides instructions for
African Americans. She says to take ownership of the property that has
been saved from destruction and transform it into a black style. She says
to support the good, while being ever mindful of the ever-present destructive forces that surround. "Salve salvage in the spin. / Endorse the splendor

splashes; / stylize the flawed utility" (2.1–3). She comments that riding above the chaos is not an easy position to maintain, but that African Americans must stay there and must "live" in spite of the difficulties. According to the poem, "Not the easy man, who rides above them all, / ...shall straddle the whirlwind. / Nevertheless, live" (2.6, 9–10). It implies that power comes from being carried forward on the wild motion of the whirlwind.

The second movement, section three, describes the antagonistic circumstances surrounding African Americans. The first three lines begin with the words "all about" emphasizing the circular and cyclical aspect of the negative forces. She lists specific places, people and things that are destructive elements in the African American community and then raises the question, "But / what must our Season be, which starts from Fear?" (3.4). Her answer is to "live," "define" and "medicate" or anesthetize the whirlwind. She instructs blacks to define their own existence and, in so doing, to neutralize some of the chaos. Arguably, the capitalized "Season" refers to Ecclesiastes, chapter three, which implies the time has come for parity. "There is a time for everything and a season for every activity under heaven" (Ecc. 3.1)."Our Season," the poem explains, "starts from Fear." Here the capitalization of the word "fear" implies the *spiritual* fear of God, which according to scripture, means "to walk in all his ways, and to love him, and to serve the Lord thy God with all thy heart and with all thy soul" (Deut 10.12). In context it cannot mean human fear of harm; Brooks' use of the word would mean walking in a morally upright way and following God's precepts. To live in the whirlwind and "medicate" it, requires that kind of fear, and cannot accommodate a natural fear of harm. Again, Brooks is bringing a spiritual dimension to the analysis of the social condition of African Americans and is commenting that a spiritual resolution holds the answer.

The third and final movement, section four, portrays the explosion of black pride and consciousness, whose time has come — the civil rights revolution. Brooks' phrase, "cracks into furious flower," says it most eloquently. She characterizes the explosion with orange to red colors and the noise and shine of war with its casualties. The passion and bloodshed bring the flower into bloom. The stanza itself is structured like a flower that opens and exposes its center. "A garbage man" who "is dignified / as any diplomat" and "Big Bessie" who "is a citizen / and is a moment of highest quality; admirable." Big Bessie, who fits the scene here is a character from an earlier poem. Wheeler posits her purpose in this poem. "In the fourth and last section of the 'Second Sermon,' Brooks resurrects the speaker of "Big Bessie throws her son into the street" at the end of Selected Poems. In the earlier piece, Big Bessie produces large but relatively lucid orders:...

Her inclusion [in "Second Sermon"] reinforces the connection between these two kinds of voices, the maternal and the preacherly" (Wheeler 4). The garbage man and Big Bessie are the embodiment of social inequity and the riot marks the time for their recognition and the resolution of racial conflict and equality. There should be respect for them regardless of their occupations. One must have pride in oneself and ones blackness. Brooks represents that it is the honorable and righteous mission of ordinary black people to bloom / speak out on civil right — as "furious flower[s]" to make the country better. Shaw relates the message of rebirth in the poem with the specific historical moment exposed in this poem and others.

> Repeated references to "time" in several of Miss Brooks's later poems provide a clue to the meaning of the spiritual rebirth of the black, as discussed in "The Second Sermon on the Warpland." Time is referred to in "Medger Evers" as "The Raw intoxicating time was time for better birth or final death" [and similarly] in "Young Africans"...; and in "Paul Robeson." All of these poems cited above deal with time in such a way as to suggest a readiness or ripeness for harvest or rebirth..., meaning that it is completely justified and appropriate for the black man not only to make his move toward rebirth now but also to continue to live throughout the whirlwind [Shaw 160–161].

The conclusion to "Second Sermon" laments that it is lonesome being the group to bring noise and attention to societal inequities, however it is necessary. According to Brooks' last line, "Conduct your blooming in the noise and whip of the whirlwind."

As previously noted, "Third Sermon" is the hinge-pin for one trilogy and the culmination of the other. In the first instance, "The Third Sermon on the Warpland ... [is] — in the very midst of both a metaphorical and a real race riot" (Malewitz 8). The poems in sequence are "Riot," "Third Sermon" and "An Aspect of Love, Alive in the Ice and Fire (An Aspect of Love)." In sum, the poems address the riots in Chicago after the assassination of the Rev. Dr. Martin Luther King. "Taking the Chicago riots following Martin Luther King's assassination as the dominant leitmotif of the collection ["Riot"], Brooks willingly records the divisions of racial conflict between whites and blacks, proponents of violent and nonviolent direct action, and men and women" (Malewitz 8).

The first poem, "Riot," focuses on the impact of the riots on the white community by focusing on one individual, John Cabot, who was "once a Wycliffe." His name has much historical significance. John Cabot (originally Giovanni Caboto). was a 15th-century Italian-born explorer who commanded the English expedition that landed on the North American mainland in 1497. He, like Columbus, was seeking a trade route to the Far East. The poem tells the reader that *this* John Cabot came from Wilmette, which is a suburb of Chicago on Lake Michigan, and that he was once a Wycliffe. John Wycliffe was a 14th-century theologian and religious reformer. He was a professor and scholar who believed that everyone should have access to the Holy Bible, so he, and his followers, produced the first hand-written English language New Testament manuscripts from the Latin Vulgate in the 1380s. His ideas of equal access to scripture and his rejection of the notion of papal supremacy were heretical in his time, but they anticipated the Protestant Reformation, which occurred two centuries later. Wycliffe died in 1384 and on May 4, 1415, the Council of Constance declared him a heretic and decreed the destruction of his writings and his body. In 1427 Pope Martin V had Wycliffe's remains exhumed, burned and cast into the River Swift. So, his body was sacrificed for his religious beliefs, martyring him. The Wycliffe translation of the New Testament is still in print. Melhem adds that the name John Cabot was "synonymous from Colonial times with prominent settlers of Massachusetts" (*Gwendolyn Brooks* 193).

Brooks' John Cabot has elements of both. He has the look of a white Anglo-Saxon Protestant, "all whitebluerose below his golden hair" (1.2). He has ventured out of his suburban life where he drives a Jaguar and drinks fine scotch and has entered a black neighborhood, exploring a new American shore. Here the blacks are not like the blacks he knows from Chicago's North Shore community of Winnetka who are "Dainty." It seems that John Cabot, and those he symbolizes, consider themselves to be reformers, liberal in their attitudes of social equality for all. However, these "Negroes" in Chicago were "black and loud. / And not detainable. And not discreet" (3.4–5). To John Cabot they are gross. And he does not want this black world to touch him. But it touched him: "In that breath / the fume of pig foot, chitterling and cheap chili, / ... (4.3–4). John Cabot went down in the smoke and fire / and broken glass and blood" (6.2). John Cabot's dying words, and the last words of the poem, parody those of Jesus on the cross. He "cried Lord! / Forgive these nigguhs that know not what they do" (6.2–3). He sees himself as a victim, but does not understand the racial attitudes that precipitated the riot. That is ironic, indeed, inasmuch as he uses the pejorative term "nigguhs," which underscores the social perspective that precipitated the riot. It must also be noted that John Cabot has the initials of Jesus Christ, so Brooks is confirming the association between the two and the sacrificial aspect of Cabot's death. Yet, the poem is about blacks taking control of their own destiny, so Brooks permits the adventurous, white liberal reformer to die, so that blacks might live.

It is consistent with the crucifixion of Jesus who died so that believers could live free and have everlasting life. "Riot" is a complicated work and Brooks establishes a delicate balance. It does not advocate violence for its own sake, rather it connects philosophically with the retribution of God expressed by Amos. "A Trinitarian motif presides, roughly (and ironically) correlated as follows: Father, the Judgment of God visited upon the blasphemous earth and its emblem, John Cabot; Son, the Incarnation and Passion of the earthly riot; and Holy Ghost, the provisional *caritas* of 'An Aspect of Love'" (Melhem 201). Consistent with that view, John Cabot had to die so that blacks could live.

Setting aside "Third Sermon" for the moment, an examination of the third poem in the "Riot" trilogy reveals a focus on individuals, also — two lovers in the black community. In the midst of the riot, two people make love — creating a spiritual oasis in the chaos of surrounding anger and violence. "An Aspect of Love" has the subtitle "LaBohem Brown." In typical Brooksian fashion she chooses an elevating and eloquent operatic first name for the African American woman speaker of the poem, coupled with a common last name to elevate the common to an uncommon place. LaBohem is the speaker of the poem. She is the teller of their tale. She is strong and clear and able. LaBohem's lover is portrayed as a proud black man: "You are direct and self-accepting as a lion / in Afrikan velvet" (4.5). The poem emphasizes the peace and calm of the lovers' encounter in the midst of the riot. Indeed, "Because the world is at the window / we cannot wonder very long" (3.1–2). There was so much going on around them that they could not tarry long after their time together. The poem begins, "In a package of minutes there is this We."

The reference to the opera *La Bohème* is apt. In the opera the main character, Mimi, dies at the end, thus separating from her lover, Rodolfo. Indeed, during this riot Ms. Brown may die after parting from her lover. "On the street we smile. / We go / in different directions / down the imperturbable street" (6.1–4). The reader is left wondering what each will encounter as they move through the riot in the community and philosophically whether their private love can function as a seed from which public expressions of love will grow. They represent the new black woman and the new black man who are born through the struggle and strife. This is the third poem in the sequence and expresses the hope of the birth of new, positive, racially conscious black citizens.

The poem also references Robert Frost's poem "Fire and Ice" in the title. Frost's poem compares the virtues of ice with fire as means of destroying the world. The poem associates the extreme opposites of fire and ice with love and hate, respectively. In Brooks' poem the lovers have the heat of the moment in the middle of the sterility, violence and destruction out-side. The speaker in Frost's poem says he would "favor fire" to end the world, however he recognizes that "for destruction ice / Is also great / And would suffice." It ends with the satirical comment that humankind will use whatever means are available to destroy the world. On the other hand, Brooks' theme of destruction in her poem is balanced with the birth of something new to replace that which has been destroyed. "An Aspect of Love" addresses the unity of the lovers and celebrates the concepts of a fresh form of black manhood and womanhood having evolved from loving themselves in a new and revolutionary way. Kent concurs, "Thus the ice and fire, as in Robert Frost's "Fire and Ice," have to do with destruction but also with creation" (238). Melhem extends the lovers creative energy to an explanation of the ultimate purpose: "Caritas is to redeem apocalyptic judgment and wrath, blood-guilt, hatred and sacrifice" (*Gwendolyn Brooks* 200). Brooks' hope lies in love. The definition of the phoenix that intro-duces "Third Sermon" replicates that philosophical perspective.

While "Riot" recreates the sensual images and the response of the prototypical white liberal and "An Aspect of Love" characterizes the union of the black man and woman who were born again from the riot, "Third Sermon" dramatizes the rioters and the details of the riots in the black community. "The Third Sermon on the Warpland" deals more concretely with a particular instance of rebirth...." It presents a number of different pictures of a riot in the black ghetto" (Shaw 161). Like any birth it is por-trayed with pain, blood and suffering, but with the beauty of new life coming forth. This progression directly parallels the third movement of "Second Sermon" with the fiery explosion of orange and red colors as pas-sion and bloodshed bring the flower into bloom.

Similar to the other sermons, "Third Sermon" also has three move-ments. The first movement of the poem sets up the social milieu imme-diately before the riots. It opens with earthy images of flowers and water and calm. That is followed by references to slave chains having been put on the shelf, the sound of which has been obscured by sweet symbolic "cookies." The metaphor is apt. Cookies taste good but lack nutritional value; their sweetness masks hunger for a short time, but they do not assuage it. When the "hunger" returns it is the rattling of the slave chains singing "A Death Song for You Before You Die" that lets blacks know they are not living full lives. Rather, they are dead because they do not have the opportunity to live. If they listened and heard the chains and the dirge, they would make their own "blackblues" music to reflect their situation and condition. The poem moves to the local black eatery on West Madison Street. People have heard about Martin Luther King's assassination and are angry. No one is eating. The people have reached their breaking point. "The poem cuts to West Madison Street where 'Jessie's Kitchen, featuring Jessie's Perfect Food' is empty.... Synaesthetic, the 'cry' of the flowering flames perfectly realizes the riot as 'the language of the unheard' (Melhem, *Gwendolyn Brooks* 196).

The second movement describes the riots that followed in Chicago. It describes young men running and looting, but they are taking things with images of blacks — culturally affirming items. "The poet enters to comment on their choice of records: eschewing Bing Crosby for Melvin Van Peeble's 'Lillie' (Lillie done the Zampoughi Every Time I Pull Her Coattail), in the album *Br'er Soul*, racially selective plunder that distinguishes them from vandals" (Melhem, *Gwendolyn Brooks* 196). The poem explains that in this riot people are running and stealing in hell. They listen to black musicians and broadcasters on the radio and receive light and heat and fertility from the sin of having stolen radios. In this passage Brooks also distinguishes "little rioters" from the big rioters who have executed a "clean riot" in which blacks were violated for centuries. Blacks had been oppressed ("long stomped") raped ("long straddled"), poor ("BEANLESS") and rejected ("Knowing no") (6.1–3). The clean riot has caused the "little rioters" to explode. This is the way, the poem asserts, the rioters light a candle to illuminate the oppression. Their candles "curse ... inverting the deeps of the darkness" (8.5). They bring the deep oppression to the surface by turning it inside out. The section uses the refrain, "The young men run," to emphasize the numbers of people involved in the riot and to depict them moving from one thing and moving toward another. The Law arrives to quell the riot. Again, Brooks uses the phrase "The Law" instead of policemen to dehumanize the officers; they are the "letter of the law" incarnate — "GUARD HERE GUNS LOADED" (9.1). The references to youth and children are framed in the poem by guards and the law. But, "Motherwoman" is dead. Her "firm virginity / as rich as fudge as if you have had five pieces" (11.5–6). This symbolic black woman had never experienced life even though she was older and a mother. She was rich with possibilities, but she was black. That movement ends with the rioter continuing with the voice of a specific young black male, Yancy, yelling, "We'll do an us!... Instead of your deathintheafternoon, kill 'em, bull!'" (13.1–3). Yancy is saying, in effect, that they will act "pro-black," not "anti-white," again projecting the positive outcome of the riot.

The third movement sets forth the pacifying role the street gangs played in defusing the riots and restoring order and peace; it also presents society's response to them. The poem lists gang members and leaders who are not participating in the riot and who "peer and purr, / and pass the

Passion over" (16.9–10) as not their domain. It was reported in the *Chicago Daily Defender* on April 9, 1968, that four Chicago gangs joined forces and printed 3,500 flyers, which stated in part,

> Little Brothers and Sisters our Moses is DEAD. But let's not destroy our hopes or his dreams for equality. We realize, we as brothers and sisters who share your grief of this violent murder, that there isn't too much we can ask of your personal feelings but let last night be the last of this destruction [Fitzgerald 1].

There is a beautiful irony in the gangs being the pacifists. Street gangs who have a reputation for violence have also been misunderstood on the Warpland. The poem relates the report of the *Chicago Sun-Times* that printed the number of violent deaths along with a phone number for readers to call to check rumors regarding the riot. The poem also reports whites questioning the reasons blacks were destroying their own neighborhood, but others understanding, "It's time. / It's time to help / These people" (17.2–3). The poem's message of a positive outcome from the riot is reinforced, yet again. The poem ends with calm, like the opening passage, but instead of beautiful water images that evolved into a revolutionary storm, "The dust, as they say, settled" (stanza 20). It is a new world.

There are places in "Third Sermon" when diction points to religion. The rioters "sun themselves in Sin" after they "go steal in hell" (stanza 6). Again, Brooks likens the poverty-ridden black neighborhood to hell. The several references to candles, curses and lighting the way certainly have religious connotations. When the gangs refuse to participate in the violence they "pass the Passion over." The capital *P* in passion connotes the death and resurrection of Christ and their embrace of the peace that Christ's passion calls for. In addition, it reinforces the death and rebirth of black people after the riot. However, a primary religious element in the poem is the presence of the Black Philosopher and the White Philosopher. Similar to the technique Brooks used in the Mecca in which there were intervening philosophers who are outside the action of the poem, observing it and commenting upon it. The Black Philosopher, who appears three times in the poem, and the White Philosopher, who appears once, give voice to black and white leadership. The way they interject their views from outside the action gives them a spiritual aspect, particularly in a sermonic piece. Notably, they are not ministers.

The Black Philosopher's first speech occurs during the first movement of the poem before the riot occurs. He advises that their slave chains have been put away and are drowned by western culture, but evidence of slavery is present and represents African Americans figurative death during life.

He states, "If you could hear it [rattle of the chains] / you would make music too. / The blackblues" (3.3–5). He is telling them to recognize their present state in the context of the history of slavery. The second speech of the Black Philosopher comes at the end of the riot. He "blares, 'I tell you, exhaustive black integrity / would assure a blackless American'" (14.1–3). At the point of his second comment in the poem he is responding to the events of the riot and does not acknowledge the undercurrents that have erupted into the riot. In his first speech he is speaking about the blackblues as the music of black people. In his second statement he wants to ensure a blackless American, which would mean a complete *whitewash* of black people to accomplish a colorblind America. Since he "blares" his statement, literally or figuratively using a megaphone, the image is one of someone riding around in a car using a megaphone to speak to the community. His shift in perspective implies that he is either out of touch with black people because of age or position, or he is presenting the view of the empowered and has been *bought* on some level. In this instance he is placing the ethical problem that created the riot on the black victims, instead of on the white perpetrators who precipitated it. The different positions he takes in the poem may also represent the different perspectives that exist in the black community. The final reference to the Black Philosopher ends the poem. It states that he "will remember" the historical crisis that brought blacks to life and triumphed over the silent social pain they experience. He will remember; he will understand the event when time gives him perspective and illumination. The Black Philosopher has gone from a pre-riot black cultural perspective to a post-riot pacifism. The portrayal of the Black Philosopher's future understanding reflects the chorus of the traditional spiritual "We Are Often Tossed and Driven": "We'll tell the story how we've overcome, / For we'll understand it by and by."

A White Philosopher is referenced during the riot as having said previous to the riot, "It is better to light one candle than curse the darkness" (8.4). The White Philosopher would seem to be affirming the riot as "lighting" the way. The proverb is also à propos to the riot because it had previously been associated with social activism. Former Illinois Governor and United Nations Ambassador Adlai Stevenson used the proverb in 1962 to praise Eleanor Roosevelt for her social activism. In addition, the metaphor of darkness for ignorance or evil is an ancient one, and as previously noted, it appears innumerable times in the Bible. It associates with an epiphany of faith, in which one figuratively "sees the light." It also alludes to the metaphor of Jesus as the light of the world, which Brooks utilizes in many poems. So, this quote, which is preceded by the line, "Fire. / That is their way of lighting candles in the darkness" (8.1–2), has religiosity, as well as socio-political significance.

"Third Sermon" has an epigraph that is the definition of the mythical phoenix, "which lived for five hundred years and then consumed itself in fire, and rising renewed from the ashes." Brooks quotes the definition however she changed the tense for the last verb from past to present to show the direct application to the rebirth of black people through the riots. Brooks uses the phoenix that symbolizes the cycle of destruction, purification and rebirth to memorialize the riot as a historical moment for black people. Melhem also relates it to the African heritage. "The "Third Sermon" carries an epigraphic definition of 'Phoenix' (from Webster's) as a 'bird in Egyptian mythology' or religion. African ancestry sparks the poetic conception, mainly of 'the Black Philosopher,' who discussed the heritage of slavery and present bondage" (*Gwendolyn Brooks* 195). Immediately before the final reference to the Black Philosopher are the lines, "Lies are told and legends made, / Phoenix rises unafraid" (18.1–2). Regardless of what is said, black people will act to change their condition in America and be reborn. "As the inscription at the beginning implies, the poem captures the spirit of the black man rising renewed from the ashes of a self-consuming fire" (Shaw 162).

"Third Sermon" also fits into a trilogy of form and function with those of the first two sermons. In addition to the three movements of the traditional three-point sermon, the three sermons share other elements of the African American sermon. The sermons, particularly the third one, are conceptually and symbolically synthesized by Shaw's notion of blacks having fallen from a glory they previously had and should still have.

> One convenient vehicle for such symbolic expression [of pent-up frustration] was the Christian religion. The whole idea of the triumph over oppression and a rebirth in glory allowed the black man to vent expression of his pent-up desires. Miss Brooks uses the Christian theme, but she also uses the War, unrequited love, and other common occurrences in black life to convey the theme of a fall from glory (77).

The opening of the title poem from *Primer for Blacks* supports this view:

> Blackness
> is a title,
> is a preoccupation,
> is a commitment Blacks
> are to comprehend —
> and in which you are
> to perceive your glory [1–6].

The three poems have important elements that bind them together. Their consistencies and similarities create Brooks' picture of the time. A review of the three poems yields an interesting set of repeated words and concepts.

First Sermon	*Second Sermon*	*Third Sermon*
doublepod seeds	blooming / furious flower	goldenrod / crazy flowers
heralding		herald
black	black	black
brothers, sisters	Big Bessie	Motherwoman
	light	light
	musical reference	musical reference
Religion: church	Bible: season / fear	Religion: passion

The seeds "for the coming hell and health together" of "First Sermon" are "blooming," and "furious" in the second, and have become saturated with the sun's heat and fertility, thus becoming explosive and emotionally unruly in the third. Melhem comments on the progression as well: "The coupling of apocalyptic and symbolic horticultural imagery, intimated here, will resound fully in 'The Second Sermon on the Warpland'" (*Gwendolyn Brooks* 142). Brooks expresses the rebelliousness of the people of the warpland by threading language of refusal through the poems. "Just as the people 'went about the warpland saying No' in First Sermon, Brooks frequently incorporates 'do not' and 'will not' constructions into her Third Sermon's prosody" (Malewitz, 11). There is the consistent note of rebellion and rejection of the *status quo*.

"First Sermon" references blackness with the words "My people" along with "love like black." The "Second Sermon" references the same with "half-black hands" that assemble oranges, which are part of the explosive imagery of the poem. "Third Sermon" has the Black Philosopher, "The blackblues," and "black integrity" to re-emphasize that it is black people who are experiencing the crisis of frustration and oppression that have erupted in the riot. "First Sermon" also addresses "sisters, brothers" then "brothers, sisters" who represent the community as a whole. The reversal of the words would imply gender equality in the struggle and in the community. In "Second Sermon" the quintessential black figure is Big Bessie. She has feet that hurt, and stands as "a citizen in the wild weed" that is the warpland. She is unrefined, but an admirable and very real part of the country. Her place and status are the embodiment of race relations in the United States. The Motherwoman in "Third Sermon" is the same sweet, strong woman who was Big Bessie in the "Second Sermon." In this one, however, she is part of the revolution and is dead. She is one to be respected, but she is part of the old order.

First Sermon intones that the spiritual war will result in a new day, in which there will be abundance and fulfillment. That notion is reinforced in "Third Sermon" with gang member Peanut a.k.a. Richard the Ranger as "A Herald." He represents the new order by bringing peace to the streets of the black community, inverting the perspective of the old order that gangs bring violence.

Light and musical references appear in the second and third sermons. The speaker calls for a church in the "First Sermon" and uses religious allusions in the second and third sermons with the capitalized words "Season," "Fear" and "Passion" that elevate the riot to a spiritual level. The references in all three poems progress in intensity, in imagery, in the evolution of the character of black people and the elevation of the activism to a spiritual war. In addition, the poems progress from building love in "First Sermon," to living in the whirlwind in "Second Sermon," and to destroying the old order and building a new nation in "Third Sermon."

Call and response is another important element of the African American sermonic rhetorical style. It involves the preacher speaking to the congregation and the congregation answering him with affirmative, traditional responses. The process is a ritual in which the audience participates in the sermon. Similarly, Brooks created multiple persona in these three poems who comment on the action and speak to the reader. Indeed all three are calling the reader (i.e., black people) to action and portraying events as a symbolic response. The "First Sermon" has a narrator who provides the exposition and advises the reader of the essence of the "Single Sermon" which is "No." Immediately following the exposition the speaker delivers the rest of the poem as the sermon that responds to and expands upon what the single word "No" means. Like a church sermon, the text is "No" and the sermon develops from that text. The opening lines of the sermon reiterate the text as reversing the river of life. The second and third movements of the poem respond to the call by describing the present and the future representations of the rebellious "No" call to black people. "Second Sermon" alternates imperative mood with indicative mood in a classic call and response pattern. For example, the end of section number three of the poem commands, "Live and go out. / Define and / medicate the whirlwind,/" and the beginning of section number four states, "The time / cracks into furious flower. Lifts its face / all unashamed. And sways in wicked grace." In "Third Sermon" Brooks inverts the traditional view of the call and response pattern. Here the people and the situation have taken the lead; they are calling and the philosophers are responding to the call of the community. The Black Philosopher's first response shows a true understanding of the situation. His second response shows his lack of understanding of the community's actions. His third response portends that he will understand in time. The White Philosopher responded to the black community call by acknowledging, "It's time to help / These People." The call and response sermonic pattern enhances the religious and cultural nature of the poems.

Although Brooks creates a coherent set of images, messages and structures among the three poems, there are important distinctions, as well. The lengths are different. The first is short (21 lines), the second is longer (38 lines) and the third is significantly longer (105 lines). All have an introductory quotation or salutation, but the function of each one is different. "First Sermon" utilizes a quote from Kwanzaa founder Dr. Ron Maulana Karenga, "The fact that we are black is our ultimate reality." Brooks acknowledges Karenga's position by defining the reality of being black in America and instructing what blacks should do. The second poem was written "for Walter Bradford," who became one of her surrogate sons. Walter Bradford was a social organizer who worked with students at Wilson Junior College, and who was instrumental in Brooks' poetry-writing workshops for members of gangs. Prefacing "Second Sermon" with the dedication to him acknowledges his social and political influence on her and makes her audience for the sermon clear — young African Americans. "Third Sermon" uses a definition of the mythological phoenix to frame the poem at the beginning and at the end. This symbol serves to emphasize her message of destruction of the old order and the rebirth and reinvigoration of the restored spirit of black people. The progression of the opening epigraphs reflects the philosophical progression of the three poems from black philosopher Ron Karenga through black activist Walter Bradford to the broad philosophical concept, symbolized by the phoenix. Brooks' message is a universal one.

While all three sermons have a variety of images and symbols, the first one has images that are more abstract and ethereal. The second has hard, labored gritty ones. Both represent the war in symbolic terms. On the other hand, "Third Sermon," which focuses on actual events, has images that are concrete and specific. The people and events are revealed like a newsreel. They unfold before the reader with intensity as the camera pans the scenes in the black community and stops from time to time to record comments from people. The first two are expository and third is narrative.

The rhythms vary as well. All are free verse, however the first is most traditional. For example, the speaker states, "But then oh then!— the stuffing of the hulls! / the seasoning of the perilously sweet!" (3.7–8). The second and third sermons both incorporate the language and cadence of everyday speech, which grounds the music of the poems in harsh reality. A "Second Sermon" passage reads, "Big Bessie's feet hurt like nobody's business," and another says, "It is lonesome, yes. For we are the last of the loud" (4.3.1). Both are conversational in diction and syntax and are similar to conversational and everyday passages in "Third Sermon" like "That was a gut gal" and the gang's "Yeah! / this AIN'T all upinheah!" (12.1, 16.15). Even the proverb "It is better to light one candle than curse the darkness" harkens to the commonplace. Kent comments on the differences in the rhythms of the speeches.

> The Meditative portions are in the "Third Sermon on the Warpland": the comments of the Black and White Philosophers and individual lines eulogizing the dead Motherwoman and commenting on the "clean riot." The passage has the ordinary speech, loose rhythms, and communal reference points that could communicate with a mass audience [237].

The rhythms provide parallel contexts for the sounds and meanings of the language. One such spot appears early in the poem. "Crazy flowers / cry up across the sky, spreading / and hissing **This is / it**" (4.5–7). Here the replication of the letter *s* duplicates and reinforces the hissing flowers and controls the rhythm. "As the field of vision expands from one [sermon] poem to the next, the formal scope extends from brief and nearly metrical to more widely various free verse lines" (Taylor 273).

When "The Third Sermon on the Warpland" is viewed in the context of either trilogy, the poem is a triumph. In the "Riot" trilogy the Third Sermon is buttressed by white rejection of African American equality on one side and African American love and renewal on the other. In the *Sermons* trilogy it serves as the culmination of the African American spirit of rebellion and rebirth. When the three sermons are read as a trilogy they present African American experiences of the turbulent 1960s and the culturally defining assassination of Dr. Martin Luther King. The strategic imperatives that are advanced in the poem are still racially relevant. Brooks chose to use the sermon genre to strengthen the spiritual aspect, not just social and political aspects, of the struggle of African Americans for equality.

"A Brief Outline Guide to Sermon Structure" indicates that the primary purpose for a sermon is to demonstrate the truth of the doctrine (Campbell 1). So, Brooks' chosen medium, the sermon genre, lends authority to her words and confirms her spiritual, poetic mission. When Brooks was interviewed by George Stavros in 1969, he asked her, "Then am I right in saying these 'Sermon' are almost apocalyptic or prophetic? They seem rather...." At that point Brooks answered, "They're little addresses to black people, that's all" (41). For little addresses they have big implications. They begin with the particular and attain the universal. They begin with the developing urgency and end with the explosive objectification of injustice and oppression. They are sermons that promise hope and love; there is the promise of hope and redemption — the Christian message.

Chapter Seven

"In Montgomery"

At the Dexter Avenue Baptist church
in History City, Martin King
gave the True Bread to his People.
  — *Gwendolyn Brooks*, "In Montgomery"

In August of 1971 *Ebony* magazine published a poetic pictorial work
that was the result of collaboration between Gwendolyn Brooks and pho-
tographer Moneta Sleet, Jr., characterizing Montgomery, Alabama, at that
time. It had been nearly 16 years since Dr. King had risen to prominence
with his speech at the Montgomery Improvement Association (MIA) meeting at Holt Street Baptist Church in Montgomery. It had been nearly 14
years since Dr. King had given his "Birth of a New Nation" sermon at
Montgomery's Dexter Avenue Baptist Church that inspired people to political consciousness and social action. It had been exactly eight years since
the historical civil rights March on Washington, and it was nearly six years
after more than 8,000 people made the freedom march from Selma Alabama to Montgomery in 1965. It had been three years since Dr. King had
been assassinated that chilly Memphis day. So, Montgomery was the heart
of the civil rights movement. In 1971 the entire nation was still alive with the
reverberations from the events that had occurred in Montgomery, Alabama.

The poem "In Montgomery" chronicles Brooks' visual, emotional
and political impressions of the city and its people through the eyes of one
who understood the pivotal role Montgomery played in the civil rights
movement. The poem refers to real people, leaders and followers, who
were active in the movement. At the core of the poem's theme is an
acknowledgment of the philosophy and sacrifice of the Rev. Dr. Martin
Luther King, and the religious foundation inextricably bound to the movement. It is a lengthy narrative poem of 47 irregular stanzas. Melhem recognizes the religiosity of the poem:

"In Montgomery" is a major work.... Rhetorical and musical repetitions from the chanted sermon bridge poetry and prose.... Like a restless wraith of the civil rights movement, tracing its faded purposes, Brooks wanders through sunny streets dominated by the 'White white white' Capital. But Montgomery's workers and doers, the subjects of her lengthiest interviews cannot energize the apathy, disguised and revealed in the dazzling light" [*Gwendolyn Brooks* 219].

The organization and development of the poem provide insight into the spiritual impact Brooks intended for the poem she called "verse journalism" (Kent 241). She begins by establishing the historical context and then interfacing increasingly dramatic religious references that rise to a crescendo at the end of the poem. It is very tightly organized.

Stanza(s)	*Section*
1–3	Setting
4	Purpose
5–8	Expectations of Montgomery in 1971
9–10	Reality of Montgomery in 1971
11	biblical Philosophical Foundation of civil rights movement
12–26	Characterizations of civil rights Freedom Fighters Statement of Theme (Verse 18)
27	Characterization of E.D. Nixon
28	Restatement of Theme
29–43	Characterization of Black Community on Sunday
44–45	Dramatization of Sermon Connecting the Civil Rights Struggle to the Holy Bible
46	Dramatization of Radio Program Playing Gospel Music and Calling for Help for the Needy
47	Final Statement of Theme Related to the Rev. Dr. Martin Luther King

The first eight stanzas set forth Brooks' purpose and present the images she expected to find in Montgomery mixed with those she actually found there in 1971. She looks for evidence of the new freedom and ethnic pride, alluding to "King-images" and "King-song," but instead she sees evidence of continued oppression and a lack of progress toward King's ideals. She sees a black citizenry displaying an apathetic attitude toward its situation. Brooks was deeply saddened by the "drowsy" attitude of blacks toward the dream of equality. In stanzas nine and ten, she introduces her theme and laments that "Montgomery is a game leg." It is no longer walking, talking and feeling freedom and the whites "are smug / are smug" about the peace that exists because of the black apathy (9.1, 8). That peace rests on the pre–King oppression of blacks.

Brooks responds to that peace by reflecting on the active engagement of the movement in stanza 11. It is a tightly woven and complex section of the poem in which she personifies blackness as one with a dual physical and spiritual mission. She frames the stanza at the beginning and the end with references to blackness that fought by physically clawing its way out of an oppressive metaphoric room by breaking through the ceiling and walls to see the light of social justice. Blackness brought light to the darkness and expanded the "room" in the poem — actions that Brooks exhorts the reader to "behold." The process of light illuminating a dark world is a concept that is repeatedly expressed in the Bible as previously discussed. Clearly, "behold" is biblical diction. It appears 1,298 times in the Holy Bible (KJV), beginning in Genesis with the commands of God, who spoke things into being with the word "behold," then to other places in the Bible where prophets and apostles use the term to focus the hearer on spiritual events and visions. Brooks used the word two times in three lines of stanza 11 to analogize the civil rights movement toward social justice in the United States with the creation of the world from the void. The analogy connected the actions of the freedom fighters to spiritual actions and visions of the Holy Bible as a rebirth of Christian ideals. In stanza 11 Brooks' established the nexus between the philosophical foundation of the civil rights movement and the Bible, which she develops throughout the poem.

But the connection the poet makes is not only that of blackness creating a biblically inspired order with civil rights; the relationship is also developed in the stanza with four direct biblical quotations, each of which has specific historical and moral applications to the Montgomery that Brooks saw in 1971.

In the first quotation Brooks admonishes the country with the words the Lord spoke to Hezekiah, 13th king of Judah (circa 715–687 B.C.) and ancestor of Jesus Christ. To understand the significance of the quote, one must look at the historical setting and character of Hezekiah. Hezekiah reigned 29 years in Jerusalem during the period of the divided Kingdom of Israel, which existed for approximately 400 years after the death of Solomon, son of David. At that time the Israelites were divided into Judah in the south (centered in Jerusalem), and Israel in the North (centered in Shechem). King Hezekiah was known as a great reformer, who abolished the idol worship that had been sanctioned under the reign of his father; he restored worship of Yahweh to Judah. The Holy Bible reports that Hezekiah often prayed and consistently consulted with the prophet Isaiah. During his reign, the Israelites in Judah were attacked by the Assyrians but were miraculously saved when a plague killed 185,000 in the Assyrian camp. The prophet Isaiah told Hezekiah that Jerusalem would be saved as the Lord had spoken these words to Isaiah, "For out of Jerusalem shall go forth a remnant,... For I will defend this city, to save it, for my sake and for the sake of David my servant (*NIV Study Bible*, 2 Kings 19.31–35). Immediately after the divine victory over the Assyrians, Hezekiah fell ill.

The quotation Brooks utilized in this poem about Montgomery, Alabama, reads in context, "In those days was Hezekiah sick unto death. And Isaiah the son of Amoz came to him, and said unto him. Thus Saith the Lord, *Set thine house in order*; for thou shalt die, and not live" (*King James Study Bible*, 2 Kings 20.1). The passage is one that is emphasized in scripture. Not only is it quoted directly in Isaiah 38.1, it is referenced again in 2 Chronicles 32.24. The passage continues as follows. After Hezekiah wept and prayed, the Lord said, "I have heard thy prayer, I have seen thy tears: Behold, I will heal thee: on the third day thou shalt go up unto the house of the Lord" (*King James Study Bible* 2 Kings 20.5). Hezekiah had been a godly king, who was praised in scripture: "He trusted in the Lord God of Israel; so that after him was none like him among all the kings of Judah, nor any that were before him" (2 Kings 18.5). Yet, his healing came after his humble submission to God. God delivered Hezekiah and gave him 15 more years.

Once Hezekiah recovered, he received an envoy from Babylon, whose mission was unstated, and showed them all the wealth of his kingdom, presumably as a show of power. Isaiah responded with a prophecy about the destruction of Jerusalem and the Babylonian captivity. He said,

> Hear the word of the Lord. Behold in days to come, that all that is in *thine house*, and that which thy fathers have laid up in store unto this day, "shall be carried into Babylon: nothing shall be left," saith the Lord. And of thy sons that shall issue from thee, which though shalt beget, "shall they take away; and they shall be eunuchs in the palace of the king of Babylon" [*King James Study Bible* 2 Kings 20.16–18].

Hezekiah had unintentionally provided the means through which his people would be enslaved in 586 B.C. after his death. During Hezekiah's final years he continued to work on behalf of his people, most notably building a tunnel to bring water into the city and thwarting the possibility of blocking the water supply by enemies — an extraordinary engineering feat for the time.

While "Set thine house in order" certainly has implications for Hezekiah's personal possessions and family, the context reveals that it extends beyond that. "Thine house" here and in the later reference in verse 16, referenced earlier, relate to his ancestral, historical and spiritual domain. The words "in order" denote putting things in their proper relation to one another. It was necessary for him to arrange things that would move the divided parts of the house of Israel toward their proper relationship. So,

Hezekiah's responsibility was to work toward the unification of Israel and the reinstatement of Jerusalem as the historical, spiritual center. The words, "set thine house in order," followed by a promise of death, evoke an urgency to do so immediately — as urgent as the need for racial unity in 1971.

Hezekiah's story has a number of applications to Brooks' poem about the state of Montgomery in 1971. Brooks presents Montgomery as the Jerusalem of the civil rights movement. It is the capital of Alabama as Jerusalem is the capital of Israel. More significantly, the history of Montgomery makes it the birthplace of the civil rights movement. It was in Montgomery that Rosa Parks' civil disobedience gave rise to the Montgomery bus boycott of 1955. Similar to the Israel of Hezekiah's time, the United States has been divided into two groups of the same people, black and white, with social differences represented by the South and the North. From within that circumstance and from that place came a godly leader who sought to unify the country based upon religious ideals. Hezekiah sought to practice religious rituals with the Jews in Israel, along with those in Judah. For Jerusalem it was Hezekiah and for Montgomery it was Reverend Dr. Martin Luther King. Both recognized the authority of God and both were humble men of prayer. Both were sickened by disease. Hezekiah almost died because of a physical disease; King died as a result of a social disease, racism. Hezekiah was healed and did good works for his people for 15 more years. King was not healed in the flesh, however in her poem Brooks evokes the spirit of the Rev. Dr. Martin Luther King as a continuing presence beyond his physical death. To Brooks it is the spirit of King that must inspire the present day citizens of Montgomery to do the work God ordained to fulfill the mission of equality for all people. The Brooks analogy can be seen further in her presentation of the apathy (i.e., mental enslavement) of some of the citizens of Montgomery in 1971. King, like Hezekiah, would not live to see their plight.

The second quote Brooks employs comes from the prophet Hosea who resided in the Northern Kingdom and was a prophet during the reign of King Jeroboam II, which was a time of material prosperity in the Northern Kingdom. Prophet Hosea, whose name means salvation, ministered from approximately 753 B.C. to 715 B.C., a generation before Isaiah and Hezekiah. Again the historical context is significant. The Israelites in the Northern Kingdom had intermarried with the Canaanites and had adopted their religious practices, which involved sexual activities and excessive alcohol consumption and they had begun to worship Canaanite deities. Such practices and others were contrary to Jewish religious practices and Mosaic Law (Perkins). Hosea's prophecies relate to God's judgment about their lack of faithfulness, which is consistent with Brooks' judgment that the people of Montgomery have a lack of faith in King's vision. Hosea reminds the Israelites in the Northern Kingdom that they are loved by God and have been chosen as His people, but he also admonishes them for having broken the Sinai Covenant. Early in the Book of Hosea he presents God's view that the Northern Kingdom would be destroyed and Judah would hold the remnant who would continue the journey of God's chosen people. "For I will no more have mercy on the house of Israel [the Northern Kingdom]; but I will utterly take them away.... But I will have mercy upon the house of Judah, and will save them by the Lord their God" (*King James Study Bible*, Hosea 1.6–7). Hosea prophesies God's wrath toward the Northern Kingdom with five messages of judgment.

The passage Brooks quotes comes from chapter eight of Hosea. The message correlates with the message expounded by the prophet Amos in "In the Mecca." In context the passage reads,

> They have set up kings, but not by me: they have made princes, and I knew it not: of their silver and their gold have they made the idols, that they may be cut off. Thy calf, O Samaria, hath cast thee off; mine anger is kindled against them: "how long will it be ere they attain to innocency? For from Israel was it also: the workman made it; therefore it is not God: but the calf of Samaria shall be broken in pieces. For *they have sown the wind, and they shall reap the whirlwind:* it hath no stalk: the bud shall yield no meal: if so be it yield, the strangers shall swallow it up. Israel is swallowed up [*King James Study Bible*, Hosea 8.4–8a].

To Hosea the Northern Kingdom was sowing empty, worthless wind instead of seeds, which would produce crops. Thus, Israel would reap a whirlwind, which is empty and destructive. Here Brooks is comparing the fruitless, unproductive "sowing" of seeds in 1971 that would not yield racial equality and social justice. Hosea said, they had "cast off the thing that is good" (*King James Study Bible*, Hosea 8.3), which was their covenant with Yahweh. Again, the breaking of a covenant can be applied to the situation in Montgomery at the time of Brooks' visit. Brooks saw the fulfillment of King's dream of social equality as a covenant to be upheld. On the other hand, Hosea also contains a message of restoration. If the Israelites were willing to repent, they would be saved. He lets them know that God has never left them, regardless of their actions; it carries a message of hope. Here too, the passage can be directly applied, because there is still hope.

The emphasis in the Hosea passage is three-fold: (1) to remind the rebellious Israelites of their responsibility to God under the covenant, (2) to warn them of the divine judgment and wrath that would ensue if they failed to listen, and (3) to advise them of their opportunity for restoration if they repented. By citing that particular passage, Brooks implies the same three-fold message for the people in the United States. Comparisons can be made between the materialism and prosperity of the two societies. The citizens of both societies failed to adhere to their obligations under their traditional religious ideals. For the United States discrimination violated the Christian religious tenet to love one another, along with others. Brooks infers that the religious ideals, like those of the Israelites, have been "swallowed up" by the culture. The quotation, which tells of the sterility and chaos that follow from the infertile plants of the blasphemous, indicates the United States is in danger of such chaos if a change does not occur. The quotation also tells of the divine retribution that will ensue if people disregard the warning. Brooks infers that the citizens of the United States, like the Northern Kingdom, will invoke the wrath of God unless they repent and return to the biblical, spiritual foundation upon which it was founded. In effect, the United States could be redeemed if it gets back to the spiritual foundation. Once again, Brooks links her social message to the Holy Bible.

After referencing King Hezekiah and Minor Prophet Hosea, Brooks quotes the words from John 13, which Jesus Christ spoke at the Last Supper with his disciples. The passage reports the following events. Jesus indicated that his time to "depart out of this world unto the Father" (1) had come. After supper Jesus washed his disciples feet to demonstrate that "the servant is not greater than his lord; neither he that is sent greater than he that sent him" (16). He noted that one of them would betray him and identified Judas Iscariot to Simon Peter. Jesus continued to explain that His death would glorify God. In context Brooks quoted Jesus, "Whither I go, ye cannot come; so now I say to you. *A new commandment I give unto you, That ye love one another;* as I have loved you, that ye also love one another. By this shall all men know that ye are my disciples, if ye have love one to another" (*King James Study Bible*, John 13.33b-35).

Application of the Last Supper to the situation in Brooks' poem revolves around the characteristics being illustrated and advocated by Jesus, such as humility, equality, loyalty and reverence for God. Even Brooks' use of that particular event implies that the situation in Montgomery was at a critical point and that a grave outcome was imminent. In addition, the specific quotation she uses, which consists of the one commandment Jesus added to the Mosaic Ten Commandments, has direct social implications. Within the text Jesus acknowledges his faithful disciples along with Judas, whom he knows to be a traitor, yet he communes with all of them and commands them to love their fellow humans. In the America that Brooks is describing, loving one another would require loving others regardless of race, ethnicity, attitude or other differences. That is the Christian principle Brooks is presenting at this point in the poem.

The final biblical quotation in stanza 11 comes from Psalm 30, which is a psalm of thanksgiving for God's intervention and deliverance from a problem. Psalm 30 has a traditional three-part structure: (1) the introduction to praise, (2) the development of the praise incorporating the reasons or praiseworthy acts or qualities of God, and (3) the conclusion of the praise in the form of a prayer (Ryken 116–117). Bratcher applies a similar three-part model specifically to Psalm 30. "Following the form of a *todah* psalm, this psalm naturally divides into three logical divisions or movements: the introduction and summary with a call to praise (1–5), narration of the experience (6–11), and the confession of *todah*, thanksgiving (11–12), with verse 11 serving as both affirmation of the deliverance and the introduction of the praise" (2). The psalm does not employ specific language to identify the problem or the "foes"; they are metaphorical. The references to the problem are indistinct.

There is substantial scholarly debate regarding the occasion and / or the structure being referenced in the subscription of Psalm 30, which states "For the dedication of the temple of David" (NIV) or "at the dedication of the house of David" (KJV). Scholars speculate whether it is a place of worship (Bratcher 4) or David's tomb (Sielaff 7) that is being dedicated, each creating a different interpretation of the problem God healed. The most significant distinction for discussion here is whether it is the problem of an individual, implying the healing of David from disease, or the problem of a group, implying the healing of a community. The number issue rests on the language of the psalm, which opens with the first person speaker yet speaks of plural foes and calls for praise from multiple people: "Sing unto the lord, O ye saints of his" (4).

Brooks' use of the quote from the psalm draws upon the community interpretation of the problem and the call for praise. The verse Brooks cites, in combination with verse four, interrupts the psalmist's presentation of the problem to testify and express praise and joy for the anticipated deliverance, and to invite others to join the praise. "Sing unto the LORD, O ye saints of his, and give thanks at the remembrance of his holiness. For his anger endureth but a moment; in his favour is life: *weeping may endure for a night, but joy cometh in the morning*" (Psalm 30.4–5). Here again, Brooks is expressing the hope for deliverance from the suffering of racial injustice and the future joy from the resolution to the problem.

Brooks chose and presented in different ways four quotations from four different types of biblical books to reinforce the unity of her message that a biblical foundation for social justice can be found in different parts of the Holy Bible: 2 Kings (history), Hosea (minor prophet), John (gospel) and Psalms (poetry). She established a strong historical analogy in the 2

Kings passage between social division and unifying leadership; she utilized Hosea's admonitions to those who were not adhering to the law to demonstrate parallels with modern society and illuminate the promise for redemption. She presented Jesus' message of love and hope for salvation in the Gospel of John, and finally presented thanksgiving and praise for deliverance in Psalm 30. Indeed, the sequence contains an implicit minisermon. The passage comments on believers breaking their covenant with God and the suffering they endured as a result of divine retribution. Through the passage Brooks suggests that people should go back to the behavioral characteristics taught by Jesus — humility, equality, loyalty and reverence for God — because Christian principles were being sublimated by society. But, she also expressed hope for redemption for society and social justice for black people, if Christians would show love to one another. Christian doctrine refers to spiritual freedom as the result of adhering to the tenets of the faith, and Brooks is embracing that spiritual freedom as well as the social freedom for black people. It is also important to note that these passages of scripture, like many of Brooks' references, are not commonly known; they also demonstrate the depth of Brooks' familiarity with the Bible.

Stanza 11 ends with personified blackness reaching for white hands, forgiving "what it would not forget" and marching on. The stanza utilizes the biblical references to align blackness with Christian doctrine, but also to make specific the elements of the analogy Brooks is making. She also reiterates her foundational assertion that the civil rights movement was demonstrating Christian principles to a society that had moved away from them. While the beginning and end of stanza 11 bracket philosophical beliefs of Christianity and the civil rights movement in society at large, stanza 12 introduces the section of the poem that highlights the varying attitudes toward civil rights among individual Montgomery residents. Some of them remember the movement and some of them go about their lives with no regard for civil rights objectives. Some of them are characterized as religious, and some are not. Brooks is demonstrating that the conflict between the philosophies and life practices exists outside and inside the African American community as well. Brooks' catalogue of residents dominates the next 20 stanzas of the poem.

Among those who are characterized with religious references is Mrs. Sallie Townsend who is 89 years old and who "serves her Lord." The character is introduced at the end of stanza 12 and then described in stanzas 13 and 14. Mrs. Sallie had a two-part philosophy of life, use "Heart's Home Liniment" (14.2) which cures everything, and to "SERVE THE LORD!" (14.6). She represents a black historical perspective by making references to her father and his optimistic prediction of change and freedom for blacks. Mrs. Sallie Townsend is the archetypal black earth mother: "She had ten children" (14.7). She is warm, loving, longsuffering and strong. Brooks describes her in the most positive terms: "She is strongsweet, a heavy honey" (14.19–20). Here Brooks is also affirming the Christian teachings she expressed earlier in the Last Supper reference. It should be noted that Mrs. Sallie Townsend is much like Mrs. Sallie in "In the Mecca" and Big Bessie in "The Sermons on the Warpland." Her character rests on a foundation of religion.

A fascinating character in the poem is the brown threshing woman whom Brooks references twice. She is introduced into the poem by a community organizer named Leon Hall, who is asking her to convene a committee to educate the black population about their rights. She is described in metaphoric terms, almost mythological terms, as she "knows / Montgomery's muddy / and weeps, out of stretchy eyes" (17.22, 18.3). This image conjures up one of a spirit rising from the river bottom. This woman knows how much has been lost with integration, particularly for the children, who have lost the community-based love of black teachers. "She weeps for the plight of black children" (18.14). Even her first person assertions assume the voice of a spirit deity: "But love is denied them. I do not deny them, / I do not push them away. I do not turn, / with love in my look, to the yellow haired" (17.26–28). Although the other characters in the list have names, she remains nameless. The brown threshing woman wants to leave Montgomery in frustration, because the circumstance and her dedication to the cause draw so much from her life. Yet, she weeps and, according to Brooks, "will speak, spurt and spar for Black children" (17.15). She exhibits Jesus' love of children. The reference in stanza 16 and repeated in 17 emphasizes the significance of this nameless "threshing" woman who says she will not assemble the committee, that she is leaving Montgomery.

Biblically many passages involve threshing, which was a male domain, but only one threshing reference involves a woman, Ruth. After her husband's death, Ruth chose to leave her native country of Moab, which worshipped pagan gods, to follow her mother-in-law Naomi to Bethlehem. She adopted Naomi's Hebrew God. While in Bethlehem, she humbled herself before her kinsman-redeemer Boaz by sleeping at his feet on the threshing floor at the end of the grain pile. The threshing floor, where grain was beaten to dehusk it, separated the usable portion from the useless shell. The threshing floor became the birthplace of the relationship between Ruth and Boaz (Ruth 2–3). Later, she became his wife. Ruth's commitment to Naomi and her conversion to the God of Israel earned her such favor with God that she gave birth to a son with Boaz, named Obed, who was the grandfather of King David. Ruth, the Moabite, was an ancestor of Jesus Christ. Ruth is one of only four women named in the genealogy of Jesus and one of only two books in the Holy Bible that is named for a woman (Matt. 1.5).

Three relevant associations are apparent between Ruth and the "brown threshing woman" of Montgomery. Her namelessness in this poem of specific names, implies that she is symbolic; she represents the spirit of the movement. Her adherence to the doctrine of the movement is strong; she still follows the precepts that Dr. King espoused. Like Ruth of the Bible who symbolized loyalty, the brown threshing woman of Montgomery was fiercely loyal to Dr. King's message. Like Ruth she is one who is metaphorically separating the grain for planting, to yield a good future crop and looking to help future generations. That refers directly to her expressed concern for the children. It points to her concern for the descendents of the African American community. She expresses a desire to leave a place (like Ruth) where the spirit is dead. Montgomery has lost the biblical and social spirit of the civil rights movement. As an ancestor of Jesus Christ, Ruth influenced people future to herself. In addition, the brown threshing woman's weeping emphasizes her empathy and her humility, which are also characteristics of Ruth and her relationships with Naomi and Boaz.

Stanza 18 has allusions to another biblical narrative — the exchange of firstborn birthrights between Jacob and Esau. The speaker, Idessa Williams recounts the historic days: "Black people came alive! / They put hands in / And pulled a Birthright out!" (18.12–14). The capital letter on "Birthright" underscores the biblical association. Genesis chapters 25 through 27 narrate the story of Jacob and Esau, twin sons of Isaac, son of Abraham, father of the Judeo-Christian and Islamic religions. Jacob came out grasping the heel of his older twin brother Esau. Later, Jacob tricked Esau into selling him his birthright for a bowl of stew. According to scripture, the birthright of the firstborn was a double portion of the father's inheritance, which included title to and possession of the land (Deut. 21.17). It also carried divine authority to perpetuate the family line in accordance with the scriptural directive that the firstborn belonged to God. In the particular case of Isaac, the line promised from God in Genesis was the line from which the Lord of humankind would come (Gen. 27.29). The most important privilege granted to the one with the birthright is the God-granted inheritance, and the inheritance Jacob took was the covenant with Abraham, which placed him as the father of the 12 tribes of Israel.

In the lines from stanza 18 cited above, Brooks is quoting the words of resident Idessa Williams, who had worked with voter registration and the Montgomery Improvement Association (MIA) during the movement.

She proudly expresses, in biblical terms, the boldness of the freedom fighters and the authority under which they seized their divinely ordained birthright — civil rights. Williams also uses biblical language as she calls for Montgomery to be roused to "passion" (19.6) and a "resurrection" (19.9) by the young people. She refers to the past achievements of the civil rights movement as a "Miracle" (19.7).

Stanza 27 pays particular homage to E.D Nixon and his influences. It is 104 lines, comprising three full pages of the poem's 28 pages. Nixon was a leader of the National Association for the Advancement of Colored People (NAACP) in Alabama and collaborated with Martin Luther King, Jr., to create MIA and organize the Montgomery bus boycott. "It was E.D. Nixon who selected Rosa Parks for attention when she landed in jail.... Rosa Parks had been a member of the NAACP since 1943 and former Secretary.... It was E.D. Nixon who called Martin Luther King, Jr., to ask whether or not the meeting [about Ms. Parks] might be held at his church" (Walters 1). E.D. Nixon was a key leader at the beginning of the civil rights movement. At the end of Brooks' characterization of E.D. Nixon she makes the dearth of present-day leadership evident in by invoking the intervention of God in the last four lines.

> Wanted:
> The Fine Hand of God:
> Marching Songs for the People, in a
> Town That Could Be (But Ain't) Your Own [27.101–104].

God is referenced again in stanza 33, in which a monologue by a resident identified as "firecracker" makes reference to contrasting Old Testament and New Testament depictions of God and Jesus.

> if we's to get anywhere.
> **Especially** since we done sent up prayers
> and been real good
> and done gone through all that sufferin
> God is a righteous God.
> He look down peaceful on all.
> But JESUS get **MAD**!
> JESUS'll get up and DO somep'm [9–17].

Firecracker, whose name connotes a spark or explosion, is making a clear statement about Christian doctrine as an active force against oppression. With the references to prayer and suffering the passage illustrates the connected Christian and social doctrines. The Old Testament / New Testament dichotomy of the passage may also symbolize the pre–civil rights/post–civil rights societal attitudes. To be sure Brooks is acknowledging the religious underpinning of the movement and is using biblical attributes of God and Jesus to demonstrate them.

Stanzas 34 through 40 continue the catalogue of individuals. Brooks provides rich description that characterizes each in a very individual way. It is a series of ordinary people expressing the condition of the black community in Montgomery. The range of attitudes and frustrations is made clear by their comments and discussion about whether or not to leave Montgomery. They acknowledge progress but they intone, "There's room for improvement" (34.7). The need for "improvement" is ironic when it was the MIA that had initiated the civil rights movement in 1955. Those stanzas do not have religious references, however stanzas 41 through the end of the poem are full of religious allusion.

Dexter Avenue Baptist Church, now named Dexter Avenue King Memorial Church, is the church at which the Rev. Dr. Martin Luther King began his first full-time pastoral assignment. During his tenure at Dexter, Dr. King hosted a meeting that resulted in the development of the MIA, became its president and initiated the Montgomery bus boycott. So, the rich history of Dexter Avenue Baptist Church made it an important stop on Brooks' tour of 1971 Montgomery. In stanzas 44 and 45, she describes the interior of the church and a Sunday service. She lines a traditional hymn, "I Am Thine, O Lord (Draw Me Nearer)" and then dramatizes a sermon of Minister Murray Branch. In this sermon his message made parallels between the plight of African Americans and the children of Israel in the Old Testament. He told them to continue fighting for equality. Brooks chose to place this call for activism in the context of a church service. Murray Branch's sermon reinforces Brooks' union of the biblical teaching and the civil rights movement.

Then the poem segues into "WABX, the Soul Station," on the radio, which is playing the song of gospel group The Soul Stirrers. Then the station plays the gospel tune "O Happy Day! (When Jesus washed, oh when / He washed ... my sins away!)" and the traditional hymn "The Old Ship of Zion!" while the announcer pleads for the listeners to feed the hungry, clothe the naked and visit the sick or the imprisoned (43.9–10). Although both songs express the joy of redemption and the reward of heaven, respectively, there is a sad poignancy — pathos — about this plea. While the listeners, like the parishioners at Dexter Avenue Baptist Church, are Christians, the solutions for community needs being mentioned are being asked of the disenfranchised black community, not the greater Montgomery community.

The song lyrics emphasize the important role religion continues to play in the lives of the black community in Montgomery while their economic and social needs are still not being met. The music in the poem heightens the music of the poem itself. "The poetic voice of the Super-Reporter unifies diverse moods and modes.... Music and rhythm blend the sermonic / prophetic, reportorial and conversational strains" (Melhem, *Gwendolyn Brooks* 218). The music and message rise to a crescendo at the end with the final rhyming couplet: "Martin Luther King is not free / nor is Montgomery."

Brooks threads multiple references to Dr. Martin Luther King through the poem to remind the reader of Montgomery's historical status and the resulting responsibility of African Americans to keep the civil rights movement alive and to affirm the value of Dr. King's sacrifice. Her concluding couplet and statement of theme, "Martin Luther King is not free. / Nor is Montgomery," makes it clear that even with Dr. King's death the mission was still alive, and Montgomery had a responsibility to move it forward. She pays homage to Dr. King as a true model of Christianity in the lines that introduce this chapter. To Brooks Dr. King introduced the "true bread" which implies that he presented a true Christian perspective. Jesus said to them, "Very truly I tell you, it is not Moses who has given you the bread from heaven, but it is my Father who gives you the true bread from heaven" (John 6.32).

The tone of the poem reflects its religiosity. It is serious; it is somber; it is prophetic. From the metaphor of Montgomery as a "game leg" early in the poem to [*untitled Reverend*] Murray Branch's call to the people, "Don't sit down on the job. Dying while still ambulatory is reprehensible" (42.2–4), the overarching mood of the poem is pessimistic and forlorn, as if the movement for which so many fought and died had been forsaken. Idessa Williams, who sat on the original steering committee of the MIA, which directed the Montgomery bus boycott, summarizes the state of Montgomery in 1971 for Gwendolyn Brooks. "The Miracle and Montgomery are dead. / "The light, it done gone out."

This poem shows Brooks' comprehensive knowledge of the Holy Bible. References to events are often those that are unfamiliar to most people. Brooks chose biblical passages from various sections and time periods in the Bible. She chose one from the North and one from the South during the divided Kingdom of Israel; she chose one Old Testament psalm and one New Testament passage. Then, she integrated specific songs from the African American religious experience. It is apparent that Gwendolyn Brooks knew her African American Christian cultural traditions. Kent concurs: "She reaches into the biblical area for expressions and rhythms that have fused themselves into black experiences" (242).

Chapter Eight

Short Poems: Depictions of God and Preachers

Force, whether
God is spent pulse, capricious, or a yet-to-come.
— *Gwendolyn Brooks BOYS. BLACK. a preachment*
— *Gwendolyn Brooks Another Preachment*

Gwendolyn Brooks' multitude of creative strategies for the use of religious allusion in her long poems and the construction of her underlying religious, philosophical theory is also evident in her short poems. From her early published poems in 1945 through those written late in life, there was a conscious religious presence in her poetry. This chapter and the following two chapters discuss selected short poems and explicate aspects of the poems that relate to specific religious elements.

Gwendolyn Brooks wrote several poems with God or preachers as central characters. They deserve particular focus here because these poems are essential to Brooks' development of statements on religion and faith. They go beyond characterization to examine doctrinal precepts. She portrays God as remote, unresponsive and inconsistent at the head of a church that does not fulfill its responsibility to its parishioners with preachers functioning as robotic surrogates and kindly enablers in a cosmic deception to keep people from knowing their lonely position in the universe. The Brooksian God has abandoned His poor, African American followers, and church leaders are perpetrating the myth of His presence by preaching the doctrine. Yet, she continuously affirms the existence of God in her poems.

In the sonnet entitled "firstly inclined to take what it is told," the first eight lines of the poem address God and characterize him in the process. In the poem, Brooks addresses God in the language of the King James Version of the Holy Bible and lists a series of positive characteristics, such as "thee sacrosanct, Thee sweet, Thee crystalline, / ...Thy beautiful center ... Thy grand, Thy mystic good" and so on (lines 1, 5). So the speaker addresses God as sacred and inviolable. In addition however, Brooks interjects less complimentary comments that God is accompanied by "wile of mighty light" and "narcotic milk of peace" (2–3). The word "wile" invokes connotations of trickery and deceit, implying that the "mighty light," Jesus Christ, is deceiving followers. "Mighty light" is a direct reference to Jesus Christ as scripture relates, "When Jesus spoke again to the people, he said, 'I am the light of the world. Whoever follows me will never walk in darkness, but will have the light of life'" (John 8.12). Brooks' use of the word "narcotic" implies numbing of the senses and addiction for believers. The use of milk as a biblical symbol appears many times in the Old Testament, most often as a symbol for prosperity and promise in the phrase "milk and honey" (e.g., Exodus, Leviticus, Numbers, Deuteronomy, Joshua, Jeremiah, Song of Solomon, Ezekiel). Milk also appears several times in the New Testament as a symbol of spiritual food for new Christians (e.g., 1 Corinthians, Hebrews, 1 Peter). "Like newborn babies, crave pure spiritual milk, so that by it you may grow up in your salvation, now that you have tasted that the Lord is good" (1 Peter 2.2–3). So, milk is a prolific biblical symbol. The implication in the poem is that Christians have been tricked into believing the promise and have ingested the spiritual *food* they have been fed. By the time the reader gets to lines six, seven and eight, God is likened to a star, distant and sad, yet "Delicately lovely to adore" (8). God is one to be seen from afar and admired, but not one who is close, personal and responsive.

The last six lines of the poem revert to the speaker who explains in the first person that s/he had been "brightly ready to believe" because of youthful frailties (9). The speaker is "Firstly inclined" to accept what s/he had been told and to fit into the neat parameters of faithfulness "To a total God" (13). The inference here is that the reality of God in the speaker's life does not measure up to the idealized expectation. This sonnet expresses that the speaker came to believe that God was what s/he had been taught as a child. The title "firstly inclined to take what it is told" makes it clear to the reader that the speaker no longer accepts what s/he has been told. "In 'firstly inclined to take what is told' the persona expresses a willingness to accept.... But God seems so far away from the world of Bronzeville" (Williams 68).*

*In the 1930s and 1940s Bronzeville was a self-contained city of blacks on the South side of Chicago. The residents were constrained to its borders by racism and poverty. The isolation was so widely recognized that the editor of the Chicago Bee newspaper sponsored a contest to elect a "Mayor of Bronzeville" in 1930 (Bolden 9–10n).

In Brooks' sonnet "God works in a mysterious way" she states the title adage and responds to it. She opens the poem by stating that a youthful eye "cuts down its own dainty veiling" (1–2) and that those who draw light or "Beam from a Book" (4) endure "modern glare that never heard of tact / Or timeliness" (5–6). The capitalized "Book" is an obvious reference to the Holy Bible and the "Beam" is an indirect reference to Jesus as light.

The cutting down of the "dainty veiling" is a biblical reference from both the Old and New Testaments in which the veil is used to separate God's essence from human sight. Moses, who was granted the exceptional privilege of being in God's presence and whose face reflected God's glory used a veil to shield his face from the other Israelites until the glory faded from his face (Ex. 34.33–35). The New Testament uses the image of the veil to distinguish the new covenant from the old. "We are not like Moses, who would put a veil over his face to keep the Israelites from gazing at it while the radiance was fading away.... Whenever anyone turns to the Lord, the veil is taken away" (*The NIV Study Bible*, 2 Cor. 3.13, 16). So, when the poem says the youthful eye will cut down its own veiling, it is saying the youth will examine God directly with its own perspective "in undiluted light" without concern for traditional teachings about the "Mystery that shrouds / immortal joy" (6–7). The most direct association is the *cutting* of the veil, that refers to the tabernacle curtain that separated the most sacred part of the Hebrew tabernacle from the outer temple rooms. That most holy place behind the curtain was accessed only by the high priests who offered sacrifices and prayer on behalf of the sinful. It housed the Ark of the Covenant topped by the Atonement cover and contained the stone tablets on which the Ten Commandments were written (Ex. 30.6, 40.3). The curtain tore from top to bottom on the day of Jesus' crucifixion, opening the way for believers' direct contact with God, hence removing the veil that covered the symbolic face of God (Matt. 27.51, Mark 15.38, Luke 23.45). Brooks' cut veiling that opens the way to see God is parallel to the divine splitting of the curtain to provide access to God by His people.

The speaker goes on to examine attributes of God. The phrase "Mystery that shrouds Immortal joy" acknowledges God's eternal aspect and heaven. The narrator speaks of the power of God to "direct chancing feet across dissembling clods," acknowledging God as a guide (80). The speaker is out from under "Thy shadows, from Thy pleasant meadows,... Thy children's air" (9, 11). Here the speaker is stating the clarity of the perception of God, but at the same time giving God ownership of the "shadows" and the "pleasant meadows," implying His complicity in the creation of the mystery the speaker has seen through. Here again is a God who is deceptive. And in the final three lines, the speaker challenges God to manifest himself or people will assume a "sovereignty ourselves" making their own heretical authority. The final lines are set up as a hypothetical "if" statement assigning God possible characteristics of "hate or atmosphere"—one negative and one formless. The lines challenge God's presence as love. "Finally, in 'God works in a mysterious way,' the persona command God to come out of hiding. 'If Thou be more than hate or atmosphere / Step forth in splendor, mortify our wolves. / Or we assume a sovereignty ourselves'" (Williams 68). The poem is an invocation, but the tone and theme imply that God is either not there or is so remote as to be unreachable. The language of the poem reflects the language of the King James Version in ironic contrast with the speaker's quest for clarity and transparency.

In "Another Preachment to Blacks" Brooks advises blacks to "force" equality, regardless of how chaotic and difficult that process might be. The chaos she describes questions God's role in the events. Not only does she question God's role, but she also questions His attributes in the poem. Is he omnipotent and totally in control, or does He allow things to happen in a haphazard and uncontrolled way? The words concede God's existence and hold God responsible, but they describe His actions, hence His character, in a way that is not consistent with Christian doctrine. The poem states, "Force through the sludge. Force, whether / God is a Thorough and a There, / or a mad child, / playing / with a floorful of toys, / mashing / whatwhen he wills. Force / whether God is spent pulse, capricious, or yet to come" (3.4–11). Clearly this representation of God is negative. It reflects the hate-filled, formless God of Brooks' "God works in a mysterious way." This portrayal of God is one whose actions are inexplicable and erratic like those of a young child. God is presented as the antithesis of the deliberate Christian deity with a perfect divine plan.

The God Brooks describes in her poems is consistent with Christian doctrine in that He is idealized "mystic good," the beautiful center, a powerful guide and is divine. Her poems demonstrate a respectful recognition of the existence of God. However, the God she describes in inconsistent with Christian doctrine in that He is isolated from people and events on earth, is not actively and methodically moving people toward good; he is unresponsive to the disenfranchised.

Brooks also wrote poems in which she characterized God's earthly representatives, preachers. One of her most poignant poems is "the preacher: ruminates behind the sermon" in which the preacher is pondering the loneliness of being God while he was preaching a sermon. Brooks spoke about her model for the poem. "We [Carter Temple Colored Methodist Episcopal Church] had a preacher who said pretty much the same thing to his congregation Sunday after Sunday. A lot of us felt that he didn't really need to concentrate, and his mind could just wander wherever it wanted to. So I had him ruminating in the poem, thinking about God" (Howe and Fox 140).

The preacher, then, is not focused on the sermon he is delivering and that sermon is rote. It is memorized and recited, not delivered from God to the church goers. Brooks is portraying a preacher who is the antithesis of what a preacher is supposed to be — called by God to be a vessel through whom a message from God will be communicated to the faithful. The poem shares his thoughts stating, "I think it must be lonely to be God" (1.1). This God is conceptualized in a very personal, human-like description. In the unimaginable realm of having no equal is the sadness of not having a friend, of never being able to look straight or lift His eyes and to have the nagging notion that "Nobody loves a master" (1.2). So, there are those who have difficulty loving God, because he is a "master." Some commentary associates that reticence with an aversion to slavery. Whether it is a reference to slavery or not, the separation between the deity and the faithful is definitely there.

> The spiritual question in the previous poem and the spiritual presence of the black church in Bronzeville introduce "the preacher: ruminates behind the sermon".... God may feel the lack of a hand to hold.... He is both remotely omnipotent and humanly deprived. God as "master" invokes the concept of "slave" and slavery adding political irony to the religious subject and skepticism to the humanist tact.... It is as if God were withdrawn into the stanzas, himself entrapped by ritual and remoteness [Melhem, *Gwendolyn Brooks* 27–28].

Though the poem speaks of God and Jehovah, its title informs the reader that the preacher is in the same lonely position. Both God and the preacher reflect a dual character. God is divine and human; He is present but distant; He is lonely, yet engenders fear in those who worship him. The preacher is preaching a sermon to his parishioners, yet having an inward personal monologue. It is no accident that Brooks uses all lower case letters in the title of the poem even though this is *the* preacher not *a* preacher. He is not afforded the capital letter denoting the respect his position would usually dictate. The duality Brooks applies to these characters is a motif she integrates through many of her religious references. They balance real against the ideal and resistance against acceptance.

In "obituary for a living lady" Brooks presented an unflattering picture of a preacher in what she terms "God's country," the church. In the poem she narrates the evolution of a young girl, who refuses the sexual advances of a young man, only to lose him to a willing competitor. The young woman finds solace and escape by withdrawing from life and living, hence dying, in "the country of God" (24). This poem is her obituary. In church country she encounters the preacher, who desires her and is plotting the time when he can make his sexual advance. In this poem the church is draining the life from the young woman who is seeking redemption, while the preacher, whose actions are parallel to those of the young man, is deceitful and sinful. She is pure; he is not. Ironically, he too is focused on her physical self, not her spirit.

Similarly, the preacher in "the funeral" is deceiving people; he is giving them "the dear blindfold." This time it is the people who are attending a funeral. He is covering their eyes so they do not see. The poem states, "These people are stricken, they want none of your long-range messages, / Only the sweet clichés, to pamper them, modify fright" (1.3–5). The preacher follows the script that continues the "tradition of piety and propriety" (2.1). He tells them, "Heaven is Good denied. / Rich are the men who have died" to anesthetize them to the pain they endure on earth and give them the hope of heavenly reward (2.3–4). Like the preacher in "ruminates," he is reciting his message. In fact, instead of delivering God's message, the preacher is breaking the commandment not to bear false witness by giving his parishioners what they want to hear as they "vaguely pray." He is shielding them from the truth. By teaching his parishioners that they will receive their reward in heaven, he is teaching them complacency in their circumstance. The poem makes it clear, however, that his purpose is to soothe them. His intentions are positive, although misguided, again expressing the duality of his character as a preacher. The image of the "dear blindfold" also suggests the image of blind justice, which also does not see or provide truth. Again Brooks integrates a social reference into a spiritual one.

It must also be noted that the spiritual leaders that Gwendolyn Brooks creates are called *preachers*, not ministers, not pastors, nor any other word that connotes a person who is tending the flock. They are giving a message to their parishioners that may or may not be beneficial to them. By using the word preachers, she implies that they are the speakers who use God's word, but who are not communicating God's message.

In "obituary for a living lady" and "the funeral," the preachers deceive an individual and a congregation, respectively. The focus expands and the consciousness is heightened for the preacher in "SONG: THE REV. MUBUGWU DICKINSON RUMINATES BEHIND THE SERMON." In the 1981 "SONG: THE REV. MUBUGWU DICKINSON RUMINATES BEHIND THE SERMON," the reader is first confronted by the contradiction inherent in the minister's apparently bicultural name and the end of the title that parallels Brooks 1945 "the preacher: ruminates behind the sermon." In the first poem the title is all lowercase, and in the second poem it is all capital letters. In the first poem the preacher is contemplating the loneliness of the hierarchical separation from God's people. In the second poem the preacher is still in a lonely position because if he is to be true to the time, he is charged with correlating the Christian message with the civil rights movement for equality for all of God's people. "'Song: The Rev. Mubugwu Dickinson Ruminates Behind the Sermon' addresses the religious and updates an early Brooks poem.... Twenty-five years later, the Protestant minister has acquired an odd (Bugwu suggests insect and vernacular bug or bother) though stylishly African-sounding given name, keeping the Anglo–Saxon one, and has become even more skeptical" (Melhem, *Gwendolyn Brooks* 209).

Brooks addresses the role of the preacher in the conflict between Christian principles in theory and the treatment of African peoples in America and Africa. His dilemma — he must preach a doctrinal message of peace to his congregation while "agitation" (lines 3, 4, and 5) against oppression is occurring in the United States and all over the world. In this poem the preacher has a social and political consciousness and is pondering the inconsistencies between his message to them to be good, knowing that "agitation" enabled African peoples to "register their science and their soil" (7) and that agitation is not consistent with a Christian mode of behavior. He recognizes that they want something to dull their senses to continue living contentedly in their circumstances. "You want brief brandy or a braver beer." And he tells them, "I wish I had a goodly word for you," but he knows, "'Be good' is the good I know. / But that will not suffice" (8–11).

Here he is recognizing that his parishioners want a "dear blindfold" like those of "the funeral," but he is conflicted. He faces, and has them face, the realities of life and the actions they will need to undertake to be free spiritually and physically. He [the Rev. Mubugwu Dickinson] recognized the political ramifications of his message in the context of oppression, and with the juxtaposition of their lot and that of other countries. He recognized the way those ostensibly preaching and teaching Christianity in Africa had deceived the people and used it to overtake them — made them "fool[s]" (Shaw 134). The poem ends with an explanation of why being good will not suffice. It lacks passion "because it is what you learned when, little and 'a fool; / you sat in Sunday School" (13–14). The Rev. Mubugwu Dickinson even associates the philosophy of being good in Christian terms with childishness.

The depiction of God and preachers in Brooks' short poems reflect the overall inconsistency she portrays between Christian ideals and doctrine, the behavior of Christians toward others in society and the doctrinal mandate to turn the other cheek when some groups are unfairly treated and oppressed in society. Brooks' distant, unresponsive God is the antithesis of the omnipresent, compassionate Father expressed in the Holy Bible. It is contrary to Christian doctrine, which provides that God will fight the battles of His children and give eternal life as the reward to those who have behaved according to His directives and have accepted Christ Jesus as redeemer. In a similar way Brooks shows the duality between the position of preacher and the realities of an individual living in the world and serving in that position. Yet, Brooks' portrayal of their conflict suggests compassion for them as they grapple with the complexities of religion in theory and in life. The reader feels the difficulties faced by the Rev. Mubugwu Dickinson as his position confines the word he can preach to this congregation. One even understands the preacher in "obituary for a living lady" who is fighting the battle between the spiritual and the flesh. Indeed it is the lonely position described in "the preacher: ruminates behind the sermon." Brooks' portrayal of God and preachers illustrates her personal frustration with religion.

Chapter Nine

Short Poems:
Sundays and Church

> And the organ-sound and the sermon
> Washing you clean of sin.
> — Gwendolyn Brooks, *Beulah at Church*

Gwendolyn Brooks also wrote short poems that explored the nature of the Sunday Sabbath and poems that reflect elements of a Sunday church service.

"Sunday Chicken" from *Annie Allen* memorializes the tradition of what African Americans refer to as the "gospel bird." Historically, poor African American families often could afford only vegetables and starchy foods on a daily basis, but they tried to have chicken on Sunday, often killed and dressed from the family chicken coop. Sunday was and is a feast day. Here Brooks satirizes the killing of the chickens with humor. "Indeed it is no more a sin," says the persona narrating "Sunday Chicken," than a cannibal "who could dote / on boiled or roasted fellow thigh and throat" (3.2–3). Yet, she associates the killing of the chicken with cannibalism, adding a serious element to the poem. She makes the negative association, yet she is anxious to eat the chicken that "should not wait / Under the cranberries in after-sermon state" (1.1–2). However, even the killing of the chicken embodied an ethical ambiguity. After all, it was killing those chickens, which were "speckle-gray, wild white ... or lovely baffle brown. It was not right. 'Sunday Chicken' shows Annie's dislike of killing anything, even the once-lovely chicken" (Melhem, *Gwendolyn Brooks* 58). In *Report from Part One* Brooks referred to chickens and other animals as "people" in the sense that they are "things of identity and response" (193). The metaphor can be extended to the idea that chickens are unthinking creatures, in this instance, waiting to be devoured. Also, from that perspective killing and cooking the chicken set up a moral dilemma to follow or not to follow the commandment against killing. Here Brooks utilizes the Sunday chicken to symbolize perfunctory participants in Sunday worship and also the conflict between right / moral and wrong / immoral Christian behavior on a very basic plane. These are the issues Brooks examined in a great many poems throughout her body of work.

Brooks also depicts Sunday as a day of peace and love. "When you have forgotten Sunday: the love story" is a poem that narrates the events of a Sunday in which a couple enjoys a quiet, simple day with relaxation, conversation and a basic dinner that mirrors dinners on other Sundays "always chicken." At the end of the day they go to bed and make love, becoming one. The poem opens and closes with the same images of "Sunday halves in bed," and "flowed into bed,... then gently folded into each other" (28, 31). That beautiful image of love portrays the peace and order that is Sunday, reflecting the Christian concept of God as the author of order, balance and completion, and Sunday as the biblically sanctioned day of rest.

Brooks also commented on the nature of the Sunday Sabbath in an early poem, "the soft man," that describes a man who enjoys the street life during the week but goes to church on Sundays. Brooks indicated in an interview, "Oh, that was about a young artist I knew, a painter who later became quite famous and hated that poem ... he was very religious. He found his salvation in religion. That was true in life and I hope in the poem" (Howe and Fox, 145–146). The character has integrated the spiritual into his physical natural world. The soft man is consistent in his participation in the church life. He never separated from his religious training, vis à vis church on Sunday.

The character has a moral standard that he applies to those he encounters, even though he is engaging in the same activities they are. Women are either "Marys [moral women] or chicks and broads [immoral women]." The men are "hep, and cats" [cool], or corny to the jive [un-cool]" and he likens the places they frequent as "garbage cans." He is casting a negative, judgmental light on them. At the same time he is affirmed at church where he is not judged because, "No one giggles where / You bathe your sweet vulgarity in prayer" (3.1–2). Here church is described in the second stanza as a "clean unanxious place." Church was a haven — a peaceful place in contrast with the language and activity of nightclubs and other evil places that are "dealing out the damns to every corner" as described in the first stanza. The soft man is seeking redemption and salvation and finds solace in church on Sundays.

Not only does Brooks contrast the characters and the setting in the poem, she also contrasts the rhythms and line structure. In "the soft man" the stanza depicting the street life has eight lines, multiple images of people and places along with two parenthetical comments "(keeping Alive)" and "(and the joint is jumpin', Joe)" (1.5–6). All of them add melodies to the motion and music of the nightlife scene. The second and third stanzas that relate to church are spare. Lines are few and short, reinforcing the clear, clean order of the church scene. The contrasts in diction, imagery and rhythm between the first and second stanzas give the poem its poignancy. The poem expresses a clear message that attending church where the soft man can be "...cool / In lovely sadness" and adhere to church values, yields personal peace (2.3–4). The third stanza, in which he is not judged but is accepted as he is at church on Sunday, is where he can let his designated softness show. Brooks uses Sundays at church as a metaphorical oasis from the convoluted, chaotic street life. It reflects the symbolic peaceful Sundays of her other poems.

One of Brooks' most complex poetic discourses on Sunday centers around a character who adopts the sabbatical nature of Sunday and the ritualistic patterning of Sunday, but who creates his own irreverent and inverted version of Sunday from his religious foundation — Satin Legs Smith. In her lengthy 1945 poem of 22 irregular stanzas, "The Sundays of Satin-Legs Smith," the title character's actions during the week are only hinted at, while his actions on Sunday define him. His life story is told in snippets as his Sunday unfolds.

Satin Legs' actions are elevated from the first two lines in which his title, "Inamoratas," has been "bestowed" (1.2) on him and his inclination has been "Blessed" (1.2). Plural for *inamorata*, "Inamoratas" means *female lovers*. It is a dubious title but carries the parenthetical note *with an approbation* or *approval*. So, his unflattering title has been blessed with a capital B. There is a spiritual elevation of his rather base, sinful, perhaps blasphemous actions, for a Sunday Sabbath. But the poem explains this seeming paradox as it progresses.

With his rising early on Sunday morning, he "sheds, with his pajamas, shabby days ... his intricate fear, the / Postponed resentments and the prim precautions" (4.1–3). The audience is told that he "designs his reign." This day — this Sunday — is the day over which he has control. During his bathing and dressing, the reader is made aware of the contrast between the aromas of flowers around his morning bath and the scents of his past: "His heritage of cabbage and pigtails, / Old intimacy with alleys, garbage pails, / Down in the deep (but always beautiful) South" (5.16–18). His closet is his fortune with brightly colored suits in colors like "Sarcastic green" with shoulder pads that are "cocky and determined as his pride" and "hysterical ties / Like narrow banners for some gathering war" (8.2–3). He is arrogant. He does not have diamonds or pearls or silver plate. Brooks uses the word "glory" (7.4) to explain what his fortune is and what it is not. It is a suggestion of the pearly gates to which he does not aspire, nor will he enter.

When he exits, he "dances down the hotel steps," letting the reader know that he lives a transient life in a hotel and that he is carrying over his Saturday night dancing into Sunday morning — a sin to some. In stanzas 14 and 15 that follow, the reader gets a glimpse of his neighborhood, which has the sounds and sights of a poor urban neighborhood, but also specifically references the Sunday behavior of others in the community. The reader is told, "He hears and does not hear" (14.2) and "He sees and does not see" (15.2). Satin Legs has suppressed the consciousness of traditional Sundays. Yet, he loiters, watching the men and women coming from church service, including "Children's governed Sunday happiness" suggesting parents teaching children to temper their behavior in honor of the Sabbath (14.4). He sees girls with "ribbons decking wornness" (15.4) and boys "Wearing the trousers with the decentest patch, / To honor Sunday" (15.5–6); women coming from church with "temperate holiness arranged / Ably on asking faces" (15.7–8); and men without wonder and joy who know hunger. Sunday for the churchgoers is a time when people dress in the best that they have, behave in the best way they know how and seek answers to the problems of life, including deprivation. Satin Legs, who is smooth and cool, has suppressed those lessons of his youth. He remembers but has redefined "Devotion" in order to forget the experiences he discusses in stanza 16: "Whether or not his mattress hurts" ... the thing / His sister did for money:... all his skipped desserts" (11–15). He "Judges he walks ... alone, / That everything is — simply what it is," not a pathway to another existence (17.6–7). Religion did not assuage his hunger or the ugly memories of what poverty did to his family.

Although "the pasts of his ancestors lean against / Him. Crowd him. Fog out his identity. / ...He quite considers his reactions his" (17.1, 2, 5). He escapes from his social situation by creating his own persona on Sundays. Miller explains Satin Legs identity crisis well.

> He cannot recognize that his own flair conceals his sordid environment.... Socially blind, perceiving them [women coming from church] clearly would help him to illuminate his own identity, because their lives illustrate the inseparability of determinism and personal choice. Their social conditions have partially governed whether their service is to God, to those well-off people requiring domestics, or to men's carnality" [Miller in Mootry / Smith 105–106].

So, he avoids the obvious and goes to an afternoon movie with different ladies "From Sunday to Sunday" (19.4). But, he has not forgotten, nor lost the innate longing for the other Sunday religious rituals.

Satin Legs inverts Christian spiritual love and makes his Sunday love carnal and self-centered. In the end he seeks the sensual pleasures of a "down home" meal at Joe's Eats with the woman for the day and a sexual tryst. This is the natural spiritual experience that is concrete for him in his world. "Her body is like summer earth, Receptive, soft, and absolute" (22.5–6) — absolute for absolution or forgiveness.(22.5–6). Brooks elevates the act to a spiritual experience. Satin Legs has created a Sunday ritual that superimposes the worldly, physical experience over the religious training, but that retains the religious framework that has been suppressed. The persona of Satin Legs has come into existence because of the disconnect between the life of the religious people he observed coming to and from church, and the realities he saw day by day. His religious reality has died in his social environment. The poem characterizes Satin Legs Smith through his actions and events. "A longer poem devoted to a portrait of a ghetto man as he attempts through highlife and other diversions to cope with impotence and inferiority, 'The Sundays of Satin-Legs Smith' looms as one of the poet's most complete treatments of spiritual death in the black community" (Shaw 66).

The reader can only speculate that Satin Legs' childhood experiences at church were like those of Beulah in "Beulah at Church," a poem from Brooks' first book of poems for children, *Bronzeville Boys and Girls*, in which Brooks pays homage to her beloved "Aunt Beulah, The Queen of my family" (Brooks, *Report from Part One* 54–55). Unlike Beulah, Satin Legs had broken loose from "the big people closing you in, / ... / Washing you clean of sin" (3.2, 4).

The poem "Beulah at Church" is a four-stanza poem with the meter and rhyme scheme of a ballad and a little girl named Beulah as a speaker. The first three stanzas set forth the rules one must follow to attend church, such as being "just clean" with "No door-screen dust upon your nose," "not [to] be loud," and to "hold your song-book — so! — " and a description of the sounds of the church service. But the message of the poem is in the final stanza in which little Beulah states, "I do not want to stay away" and "It feels good to be good" (4.1, 4). She feels comfortable and joyful in the environment and activities of church. "At church, Beulah is surprised by joy while harnessed in by extreme cleanliness and adults" (Kent 121). Beulah's time at church is happy.

Brooks includes elements reminiscent of church services in a number of other poems in a variety of ways. In poems that do not have an explicit religious or moral lesson, she sometimes utilizes diction that connotes religion or that reflects the Bible for reasons specific to the poem.

A poem that demonstrates Brooks' effective use of religious diction is "A Farmer." In that poem a farmer has cancer but is out in his field moving "reverently" through the furrowed rows. Immediately, the reader knows that this farmer is a spiritual person. She says that at times he "Is very close to the meaningful sweetness of things. / Altering the earth with glory" (1.3–4). The use of the word "glory" lets the reader know that his work is in tune with God's work. It elevates his work to the divine. He is cultivating the fields that he has cultivated the year before. The reader appreciates the repetition of the life cycle in the context of the farmer's dying. His body is a metaphor for prayer as he kneels to inspect his plants. The images are soft and warm and loving. The sun is hot. Brooks presents his work as worship. The motif is pastoral.

Another example that incorporates worship into the language of a poem is "The Wall," which commemorates a gathering of black people around a wall with a mural. "'The Wall' is a poem about the celebration of the Wall of Respect, the side wall of a typical ghetto tenement building in Chicago on the corner of 43rd and Langley on which is painted a mural depicting black heroes and black pride" (Shaw 150). The poem is the second in a pair of poems entitled *Two Dedications: I The Chicago Picasso* and *II The Wall*. The poems commemorate the unveiling of two works of art: the first an abstract steel sculpture for the city of Chicago, and the second, a mural on the wall of a building in a poor area of the city, which reflected in concrete detail the community around it. The first unveiling was attended by the mayor and 50,000 people, while the second one less than two weeks later, was attended by the community, which was represented on it. The contrast between the imagery in the poems is sharp. The first was abstract and cold, generating a formal response; the second was concrete and warm, generating an informal communal response.

According to Brooks, people come "Humbly" and "All / worship the Wall" (6.1–2). Her selection of the word "worship" expresses a great deal. It shows the spiritual nature of the community; it implies connectedness among the community group versus the crowd image of the first dedication. The second group's humility, a virtue noted in both Old and New Testaments, also connotes reverence. Worship expresses the notion that those at the wall were giving the mural praise and adoration. Brooks also refers to the wall in stanza 7, line 11, as a "still Wing," one that has the capacity to elevate this community with its validation and affirmation. Again, the capital *W* elevates the image to a spiritual level.

The symbolism of the wall is intriguing. The title and the emotion of the event suggest an analogy with the Western Wall (called the Wailing Wall) in Jerusalem, which is the remaining wall of an ancient temple and has religious significance for both Jews and Christians. Brooks' use of the word "worship" reinforces the notion of prayer at the wall. Jews pray at the wall as the nearest point they can reach to the Temple Mount, which is controlled by Muslims. Also revered by Christians, the wall may be a remnant of the temple where Jesus overturned the tables of the money changers, which was destroyed then rebuilt by Herod the Great (Matt. 21.12, Mk. 11.15, Coogan 39). So, Christians also pray at the wall. Analogies can be made for both. The idea of a poor African American community praying at a site that *represents* their spiritual goal, but is not the goal itself, is a clear comparison. The association of prayer at a site where those who take advantage of the poor for financial gain were castigated by Jesus is also applicable here. Brooks introduces that idea in poem after poem, notably in "In the Mecca." The alternative name for the Western Wall adds to the symbolism of the wall in Brooks' poem. The name Wailing Wall, with its Holocaust association, further enhances the implicit anguish of those in poverty-ridden urban ghettos, even though this is an occasion for celebration.

Worship services include direct references to the Holy Bible and Brooks also wrote short poems that incorporated those references as well. One type of biblical reference that Brooks often utilizes in long and short poems is the name Mary and variations of it (e.g., Mary Ann, Marian) in ways that reflect women named Mary in the Bible. As previously noted, she used the name Mary in "the soft man" to symbolize moral behavior. In Brooks' poems there is Old Mary who has found inner peace and is no longer pained by her inability to fulfill the dreams of her youth. There are "delicate Melody Mary," "the three Maries" and Marian all of whom have created personal oases in the midst of the roach-infested and difficult environment in "In the Mecca," again signifying their untainted spiritual peace like the biblical Marys.

The name Mary holds rich religious associations. Six women in the New Testament are named Mary: The first is Mary of Bethany, sister of Martha and Lazarus, who anointed Jesus' feet with expensive oil (Lk. 10.39) as an act of sacrifice, humility and devotion. The second is John Mark's mother Mary, a well-to-do Jerusalem woman, who courageously opened her home for Christian worship during the era of Christian persecution by Herod Antipas. In fact, when Peter was released from prison, he went to Mary and asked her to alert other Christians of his release (Acts 12.12–17). Another is Mary of Rome (Rom. 16.6) who was among the group that carried Paul's epistle to the church at Rome and is noted to have worked very hard for the developing Christian church. The fourth, James and Joses' mother who is also called "the other Mary," was among the women who had come with Mary Magdalene to Galilee to care for Jesus' needs during and after the crucifixion. She also was at the tomb with Mary Magdalene (Matt. 27.28). She may have been the Mary called Clopas' wife mentioned by John. There were three women named Mary at the cross of Jesus. "Jesus' mother stood beside his cross with her sister and Mary the wife of Clopas. Mary Magdalene was standing there too" (John 19.25). All of them exemplified Christian virtues that can be seen in Brooks' characters, but the two most prominent women who serve as specific models in particular Brooks poems are Mary the mother of Jesus and Mary Magdalene.

In Christianity then, there is a strong association of the name Mary with innocence and spiritual purity, relative to the legend of her birth and the virgin birth of Jesus. In the case of Mary Magdalene the association is one of salvation for the reformed sinful. Brooks' use of the name Mary certainly drew upon the experienced Mary Magdalene's traits, as well as those of the innocent Mary, mother of Jesus.

Brooks engages the pure, spiritual symbolic associations with the biblical Mary, mother of Jesus directly in "A Penitent Considers Another Coming of Mary." The poem queries whether Mary would be willing to give birth to a second Savior and Prince of Peace to redeem this modern, violent world, if she were to come to earth a second time. The poem describes the hypothetical second Savior as sad in the face of the hostility in the air. Yet "Mary would not punish men (3.1) by refusing to provide the second Savior because she would forgive humankind. By assigning her the capacity to forgive humankind and to participate in the decision about whether or not to "furnish" (1.4) the second Savior, Mary is spiritualized to a level of near divinity. Brooks' Mary is a loving "Mother" (1.2) of all humanity, not just the Mother of Jesus as evidenced by a capital *M*.

The concept of the Virgin Mary giving birth to Jesus through the power of God's Holy Spirit certainly incorporates the view of Mary as a vessel through which God's will was done. But that does not present Mary herself as a divine being as she is in this poem. The Holy Bible offers little information about Mary before her betrothal to Joseph, her visit to Elizabeth during her pregnancy, the events of Jesus' birth and her devotion to her son during His life. There are sources however that assert that Mary was chosen before her own birth and groomed by God to a unique spiritual level for her mission. They support Brooks' presentation of a woman with the divine authority and religious decision-making prowess to be the rather modern Mary characterized in "A Penitent Considers Another Coming of Mary." One such source is the non-canonical Infancy Gospel of James, allegedly written by James, brother of Jesus, that names Anna and Jaochim as the parents of Mary. The text and tradition hold that Anna prayed for God to give her a child whom she would pledge to the Holy Temple. She was blessed with a girl, Mary, whom she presented to the Holy Temple at the age of three and where she remained and was taught religion until she returned to her parents at the age of 15, just in time for her divine mission. Although girls were not usually taught religion, it is written that Mary was unique in the eyes of God (Kirby 1–2).

While scripture offers little detail about the life of Mary, it tells more about the Mary called Mary Magdalene because she was from the town of Magdala. She was a key follower of Jesus Christ. Some would say she was the other disciple. While there is conjecture about her, some clear, specific statements are made about her in scripture that make her one of the most admired women in the Bible. She became a follower of Jesus and led women followers in financing Jesus' work. "Jesus traveled about from one town and village to another proclaiming the good news of the kingdom of God. The Twelve were with him, and also some women who had been cured of evil spirits and disease: Mary (called Magdalene) from whom seven demons had come out,... These women were helping to support them out of their own means" (Lk. 8.1–3 *NIV*).

Mary Magdalene had been a sinner, possessed by seven demons of Satan. She is sometimes depicted as the unnamed prostitute who washed Jesus feet with her tears but the Bible does not attribute specific sins to her by name (Lk. 7.37–50). Whatever her specific prior sins, she was transformed by Jesus Christ into a woman of faith who had the privilege of being the first to see Jesus after the resurrection: "When Jesus rose early on the first day of the week, he appeared first to Mary Magdalene, out of whom he had driven seven demons" (Mk. 6.9). He charged her with alerting the disciples. "Go instead to my brothers and tell them, I am returning to my Father and your Father, to my God and your God. Mary Magdalene went to the disciples with the news (John 20.17–18). So, Mary Magdalene was a very human character, rich with the moral dilemmas of life, and she was victorious over evil by changing her behavior. Brooks applies Mary Magdalene's complexity to the central character in "Gang Girls."

Brooks' empathy for girls in gangs is communicated to the reader immediately by her use of the name Mary Ann, the central character of the poem, "Gang Girls." At the beginning of the poem, she indicates, "Gang Girl are sweet exotics." And that Mary Ann has dreams of better places than those to which gang membership limits her. To Brooks "Mary is / a rose in a whisky glass" (2.1–2). She represents beauty and love even though she is in a decadent environment. Yet she is isolated, insulated from it. She can see out; she can be seen, but she is not integrated into it, connoting a certain innocence. Mary moves through difficult times in which her one bright spot is what her Ranger lover brings her — stolen diamonds. In return she drinks with him and has sex with him. The sex is not coupled with love; it is currency, which she expends, emotionally removed from the act, watching him, hearing him call her name, "Mary, Mary Ann!" Mary, the gang girl, has settled for less; she is a prostitute, like the young Mary Magdalene. She exists in the gang lifestyle, but she is not of it. The combination of innocence, impacted by a life in poverty, suggests the character of Mary Magdalene. Brooks presents Mary Ann with a character that can be redeemed or saved.

In addition to referencing places, people and events from the Holy Bible, African American church services include traditional music. Brooks incorporated references to traditional African American spirituals as auditory imagery in poetry. Melhem indicates, "...whether in the ballad, a poem meant to be sung, in the blues, or in the lyrical sonnets (as most of the 'Gay Chaps' sequence). Brooks gathers the several strains — religious, chiefly the spirituals [W.E.B.] DuBois refers to as 'sorrow songs,'" (*Gwendolyn Brooks* 21). A prime illustration is the poem "of De Witt Williams on his way to Lincoln Cemetery." In it Brooks adapts the line from the old, familiar spiritual "Swing Low Sweet Chariot" as "Swing low swing low sweet sweet chariot" and couples it with "nothing but a plain black boy" as a refrain. Brooks' adaptation of the line creates a more upbeat rhythm than the traditional dirge-like pace, but still grounds de Witt's funeral imagistically and symbolically in the African American church. In addition, she contrasts references to dance hall music with the religious music to create the contrast between the title character's big city lifestyle in Chicago with that of his roots in Alabama. The audience is told "Don't forget the Dance Halls —/ Warwick and Savoy, / Where he picked his women, where / He drank his liquid joy" (stanza 5). The poem chronicles his life and his trip in the hearse to the cemetery. He was a black "everyman" who migrated from Alabama to Chicago. He is on his way to Lincoln Cemetery to be taken up by the sweet heavenly chariot after an ordinary life with city-street pleasures.

The couplet that opens with the line from the song "Swing Low Sweet Chariot" appears in the poem twice. Each time, it is preceded by his four-line epitaph, in which the first two lines narrate his being "born in Alabama" and "bred in Illinois." Each time the epitaph appears there is variation in the opening words. The final lines, "He was nothing but a / Plain black boy" are repeated verbatim. In the opening stanza the first two lines are introduced with "He was." One may imagine a solemn speaker of those words, perhaps a clergyman, but the second time, the quatrain begins with the verbs "Born" and "Bred" which increase the pace, change the rhythm of the poem and create a contrast in voice that changes the image of speaker to that of a worldly person. That subtle, but effective change in voice for the second speaker creates an image of one who frequented those dance halls referenced in the fourth stanza, along with de Witt Williams, and replicates the fast rhythm of that music in contrast with the slow cadence of "Swing Low Sweet Chariot."

> The first one can be thought of as read by a minister, relative, or good Christian friend over the body of the deceased. The second one seems to continue the sentiments of the first. The first line, for instance, is from a Negro spiritual of funereal and redemptive content. It has been changed however, made jazzy like Louis Armstrong's swinging "When the Saints Go Marching In." The speaker here, a real street buddy of De Witt's introduces a joyous, urban individuality into the sadness of the funeral" [Williams 212].

Although de Witt did not live a pure, spiritual life, he is cleansed spiritually by the words and cadence of the poem. The music provides the setting for the character and the events of his life and his death. The lyrics set a reverent tone for the poem and communicate the appreciation and spiritual elevation of the everyday lives of those men he symbolized; de Witt Williams is the archtypical black man of his day who found the joy he could in his circumstances. Brooks' de Witt Williams celebrates the nobility of a common black man whose reward came after his death. The result is so lyrical that famed jazz musician Oscar Brown set the poem to music.

The atmosphere of Sundays and church, augmented by the language of scripture and traditional music would be incomplete without the sermon — the preached word. Brooks included the sermon genre in her poems. The three sermons on the Warpland, discussed in-depth in chapter six, are notable examples, but she also wrote shorter poems in that mode. In such poems the narrator-persona of the poem assumes a position of authority and uses direct address and imperative mode to deliver a message to the poem's identified audience about how to live. Their tone is instructive and pedantic.

In 1980 she published a volume entitled *A Primer for Blacks*, which was comprised of three poems calling for African American solidarity. The title makes the instructional mode of the contents clear. The poems included a title poem and two others, "Those of my Sisters Who Kept Their Naturals" and "Requiem before Revival." Brooks' intention to assume a sermonic tone is not only evidenced by the mode of address, but it is also expressed in some poems by the titles. Among those in which she utilized a sermonic aspect, were two poems with the word "preachment" in their titles. In 1972 she published "BOYS. BLACK. A Preachment" and in 1981 she revised it as "Another Preachment to Blacks." Both were minisermons. According to Kent one of the reasons Brooks reworked the poem was because she said the first one was too "preachy" (253).

"BOYS. BLACK. A Preachment" first appeared in *Ebony* magazine and later was included as the final poem in Brooks' volume *Beckonings*. All of the poems in the volume focus on black solidarity and black pride in an unwelcoming society. The poem "BOYS. BLACK. A Preachment" is a sermonic call to action for black males. It appeals to them to move forward into territory that has been denied to them to bring about a new era for African Americans. The poem urges them to move quickly and to push forward against the opposition they meet. In Brooks' words, "Be brave to battle for your breath and bread / Your heads hold clocks that strike the new time of day. " (1.2–3). The narrator tells them to move,

> Up, boys. Boys black. Black boys.
> Invade now where you can or can't prevail [2.1–2]
> In the precincts of a nightmare all contrary
> be with your sisters hope for our enhancement
> Hurry.
> Force through the sludge [4.1–4].

Not only does Brooks utilize the conventions of the sermonic genre, but the content of the preachment poems also has religious references, imagery and symbolism. After expressing love and trust in young males in the beginning of "Boys Black. A Preachment," the speaker says at the end of the poem,

> Take my Faith.
> Make of my Faith an engine.
> Make of my Faith
> A Black Star. I am Beckoning [7.4–7].

Although her direct reference is that she has faith in the boys themselves, the capitalization of "Faith," not once, but twice, certainly adds religiosity to the word. In addition, "a black star," with which the narrator is "beckoning," functions as a symbolic juxtaposition of the star of Bethlehem and the name of visionary Marcus Garvey's shipping line.* This black star is

---

*The Black Star Line was the steamship company operated by Garvey and the Universal Negro Improvement Association (UNIA) from 1919 to 1922. The Black Star Line was to be the UNIA's vehicle for promoting worldwide commerce among black communities. In Garvey's vision, Black Star Line ships would transport manufactured goods, raw materials, and produce among black businesses in North America, the Caribbean, and Africa, and become the linchpin in a global black economy ("People and Events: The Black Star Line").

an image in the heavens that the speaker summons as a source of spiritual and cultural power to generate forward movement. These lines pray for an unnamed power to transform the speaker's religious faith into a beacon for African Americans — a black star shining toward Africa. The simultaneous references to the Black Star Line and the reference to the concrete image of an "engine" ground the spiritual objective in an earthly, social one.

> It [BOYS. BLACK.] has a prophetic tone and urgency and reflects anxiety regarding blacks' failure to retain the high level of consciousness they had achieved, a matter that would be more fully expressed by other poems in *Beckonings*. Subtitled "a preachment," the poem begins with the urgency of a mother calling her sons abruptly into action [Kent 248].

The poem also focuses on the need for African Americans to recognize their African roots. After calling the black boys to action, she tells them, "Boys, in all your Turnings and your Churnings, / remember Afrika" (5.7–8). Even her spelling emphasizes the staccato rhythm and sound of a native speaker of an African language pronouncing the word "Afrika." It has the oral aspect of a sermon. The poem that she called "Another Preachment to Blacks" was published in 1981 in *To Disembark*. At the core of both poems is a sermonic tone that affirms the "Afrikan" ancestry of African Americans. "BOYS. BLACK. A Preachment," a call to warriors, and "Another Preachment to Blacks" tell the audience that their voices, "your singing" ("Another Preachment" 1.1; "BOYS. BLACK" 2.9), the rhythms of the heart, "pulse" and "booming" ("Another Preachment" 1.2; "BOYS. BLACK" 2.10) implying drums, both musical and talking, all "call ... AFRIKA" (1.4). She chides blacks for "singing" and "booming" about "AFRIKA" while knowing little about it.

The language of the poems also reflects religion. The word "Call" has a religious denotation as well, particularly in the context of a self-proclaimed preachment. A call is a communication from God to undertake a spiritual mission. Those internal / spiritual and external / physical African American life elements call *to* Africa, as well as reflect the call *from* Africa, to the spirit of African Americans, which Brooks presents as the "temples of your Power" ("Another Preachment" 1.3; "BOYS. BLACK" 2.17). The play on the word "temple," which in the physical sense connotes the mind and in the spiritual sense the place of worship, brilliantly expresses the mind-body-soul spiritual connection between African Americans and the African motherland. Further, they assert that the capitalized "Power" of African Americans is in their African-ness — in the unity of the bloodline. The poems go on to expose the nature of the sameness between Africans and African Americans that has been diminished by time and historical circumstance. While she acknowledges the lack of knowledge and "our tiny union" ("Another Preachment" 1.7; "BOYS. BLACK" 2.21–22), she describes the connection as "dwarfmagnificent." Further she explains that it is an active and uncomplicated reality of African American experience, "the busysimple thing" ("Another Preachment" 1.9; "BOYS. BLACK" 5.23).

In the preachments, Brooks speaks of blind leaders and blind followers. She warns them against the "imitation coronations" ("Another Preachment" 4.1; "BOYS. BLACK" 5.3) of leaders and the "courteous paper of kingly compliments" ("Another Preachment" 4.3; "BOYS. BLACK" 5.5), both of which would be given by whites and would inhibit the achievement of equality. Her mandate is for them to "Force through the sludge" ("Another Preachment" 3.4; "BOYS. BLACK" 4.4) to reach the goal of equality.

Both versions of the poem have the same purpose and the same mode of expression, but there are differences, two of which should be noted here. The stanza that ends "Another Preachment" is the next to the last stanza of "BOYS. BLACK A Preachment." In addition to minor wording changes, she changes one word "ATTICA" to "AFRIKA" in the later poem, and changes the placement of the two final lines of "BOYS. BLACK A Preachment" to make them the introductory lines of the correlative stanza in "Another Preachment." The stanzas read:

"BOYS. BLACK. A Preachment"	*"Another Preachment"*
Beware	Beware the
the easy griefs.	easy griefs, that fool and fuel nothing.
It is too easy to cry "ATTICA"	It is too easy to cry "AFRIKA!"
and shock thy street,	and shock thy street
and purse thy mouth,	and purse thy mouth
and go home to thy "Gunsmoke." Boys,	and go home to thy "Gunsmoke," to
black boys,	thy "Gilligan's Island" and the NFL
beware the easy griefs	[5.1–7].
that fool and fuel nothing [6.1–9].	

When the first version of the poem was published in 1972, the September 1971 Attica prison riot was a recent memory for all Americans.* The meaning of the stanza with the Attica reference reflects the time and implies

*The Attica Prison riot was a four-day stand off during which prisoners took control of the prison and held hostages. They presented a list of demands for reforms (e.g., more than one shower a week and more than one roll of toilet tissue per month per prisoner. It was a time of tremendous racial tension in the United States, especially in the prisons. Attica prisoners alleged that the 383 all-white corrections officers were openly racist against the inmates who were 54 percent African American and 9 percent Puerto Rican at that time. The riot occurred less than a month after the death of Black

that some African Americans were paying lip service to fighting racism by making shocking statements, but they were not actively doing anything to ameliorate it. In the second version of the poem Brooks still chides the African Americans who are not actively and effectively working against racism and inequality, but this time alludes to them shielding their inactivity by boasting of Afro-centrism although they are unenlightened about Africa, in fact. The change reflects the culture of 1980 just as the Attica reference reflected 1971. In both cases she portrays those whom she is addressing as living entrenched Americanist lifestyles behind the façade of African American consciousness. In addition the Africa reference in "Another Preachment" warns African Americans who were making social strides to avoid becoming so much a part of American culture that they forgot their heritage. Brooks' revised preachment broadened the audience beyond young males to include all African Americans.

Brooks expresses the contradiction of their existence by juxtaposing the language consistent with that of the King James Version of the Bible with symbols of pop culture. The religious language implies a worshipful attitude and mental focus on the television shows and sports of their everyday lives. Even the idea that one would "purse thy mouth" ("Another Preachment" 5.5; "BOYS. BLACK" 6.5) portrays the silence as a religious act showing faith in the U.S. society. She warns them of those "easy" ("Another Preachment" 5.2–3; "BOYS. BLACK" 6.2, 8) things that "fool and fuel nothing" ("Another Preachment" 5.2; "BOYS. BLACK" 6.9).

The change in the placement of the stanza changes the tone of the ending of the poem entirely. In "BOYS. BLACK" the final stanza is one about love and faith, which ends the poem on a reverent and prayerful note. In "Another Preachment," on the other hand, the tone at the end of the poem sharply contrasts with that of the earlier poem because the "Beware" stanza is the final one. There is anger; there is tension; there is an uneasy feeling generated from the warning. Even the repetition of the biblical word "thy" intensifies, even exaggerates, the focus on the activities that will only lull them into complacency. The subliminal tone is one of anger and frustration, and that is effectuated with the repetition of the word "thy." The fact that Brooks uses it three times in the first version

[continued] Panther member and author George Jackson at the hands of prison officials at San Quentin State Prison in California, which exacerbated the tension.. After the four days, Governor Nelson Rockefeller ordered the New York State Police to recapture control of the prison by force. The result was the death of 29 inmates, 10 corrections officers and civilian hostages and serious injuries to 80 others. After a lengthy lawsuit by the families of the victims, the New York State settled with 12 million dollars to the families of the prisoners and 12 million to the families of the nonprisoners in 2004.

and then four times in the second version shows her particular attention to making certain the audience reading the poem would understand its importance to the poem.

As the poems discussed in this chapter attest, Brooks expressed her reverence for Sundays and the traditions of the Christian Church in the sermonic genre, religious language and content of her shorter poems, just like she did in her long ones.

Chapter Ten

Short Poems: Religion and Contradiction

At home we pray every morning, we
Get down on our knees in a circle,
Holding hands holding Love,
And we sing Hallelujah.

Then we go into the world.
— Gwnedolyn Brooks *Religion*

Brooks' short poems, like her long ones, also show her concern with issues, ambiguities and contradictions associated with religion. In some poems she uses religious language, imagery and symbolism to point up ideas opposite religious ideals. In most poems she uses those elements with traditionally associated meanings to define true Christian morality in common situations. Brooks' poems define Christian love, and postulate that Christians were not demonstrating it in their daily lives. She also focuses on issues that demonstrate contrasts between church doctrine and societal religious practices by individuals, with special emphasis on ethical contradictions shown by attitudes toward African Americans. This chapter will examine four poems that illustrate the approaches she used to expose those contradictions in her poems.

The poem "A Lovely Love" published in 1960s *The Bean Eaters* integrated biblical references, like the dramatic foil, to emphasize features antithetical to them. The poem characterizes a forbidden love relationship — perhaps forbidden because of age or race. The reason the relationship is not socially acceptable is not explicitly stated but it is described fully and richly for the reader. In the first eight lines the sonnet advises the reader that the lovers seek "alleys" and "darkness" to meet. Yet, like the repetition of the phrase "Let it be..." implies, it is a beautiful experience for them to be together and they want the relationship to exist. Brooks continues the contrasts with "Hyacinth darkness" which places a beautiful flower in darkness where it cannot be seen. Further, it associates with the Greek mythological Hyacinthus, who was loved by Apollo but accidentally struck and killed by Apollo during a discus match. Legend says the hyacinth flower formed from his blood. That relationship ended in death (www.greekgods.org). In Brooks' poem "petals fall" and there is a "kiss" that *scrapes* the speaker. The softness of the petals and the sweetness of the kiss are subverted by the foreshadowed painful demise of their relationship. The imagery of the falling petals and surroundings that include the words "rot" and a "splintery box" connote decay and decline. Even the janitor's splintery box symbolizes a wooden coffin for their ill-fated love relationship. Yet, on the surface, it is lovely. The lovers have release, kindness and smiles, symbolically suggesting a satisfying sexual encounter albeit in a dark and dreary place. This relationship is physical.

The shift in sonnet lines nine through 12 infuse biblical references to enhance the physicality of the relationship by expressing that it is the antithesis of spirituality. The lines read,

> That is the birthright of our lovely love
> In swaddling clothes. Not like that Other one.
> Not lit by any fondling star above.
> Not found by any wise men, either. Run.
> People are coming. They must not catch us here.
> Definitionless in this strict atmosphere [9–14].

Those lines have several biblical references that are important to the poem's interpretation.

First, there is the reference to the birthright, the word embodying the source and the privilege to engage in this relationship. The association with Jacob-Israel's birthright is two-fold. Like Jacob's birthright, this clandestine love has been *stolen*, tainting its authenticity. On the other hand, like Jacob, who became the father of the 12 tribes of Israel, this relationship is also the beginning of a new order. Here the speaker says, "That is the birthright of our lovely love." It is still beautiful to the lovers.

The speaker describes their love "In swaddling clothes." While it is a direct reference to the birth of Jesus, the word "swaddling" also refers to something that is restricting, and this clandestine "lovely love" is confining and limited. It has no future. Brooks reinforces the limited nature of the relationship by contrasting this "birth" with the "Other one"—capitalized to relate it specifically to Jesus Christ. The reference to Jesus "in swaddling clothes," the inversion of the Star of Bethlehem to a "fondling star" and the declared absence of the wise men signifies that the love relationship is in an early stage, that it is physical and that it is neither sanctioned by spirituality nor by society. Bolden says it well: "The lovers are not permitted the ethereal meaning accorded the two celestial figures of the stable, nor will men come bearing gifts from afar.... Finally, in the closing couplet, the young couple yields to the reality of their environment and the fact that the allusion to a higher religious birth is not to be their own" (127). The directive to "Run" to avoid being caught, places the situation in perspective. The relationship will not prosper, yet the lovers had a moment of order amid the chaos.

Brooks' *Selected Poems* concludes with poems grouped as *A Catch of Shy Fish*. Here Brooks incorporates a very traditional Christian concept and symbol to define the group of poems. The catch of fish is a direct reference to the New Testament commission Jesus gave His disciples to make them fishers of men by vesting them with the spiritual authority to gather converts (i.e., fish) in the net of Christianity (Matt. 4.19, Mk. 1.17). Each poem in Brooks *A Catch of Shy Fish* is about a poor, African American person or couple who aspires to a spiritual plane beyond what their circumstances would provide. Thus, she extends the metaphor although she describes them as "shy."

The relationship between the symbol of the fish and Christianity is a strong one. It is traditional and significant because of scriptural references and historical use. Jesus fed the multitudes with five loaves and two fish (Matt. 14); Jesus provided a net full of fish when the disciples cast their nets on the right side of the boat (John 21). The most important biblical reference is the meal the resurrected Christ ate with His disciples, which consisted of fish (Luke 24.42.43). Consistently, early Christians would scratch a fish symbol on the ground in the catacombs in Rome as a means of distinguishing friend from foe during the first century. In addition second century Greek theologian Clemens (St. Clement of Alexandria) noted that the letters of the Greek word for fish made an acronym for Jesus as follows (seen in Avey).

Greek word for fish, IXΘΥΣ (pronounced Ichthys)

I	X	Θ	Υ	Σ
Iota	Chi	Theta	Upsilon	Sigma
Iesous	Christos	Theou	Yios	Soter
Jesus	Christ	God's	Son	Saviour (Seiyaku)

That solidified the tradition, and the Ichthys / fish symbol has been an icon for Christians until the present time. Melhem concurs.

> The participants display a modest but persistent valor, even when it is misplaced.... This innocence, to a degree, makes them "fish" in the traditional Christian sense, which points toward their redemption and

their self-entrapment.... The net, ... is also that of universal love, Brooks' major theme of caritas, and recalls the invitation by Jesus to Peter and Andrew, "Come ye after me, and I will make you to become fishers of men" (Mark 1.17). While it is a more subtle Christian reference, it is a substantial one [*Gwendolyn Brooks* 143].

Another Shy Fish poem is about a couple whose relationship is not sanctioned by society, "Spaulding and Francois." It is another poem in which the religious imagery and symbolism are essential to the experience of the poem and one that illustrates how Brooks uses religious imagery and symbolism to sculpt a work. The poem has three stanzas. The first stanza provides the setting in which the couple is enjoying "Things Ethereal"—spiritual joys during the night. The capital letters provide emphasis however with the religious language in the other two stanzas, and one must conclude, they also add religiosity to those words. The two-line stanza includes the words "cool silver in their dream" creating an image of moonlight. The second stanza speaks of wind tangled among "bells" inferring church bells, "spiritual laughter" that is hushed, "the happiness of angels" and "angels' eyes, soft, Heavy with precious compulsion." All of those images create a vision of a spiritual love experience that has been elevated to a religious experience. The tone of those verses is hushed and serene, like the tone of a church service. The third and final stanza, however, shatters the serenity as people "will not let us alone." There is an implied judgment by others who "will not credit, condone / Art-loves that sun / Them" who are parenthetically "moderate Christians rotting in the sun" (3.1–4). The play on the word "sun" for Son communicates a clear message about decadent, judgmental, inflexible Christians, who fail to recognize or understand a love that is ethereal — a love whose description here symbolizes Christian love. All three stanzas end with religious imagery and the very message of the poem is developed through the religious images and symbols. Hansell agrees. "Obviously, from the artists' point of view, what the people want seems contemptible, 'moderate Christians rotting in the sun' is a description full of contempt" (Mootry & Smith 72). Melhem expands upon that notion.

Because their Christianity is inadequate and hypocritical, the sun (Son implied) cannot sustain them. Sun becomes an antithetical image and takes on apocalyptic significance. The couple's moon imagery, inferred, counters that of the sunlit People. If the latter were sincere — to pursue the biblical analogues — the sun would not smite them by day, as the moon at night does not disturb Spaulding and Francois (See Psalm 121.6) [*Gwendolyn Brooks* 149].

Brooks displays dissatisfaction with the conflict between Christian doctrine and religious practices of Christians in this poem. Brooks' message that

Christians are not behaving like Christians should behave is included in her poems for children, as well. The opening quatrain from "Religion," which introduces this chapter is an example.

"Religion" is about a family that practices Christianity in a ritualistic way but does not adhere to the tenets of the faith. Brooks sets up the ritualistic aspect by creating parallel lines as the first quatrain and the last quatrain of the poem. Except for the one-word change from "morning" to "evening" the words are the same. The middle of the poem however, which follows line five, "Then we go into the World," exposes the sinful activities in which the family members engage. The father and mother are unfaithful to each other with lovers; the brother and sister take weapons to school and spend time with an unsavory person on the schoolyard while eschewing the education the school is offering them. Then they all come home and engage in the ritual of praying on their knees in a circle and singing "Hallelujah." All of them are hypocrites, and the title, "Religion," is ironic, even sarcastic, in context.

A poem that vividly expresses the philosophical and political contradictions Brooks saw between Christianity the religion and Christianity the life practice is "The Chicago Defender Sends a Man to Little Rock." The poem is Brooks' response to the events surrounding the integration of Little Rock Central High School.

In 1954 the United States Supreme Court declared public school segregation unconstitutional by the Brown v. Board of Education of Topeka, Kansas, decision and followed the decision with a mandate in 1955 that states desegregate "with all deliberate speed." Like many school districts in the south, school officials in Little Rock, Arkansas, resisted desegregation and created a system in which black students were interviewed for admission, deemed unacceptable and rejected. As public pressure intensified, school officials interviewed 80 students in 1957 from which they accepted nine black students to attend Central High School. When the students arrived on September 3, 1957, they were met by a mob of whites, who yelled racial slurs, threw things at them, spat on them and threatened their lives. Segregationist Governor Faubus ordered the Arkansas National Guard to keep the nine African American students from entering the building. On September 20, 1957, Federal Judge Davies ordered Faubus to remove the National Guard to allow integration to take place, but Faubus defied the order. President Eisenhower sent more than 900 paratroopers and federalized the 10,000 National Guard troops to ensure the school would be open to the nine students in accordance with federal law. Finally, on September 23, 1957, the Little Rock Nine entered the school. U.S. Army units were stationed at the school for the balance of the academic year to guar-

antee the students' safety, but they could not thwart the attacks and indig-
nities the students suffered that year. Governor Faubus shut down Central
High School for the 1958–59 academic year to avoid integrating it. When
the school re-opened in 1960, only two of the nine black students were
admitted and they graduated in 1961. The events sparked a national ref-
erendum on states' rights, civil rights and racial equality unmatched in
U.S. history. Little Rock Central High School is now a National Historic
Site and civil rights museum and the Little Rock Nine have a significant
place in the civil rights movement and the history of the United States.

In Gwendolyn Brooks' poem she uses a reporter-narrator to examine
the paradox of the white residents of Little Rock as ordinary people who
become an angry mob of adults who assaulted the young students. Many
people throughout the country, especially in the north, were appalled and
angered by the attack on the students and thought the people of Little
Rock were somehow different from everyone else. Ostensibly, the reporter's
task is to tell their story — to explain their behavior. However, he is per-
plexed, "I scratch my head, massage the hate-I-had [for the angry residents]
... Because there is a puzzle in this town.... They are like people everywhere"
(9.1, 4–7). Through this character Brooks subtly, but categorically illustrates the transformative power of racism to generate hatred in otherwise
God-fearing people.

While Little Rock, Arkansas, is the physical setting for the poem,
Brooks uses religious references as a spiritual setting or context in which
to set up the moral paradox. She uses religious references to establish the
religious habits of the inhabitants, such as attending church and celebrating
Christmas. She comments on the tainted core of their religion and, at the
end of the poem, spiritualizes the victimized Little Rock Nine. Here again
she expresses the conflict between religious principles and ethical social
behavior.

While Little Rock is geographically accurate, the name Little Rock
is imbued with religious associations that enrich the meaning and symbolic
intensity of the poem very directly. There are numerous references to the
word "rock" in the Bible. The Old Testament often uses it to reference or
symbolize God. For example, 2 Samuel 22.3 says, "My God is my rock,
in whom I take refuge, my shield and the horn of my salvation." In this
instance the rock is a metaphor for God. God issued water from a rock
when the Israelites were in the desert (Ex. 17.6, Num. 20.11). Here God
uses the rock to give life. Among New Testament references to the rock
are passages that use the rock metaphor for God in the context that God
can trip someone who is moving through life without having accepted the
Gospel (Rom. 9.33, 1 Pet. 2.8). It is also used to symbolize the sterility

and infertility of a religion without Gospel roots (Luke 8.13). The rock reference in Brooks' poem relates to a deviation from religious truth. All three associations are à propos. If indeed this is *little* rock the residents lack godliness; they have received only a small portion of that which God provides. Therefore they have tripped over their religion and have fallen away from religious truth. Melhem extends the metaphor even further. "The 'Little Rock' of little faith objectifies into the small rocks thrown at the children" (*Gwendolyn Brooks* 113). With Gwendolyn Brooks' demonstrated knowledge of scripture and poesy one must presume she intended to bring all the richness of the rock symbol to the poem.

As the reporter-narrator observes the activities of the townspeople, religious allusion winds through the poem showing the layers of the small-town USA lifestyle. Brooks establishes the tone and moral setting early in the poem with the people singing "Sunday hymns" and "after testament and tunes, / Some soften Sunday afternoons / With lemon tea and Lorna Doones (4.1–3). The citizens have attended church, and they have a genteel demeanor. Then the poem moves from Little Rock at Christmas to Little Rock in July with baseball and open air concerts. She portrays the women of 1957 Little Rock in a subservient role. Making love is done as a "kindness" or "In azure / Glory with anguished rose at the root" (7.5–6). The reference to azure Glory conjures up associations with heaven with the blue sky and capitalized "Glory," yet the rose, which represents love, is anguished at the root. The contrast between the rose and the root symbolizes the inconsistency between what is presented as spiritual, Christian love and the ugly truth lurking beneath. The Christian love of the Little Rockians is not real; it is growing from an agonizing source. It has deviated from the essence of Christian doctrine, which is love based on peace and brotherhood.

Against the passivity and order of ordinary life and ordinary people in Little Rock, the reporter attempts to understand the "hurling spittle, rock, Garbage and fruit" (11.1–2) they are throwing at "bright madonnas" (11.4) and "brownish girls" (11.5) and "a bleeding brownish boy" (stanza 12). The African American children are presented as pure and Christ-like in their bleeding. Brooks reinforces the alignment of the victims of Little Rock's violent anger against the students with the Pharisees violent anger against Jesus in the last line of the poem: "The loveliest lynchee was our Lord" (stanza 14). In the voice of the reporter-narrator, Jesus was Lord of all of them. Although Brooks and some critics later lamented the use of that final line as the weakest in the poem, it is an effective ending in that it strongly characterizes Brooks' purpose and theme. She exposes the incongruity between the alleged Christian church principles of the citizens of

Little Rock and asserts the tragedy as one of universal, eternal proportions. Melhem comments on the religious aspect of the poem.

> The "Chicago Defender" is a deeply religious poem about school integration; from title to imagery to scansion and rhyme, a Christian symbolism prevails.... Although the narrative images feature whites, ambiguity — culminating in the black and white religious images — is a thematic strategy ... the final equivalency between the lord and the black children as lynch victims [is] structurally inevitable [*Gwendolyn Brooks* 109].

Bolden addresses the strength of the final line and its function in the poem as well.

> The final line,... recaptures the earlier hints of the religious rituals of a people who "sing / Sunday hymns," adhere to testament and tunes, and who "love," yet who, by contrast are still grappling with the notion of social equality.... In conjunction, the two stanzas are mindful of the lynching of Christ, yet in an ironic antithesis of interpretation, also function as an unfortunate statement on the historic potential for the tenets of Christianity to sit comfortable along side the cruelty of lynching [157].

"Chicago Defender Sends a Man to Little Rock" can only be understood with an appreciation of the way race can function as a catalyst to transform everyday American Christians into crass, violent, race-warriors who attack others, even lynch others while espousing the church values they hold forth on Sundays. Religious traditions and real life collide in Brooks' poem like they did in Little Rock, Arkansas, in 1957. The contrast between the religious allusions and the social setting builds the tension and develops the message of the poem.

As the foregoing discussion demonstrates, Brooks uses contrast and contradictions between religion and social ethics as tools to develop her messages. She extols the Christian ideals of love, peace, charity and justice like a preacher. It has been said, "There is no need for a prophetic word in the absence of contradiction. Prophets emerge only from 'gap' situations: the gap between poverty and plenty, injustice and justice, war and peace, sin and righteousness. The historic reality of existential dehumanization against the recognition of essential dignity demands a word from the Lord" (W. Jones, 6). Brooks focuses on the gap and the contradictions; she presents the necessary "word from the Lord."

Conclusion

The foregoing discussion set forth in detail where and how Gwendolyn Brooks used religious allusion in her poetry. As chapters three through ten demonstrate, her poetry is dense with such references. She used Old Testament quotes and parodies reflecting specific biblical passages, such as the "hungry tooth" and those from the 23 and 30th psalms. She included references to specific events such as the burning bush, Hezekiah's healing and Jacob's surreptitious acquisition of the family birthright. She incorporated the messages of Old Testament prophets, such as Hosea and Amos, and related them to modern time. Nor did Brooks ignore the New Testament in her work. She referenced Jesus' birth, the splitting of the temple veil, the Last Supper, his meal of fish after his resurrection and his commission to his followers. Brooks adopted the sermon genre in certain works and brought traditional church hymns into others, specifically "Swing Low Sweet Chariot," "I Am Thine O Lord" and "O Happy Day." She characterized Jesus Christ and even God himself.

It is apparent from the previous chapters that Gwendolyn Brooks had an unusually rich knowledge of the Bible. She stated in her own words, "Everyone should read the entire Bible to be educated" (Howe and Fox 143). She demonstrated her impressive Bible education by referencing passages and events in the Bible that are not generally known to those who are not serious students of the Bible. For example, her phrasing at the opening of "In the Mecca" that paralleled Matthew 1.18 (KJV) is an obscure reference. In the Amos passage of the Mecca poem, not only did Brooks re-present the message of the book of Amos, but she also paralleled its structure and development, again showing deep familiarity with the text. It appears that Brooks was quite knowledgeable about the specific period in the eighth century B.C. when the Israelites were divided into the two kingdoms, north and south, when both Amos and Hosea, whom she referenced, prophesied to the Northern Kingdom of Judah warning the people to turn back to God before it was too late. Both prophets chastised people for being materialistic, selfish and immoral. Both prophets reinforced Brooks' message that godly, Christian behavior toward others in society embodies equality — true democracy. It is also significant that she chose minor prophets Amos and Hosea to emphasize instead of major prophet Isaiah, who is from the same period and who wrote similar warnings. Isaiah is much more frequently quoted and referenced because of his messianic prophesies. She also used Hosea's message in her "In Montgomery" poem and used the whirlwind motif described in the book of Hosea in the "Sermon[s] on the Warpland." And certainly, the quoted biblical passages of "In Montgomery" that reference Hezekiah (who was King of Judah during the same period) and Psalm 30 are not among the most often quoted biblical passages.

Brooks also uses enough references to heaven and hell to manifest recognition of them in the traditional religious sense. In "The Anniad" the contrast between peace and war is presented as Heaven and Hell; "De Witt Williams on His Way to Lincoln Cemetery" was going to Heaven after living in the hellish world. In the "Sermon[s] on the Warpland" societal destruction during judgment is presented as Hell. While she makes no explicit statement about Heaven and Hell in those poems, she does acknowledge them expressly in "hunchback girl: she thinks of heaven" and the poem "when I die." These poems affirm the idea of a heavenly reward after a life of suffering. "Hunchback girl: she thinks of heaven" addresses God directly. The sadness the young woman feels as she goes through life with the averted stares of passersby and without the benefit of a straight back is reflected in the poem as she contemplates Heaven as a straight place: "Out of coils, Unscrewed" (7–8). There she will be rewarded with straightness. In heaven, the girl in the poem muses, "I shall walk straightly through most proper halls. / Proper myself, princess of properness" (9–10). Similarly the man in "when I die" will receive a reward after a life of loneliness and poverty. He is "one lone little short man / Dressed all shabbily," but when he gets to heaven the angels will kiss him, he'll wipe his tears away and he will have girls waiting for him to make him happy (1.3–4). Both characters are looking forward to heavenly rewards.

Gwendolyn Brooks' poetry has so many religious allusions that are so deeply engrained in so many ways that they cannot simply be crafting tools. The proliferation of those references and their integral role in developing the form and content of her poems make it clear that their meaning and associations are very important to Brooks. The references construct a literary design that highlights the positive aspects of Christianity. She equates true democracy and social justice with Christian ideals. In addition, she advocates the active pursuit of Christian ideals by citizens as a means of creating a true democracy in the United States.

Analyzing her religious allusions is key to decoding the poetic intentions of Gwendolyn Brooks. In order to engage such a discourse one must establish a conceptual lens through which to view the body of work. While the Ten Commandments or Mosaic Law (Ex. 20.2–17, Deut. 5.6–21) set up the foundation for the Judeo-Christian belief system, it is the New Testament teachings of Jesus Christ that build on Mosaic Law and reveal the tenets of Christianity, the New Covenant. Thus, this discussion will center around: (1) Christine doctrine, (2) Christian characterizations of God and Jesus Christ and, (3) Christian love and Society. Those points frame the religious ideas present in Brooks' poetry.

Christian Doctrine

Many denominations hold various interpretations of Christianity, but a broadly acknowledged statement of faith is the Apostles' Creed, which is affirmed in most Christian churches, regardless of denomination. It sets forth a specific set of beliefs that reflect Christian doctrine. The Apostles' Creed, sometimes called the Affirmation of Faith, was not written by the Apostles but is consistent with their teaching as it is recorded in the Holy Bible (e.g., 1 Cor. 8.6, 15.3–4, 1 Tim. 3.16). It existed in various forms from about A.D. 200 to 750. "The text accepted today is identical to what was written in 750 by Pirminius, who lived in what is now Switzerland" (www.christianodyssey.com). So these doctrinal statements constitute an excellent summary of the primary tenets of Christianity for this discussion. One translation of the Apostles' Creed states:

> I believe in God the Father Almighty, Maker of heaven and earth, and in Jesus Christ, His only Son, our Lord, who was conceived by the Holy Spirit, born of the Virgin Mary, suffered under Pontius Pilate, was crucified, dead and buried. The third day he arose from the dead and ascended into Heaven and sitteth on the right hand of God the Father Almighty; from thence he shall come to judge the quick and the dead. I believe in the Holy Spirit, the church universal, the communion of saints, the forgiveness of sin, the resurrection of the body and life everlasting. Amen [Henning, 503–504].

In addition to being a belief system stated by the Apostles' Creed, Christianity unites a community of believers who aspire to live a way of life that is guided by God, taught and modeled by Jesus and implemented through the power of the indwelt Holy Spirit.

Even though Brooks' personal disillusionment with the attitude and behavior of self-proclaimed Christians created a conflict, which Brooks did not publicly resolve, she did, however, analyze it again and again in her work. And, she consistently presented moral behavior in Christian terms. This text is asserting that Gwendolyn Brooks' poetry, when viewed collectively, presents the guiding principles of Christianity as ideal, making her (whether intentionally or unintentionally) a proponent of the Christianity. A discussion of the doctrinal elements expressed in the Apostles' Creed and their relationship to religious references in Brooks' poems illustrates this point.

Christian Characterization of God and Jesus

Summaries of the characteristics of the Christian God, mentioned in the opening of the Apostles' Creed, provide a more detailed depiction.

> The Christian Godhead is supremely powerful and knowing.... Even though God is the creator of the universe, people can still have a personal relationship with him, so powerful and knowing is he..., he wants us to think of him as our father and talk to him like we'd talk to a loving father. Prayer is just the process of talking to God..., so if we have a request, we should not hesitate to ask God to help us, and he'll grant our request if it's in accordance with his will [broadcaster.org.uk].

Another commentator states,

> Christians believe in one God, who created the universe and all that is in it.... God is entirely spiritual. That is, he exists in a sphere outside the normal physical universe.... Christianity conceives of God as ... personal, [one] who is capable of affecting and being affected by others. This is implicit in the concept of God as Father,... God cares about and interacts with the creation. Human beings are responsible to God. As the creator, God is responsible for the world and its history.... God is thought of as continuously sustaining the world [geneva.rutgers.edu/src/Christianity].

Both summaries attribute similar traits to the Christian omniscient, omnipresent and omnipotent God. God is creator of the universe and is eternally responsible for humankind with whom he has a personal fatherly relationship. God listens and grants requests that are consistent with His divine plan. He abhors sin and punishes sinners. He disciplines sinful believers to refine them and make them better. God is love, which he demonstrated most monumentally by sacrificing His son, Jesus to save the sinful world.

The God of Brooks' poetry is consistently immortal, powerful, and all-knowing. He is shown to be responsible for what happens in the world and is capable of changing the world. The attributes of God presented in "firstly inclined to take what it is told" and "God works in a mysterious way" acknowledges God as spiritual, eternal and powerful. In those poems God is shown to be capable of guiding people through the obstacles of life on earth. The God in "The Preacher Ruminates behind the Sermon," who is tired of looking straight, and the snickering God overseeing the Mecca both exhibit human-like feelings and behavior. In the poems he is anthropomorphic, making it easier to relate to him as a father figure. Brooks presents God with the power to change the world. In "In Montgomery" the narrator asks for "the Fine Hand of God" (27.103) to fix the waning civil rights movement there. Further "In Montgomery" asserts, "We ... been real good / and have gone through all that sufferin'. / God is a righteous God (33.12–14), alluding to a fatherly relationship with God who will reward children who have been good. It also suggests God's justice and reward for the faithful. Just the reference to prayers, as requests of God, rests on the premise that God hears prayers and responds to them. The implication is that God is responsible for sustaining humankind.

Christian doctrine holds that God showed his supreme love for humanity by sending his son to die on the cross for the sins of humankind so humans can be reconciled with God and have the opportunity for eternal life with him (John 3.16). Brooks expressed the idea of God punishing the sinful and disobedient directly in Alfred's poem-within-the-poem, "In the Mecca," in which she alleges that America will reap dire consequences for failing to treat African American citizens fairly and equally. The first lines of the Mecca poem, which reference the Christian idea of a fall from grace also suggest the negative consequences of operating outside of God's favor.

> Because God is a God of justice who considers that sins need to be punished, we would all be destined to go to hell in the natural course of events,... However, God sent his son Jesus to earth, to live as a human being and die to take the punishment for our sins.... Jesus was taking the punishment for sins, so that those who become his followers can receive forgiveness, since Jesus has paid the penalty. This is an indication of God's love for humans.... Christians believe that Jesus rose from the dead.... Then he is reported to have risen into the air,... an angel appeared and told them that Jesus would one day return, as Jesus himself had also said he would. When Jesus returns, it will not be as a child again; he will come back to judge the world. People who have done evil and rejected him will go to hell, but people who have been reborn by accepting his death on the cross for their sins and being regenerated into better people by the Holy Spirit will go with him in his kingdom [broadcaster.org.uk].

The Apostle's Creed states, Christians believe "in Jesus Christ, His only Son, our Lord."

> Christians see Jesus as in some sense embodying God.... Jesus is seen as a vehicle for God to be present ... there is both a distinction between Jesus and God, and an identification of Jesus with God.... The other thing is that Christ is seen as "pre-existent." That is, creation was done through him, who was always with God and in fact part of him....* The Bible says that the birth was miraculous. Jesus' mother was still a virgin. Thus God was responsible for the birth. But not physically ... a person who would suffer on behalf of all of us, bearing the punishments that we deserved because of our sins. As a result, we would be reconciled to God ... Jesus died, then began appearing to various of his followers, helping them understand the significance of his death and resurrection.... Christ died to seal our forgiveness by God. We are expected to respond by forgiving each other, and acting as a force for reconciliation in the world [geneva.rutgers.edu/src/Christianity].

Brooks incorporates all of those aspects of Jesus as the Christ in her poetry. To begin she adopts the purity of the Virgin Mary in her various Mary and Mary-derivative named characters. Indeed, "A Penitent Considers Another Coming of Mary" portrays Mary with divine qualities, as previously discussed, correlating with the concept of the virgin miraculous birth. "Emanual's Nightmare" also references Mary, mother of Jesus.

Brooks' characterization of Jesus is also consonant with the traditional attributes of Jesus. She used the name Emmanuel, "God with us" (Matt. 1.23) and says he was "born out of the heaven, in truth" ("In Emanual's Nightmare" 5.6). to reference Jesus in "Emanual's Nightmare," illustrating the concept of Jesus as the incarnation of God. Reinforcing the association with hope and love, Jesus "played on the heavy hope of the air / And loved our hearts out!" (6.3–4). At the end of the poem it is clear that Jesus had the power to stop the fascination the people had with war, but chose to let them have what they want, again like a loving parent. Also, at the end of the poem Brooks called Jesus God's Son, revealing his distinct identity as well. In "In the Mecca" Brooks' Jesus is questioning whether his philosophy of love is really working. Brooks makes a clear distinction between God and Jesus in "In Montgomery" when the narrator says, "God is a righteous God. / He look down peaceful on all. / But JESUS get MAD! / JESUS'll get up and DO somep'm" implying that Jesus would better understand the human condition and have a more human response than God (33.14–17).

---

*In Bible passages narrating Creation (Gen. 1.26, 3.22) and the building of the Tower of Babel (Gen. 11.7) both quote God using the plural pronoun "us" denoting at least one other presence with Him. To Christians "us" includes Jesus and the Holy Spirit.

In combination belief in the virgin birth and in the death and resurrection of Jesus corroborate Old Testament prophecy, and provide scriptural authentication for Christianity as the religion of the Messiah, or Christ. In addition, the Bible records that Jesus ascended into heaven by going up into the air, but will return to judge the world in a second coming (Acts 1.10–11, Matt. 25.31). All of those points are evident in Brooks' poetry. "Emanual's Nightmare" shows Jesus descending through the air paralleling scripture.

The similar characterization of Jesus is not the only aspect of Jesus evident in Brooks' work; she also incorporates the concept of repentance followed by redemption as the hope of humankind. That is the "good news" of the Gospel of Jesus Christ. The message of Jesus Christ is a message of hope for those who are doing wrong, to repent of their sins and accept Jesus as Savior, which will facilitate a spiritual rebirth and grant the opportunity for reconciliation with God. The hope of restoration to *spiritual* morality to generate *social* morality is threaded throughout Brooks' poetry. Time after time she decries the ill treatment humans perpetrate on one another, whether in war, in cities or in individual attitude. Indeed Brooks' concern for the downtrodden follows the message and model of Jesus Christ. The radio announcer at the end of "In Montgomery" is pleading with his listeners to help those in need. Yet, Brooks often combines the message of helping the oppressed with the notion that a positive change can make things better — hope. There is the hope at the end of Amos' passage in "In the Mecca" poem. There is the hope that the cynical Loam Norton expresses at the end of his parody of the 23rd Psalm when he allows for the possibility of reaching heaven. There are the gangs who served as pacifiers and mediators in the violent aftermath of the Rev. Dr. Martin Luther King's death in "The Third Sermon on the Warpland" as living symbols of hope for peaceful resolution of social unrest. All of those references imply absolution for the penitent, restoration and reconciliation with God as the ultimate hope — eternal life.

Christian Love and Society

Because the words are deemed God-inspired, hence spiritually authoritative, the Holy Bible provides the external guiding principles for Christians. The Holy Spirit, internal to the Believer, provides guidance and warnings that govern day-to-day morality and ethics for individuals and members of the church. Brooks' poetry also focuses on human behavior in the context of social conditions. Some poems present specific principles of Christianity as themes and affirm Christian doctrine explicitly, while others do so implicitly. A dominant Christian concept evident in Brooks' poetry is the Christian ideal of spiritual, humanitarian love and equality — consistent with her expressed personal religion of *kindness*. The specific Christian principles that Brooks presents emanate from Jesus' commandment to "love your neighbor as yourself." Jesus' ministry focused on the poor and disenfranchised and he sought to help them change their spiritual and social condition. There is a natural application of the religious doctrine to social doctrine as individuals treat other people and other groups in a Christ-like, loving way.

> Christians live in community. Jesus described himself as a vine, with us as the branches. It is not possible to be united with him without also being united with other Christians. The motivating force behind the Christian life is love. Since love is a personal relationship, there is no way to grow in love other than to be with others. This Christian community is called the "Church." ... The term "communion of saints" [in the Apostles' Creed] refers to the unity of all of Christ's followers, living and dead [geneva.rutgers.edu/srd/Christianity].

Christianity adopted the ancient Greek definitions for types of love: *eros* (love that is desire, often sexual), *philial* (love of family or group), *caritas* (love for the well-being and destiny of other people) and *agape* (love for the earth, all living things and the universe). The Greeks believed that all responsible members of society should work toward caritas love because all members of society are interdependent upon one another. Caritas love was viewed as essential for the survival of individuals, society and the world. They also believed that caritas love matured virtue, integrity and emotional well-being. So, each individual who expresses such love is enriched. Although the Greek term *caritas* predates Christianity, the concept is parallel to Jesus' teachings of peace, love and charity. In Christian theology, caritas/agape love (caritas) is held as the perfect model for the human spirit because it both glorifies and reflects the nature of God (New World Encyclopedia.org).

Representations of that ideal peace, love and charity are core messages in much of Brooks' poetry, and the religious references support them. She explores caritas from the perspective of God's actions and human responses to Christian teaching of caritas and how people apply or fail to apply it to everyday life. "In the Mecca" condemns the lack of caritas shown by the legal and criminal justice system and by the neighbors who live in the Mecca building. The people are impoverished, but not just monetarily, socially and politically. They are impoverished spiritually and morally, as well. Their inability to "love your neighbor as yourself" results in the death of the innocent, spiritual Pepita — who is their future. The murderer is a neighbor. Although the neighbors have few financial resources, each of them could volunteer to help with the search or do something to help and support the family. However, the residents show no concern for Pepita or her family Similarly, the police show no concern. Each character is focused on him- or herself. Although there is clearly a message about the treatment of poor people, specifically those who are African American, and a message about the impact of poverty, it is also more broadly applicable to attitudes of people toward others who are in need.

Another poem that decries the lack of caritas is "The Chicago 'Defender' Sends a Man to Little Rock." In that poem Brooks is looking at individuals again. This time she is specifically targeting the white Christians of Little Rock and how their racism distorts their spirits and blinds them to the essential tenets of Christianity — peace, love and charity, such that they behave in a violently anti–Christian way. Again, caritas is missing. They show no love for the young black children who are going to school. They show no understanding of the black people who are their neighbors and fellow human beings. They show no understanding of their interconnected destiny — only hate. In these and other poems, as well, Brooks reinforces the Christian belief in caritas — Christian love.

From her early poems, such as "A Sabbath Prayer," "Forgive and Forget" and "The Squirrel," to later ones like "In Montgomery," Gwendolyn Brooks acknowledges the existence and power of God. In interviews when she specifically denies having religion, she comments that she would say a prayer to "Dear" for safety at the beginning of a trip on a public conveyance (Hull and Gallagher 102). She acknowledges God's existence in poetry and in life. But her keen sensitivity to others and her understanding of Christian love raised a troubling philosophical question that she explored again and again in her poetry. If caritas is truly a reflection of God, then God's actions are loving and kind toward all people. Why then does God allow suffering and injustice to continue? Why are innocent people victims of evil when God has the power to stop it?

To explore the answer in her poems Brooks makes an essential conceptual dichotomy between God's *existence* and His *presence*. While Brooks' poems do not question God's existence or His power, a number of her poems question God's presence in the lives of the disenfranchised and innocent in society. The poem "firstly inclined to take what is told" is an example (see Chapter Eight). In that poem Brooks' persona questions whether the earlier lessons s/he has been taught about God are true because God is so far away from the everyday lives of black people in Bronzeville. In "God works in a mysterious way" Brooks expresses various natural and mystical evidence that reflects shadows of God, but she asks God to show himself clearly. Again, she is presenting the idea that God is distant and unseen.

In "BOYS.BLACK. A Preachment" and again in "Another Preachment to Blacks" the speaker in the poems question God's presence for the needy, but s/he also questions His manner and His attitude. The poem puts forth two possibilities for God. Either He is completely committed and present, or He is capricious and arbitrary in his dealings with people. That question correlates to another one Brooks raises, "Why does God allow suffering, injustice and evil to exist in the world and affect the lives of innocent people?" In a 1990 interview with Susan Howe and Jay Fox, Gwendolyn Brooks asked the following question and offered an answer.

> But it has been said that God is all powerful. If that is true, why can't He or She — someone so powerful — put a stop to such evil?... I surmise that each one of you has done what I have done. You have told yourselves things that will make it possible for you to go on. What I have decided is that what I must do — what I have been doing most of my life, ever since I became conscious of need — is to be kind to people. Kindness is my essential religion, and I have governed my life by the light of that religion. I feel that no matter what the "truth" is, I can't go wrong with kindness [Howe and Fox 148].

Even when expressing her doubts Brooks acknowledges God's existence and her comment about kindness actually dovetails back to caritas or Christian love, which can be characterized as kindness.

Brooks' poetry also questions the role of preachers in the lives of their congregants, which has also been discussed in chapter eight. Sermons are designed to share biblical messages and show their applicability to daily life. In Brooks poems, such as "the funeral, obituary for a living lady" and 35 years later in "SONG: THE REV. MUBUGWU DICKINSON RUMINATES BEHIND THE SERMON," she presents the minister as one who is blindfolding people so they do not see their true condition or the true nature of their religion. In these poems preachers were part of the perpetuation of a passive response to suffering and are a hindrance to the movement to elevate the condition of the poor, a significant philosophical hurdle for Gwendolyn Brooks.

She pondered poetically whether religion is a help or a hindrance to equality for poor black people. She addressed the question directly in the poem "Shall I Prime My Children, Pray, to Pray?" Is religion going to help? The poem is from *The Womanhood: Children of the Poor* poems and the first line question raised by the speaker in the poem is a question that Brooks raises in several poems. Will the prayers of poor people be heard?

The sonnet implies that religion does not provide as it promises, so religion is blinding believers with its promises. The final five lines tell the children to "revise the psalm, sew up belief / If that should tear" and that the mother speaker in the poem is "Holding the bandage ready for your eyes."

> When speaking of the series of sonnets, Shaw commented on this poem as follows. A third poem, "And Shall I Prime My Children, Pray, to Pray?" illustrates another attempt to solve the problem of girding children of the poor for the pitfalls and dead ends of life's labyrinth. Specifically, the parent is questioning the efficacy of religion and whether or not the rigors and inhibitions are worthwhile. The parent's negative terms for referring to religion suggest that he himself is not a believer but is willing to try religion as an answer for his children" [Shaw 113].

Smith also offers an insightful critique of the poem.

> The word "prime" is an elliptical expression that implies teaching at a primary level; when combined with the two accented words in the line, "pray, to pray," it becomes an alliterative but sarcastic answer to the question. In the second line, "mites" is both a reference to insect pests and a diminutive qualifier for "children" as well as an ingenious reference to the small boxes used for special, Sunday school offerings.... In the third line, "spectered" connotes the mysterious, ghostly nature of Christian mythology, while "crusts of penitents' renewals' suggests bits of the sacramental wafer as well as the more domestic image of a nearly empty food closet. Moreover in keeping with the mother's pessimism about religious belief, "all hysterics" infers an emotional catharsis that, "for a day," accompanies the children's intense religious worship.... The word "lights" signifies both religious enlightenment and self knowledge, but ironically the mother instructs her children to confine their self-knowledge in the "jellied rules" of their religious training. This spiritual food, like the earlier "crust," does not, however respond to the basic need of the poor children for nourishment [172].

Central to the question Brooks raises about whether religion is a help or a hindrance to the disenfranchised, is the conflict between the essential Christian theory of caritas and the practice as it is shown in the behavior of Christians and others in society. It is the response of others that can manifest God's provision for them. That inconsistency and the conflicts that emanate from unchristian behavior by Christians is the subject of a number of poems and references. The couple in "Spaulding and Francois," for example, is intruded upon by "moderate Christians rotting in the sun" (3.4). The conflict is represented in that poem, like others, as a perversion of Christian ideals to support self-centered views and behaviors. Gwendolyn Brooks' poetry explores the discrepancies between *apparent* versus *actual* morality and good versus evil, among others. Miller views the antithetical elements Brooks sets up as the poet opposing the id (which governs instinctual and immediate satisfaction) to the superego (which obviates unacceptable desires and monitors moral restrictions). "Often when she draws upon Judeo-Christian, historical, and folk sources, through the ornate style or through the vernacular, she opposes the id to the superego, balancing the contradictory tensions which inform human existence" (Miller, *Define ... The Whirlwind* 159). Miller's psychoanalytic conceptual frame aligns with the religious one asserted here. Satin Legs Smith illustrates the inversion of Christian practices to accommodate his id. He satisfies his physical needs on Sunday with his own version of religious ritual. When extrapolated to social interaction and social policy, the conflict generates an inversion, even perversion of Christian behavior, like that Brooks explores in "The Chicago *Defender* Sends a Man to Little Rock." The self-identified Christians exhibited violence, hate and selfishness, instead of peace, love and charity.

Unchristian behavior of whites toward African Americans is the subject of some of Brooks most moving poetry. To Brooks a lack of caritas creates a society in which individual people do not view one another's needs as important, nor do they seek to meet them. Inequality and social injustice are the result. One poem in which Brooks strongly expresses the concept of social oppression as contrary to God's morality is "Riders of the Blood-Red Wrath."

> The poem title alludes to John M. Synge's one-act play *Riders to the Sea* (1904) in which a mother loses her sixth and last son to the sea. Struggle against the environment is natural and fatalistic in Synge, man-made and vulnerable in Brooks. The "Blood-red Wrath" implies a revolutionary animus, yet it also convey the wrath of God.... The title invokes the vision of St. John the Divine of the Second Coming in which the Lord, "Faithful and True," is clothed with "a vesture dipping in blood" (Rev. 19.11–13)" [Melhem, *Gwendolyn Brooks* 135].

The poem, written in 1963, is lengthy; it has 89 lines, and is conventional in form. The language and content are complex and politically powerful. It is a poem that Brooks discusses at length in "Marginalia," her appendix to *Report from Part One*. A brief summary of her comments follows: The riders are the Freedom Riders* and "all related strugglers for what is reliably

---

*In 1961, the Freedom Riders set out for the Deep South to defy Jim Crow laws and call for change. Despite being backed by federal rulings that it was unconstitutional to segregate bus riders, they were met by hatred and violence — and local police refused to intervene when white supremacists attacked them. But, the Freedom Riders' efforts transformed the civil rights movement (Gross 4).

right" (187). The segregationists watched the strugglers, but did not see the pent up anger and emotional energy required to hold the "fury" in check. In the poem the rider goes on to say that he still loves this country and that he still "stand[s] for its stated principles." As the poem proceeds, stanzas three and four show that the segregationists have forgotten their civility and "commit crimes against God himself" and "injustices that would have offended great Christ" (188). Brooks continues by citing her passage that states that democracy and Christianity begin with the freedom riders; assuming the voice of the rider from stanzas 11 and 12, she says, "And as for my Freedom Ride — both figurative and physical — it shall go on interminably; it shall go on until it is no longer necessary,... which is in the interests of love in the largest sense, will ride on into whatever awaits us at whatever Cavalry" (189).

Brooks' pro–Christian perspective is apparent from her comments. First she indicates that the crimes of the segregationists are against "God himself." Again, she invokes the existence and presence of an omniscient God who will judge human beings. She also refers to "great Christ," recognizing the divinity of Jesus and his biblically ordained role as judge of humankind. The poem has two references to the violent attacks on the Freedom Riders as a crucifixion — "my Cavalry" and "my continuing Cavalry" — letting the reader know that Brooks is portraying their victimization as a spiritual, anti–Christian violation. On the other hand, she says the Freedom Riders are working in the interests of "love in the largest sense" meaning caritas, which is the essential tenet of Christianity. The poem's statement, "Democracy and Christianity / Recommence with me," epitomizes Brooks' philosophy in a most succinct way (10.1–2). For Brooks the two ideals are bonded. One cannot have democracy without having love for one's fellow human beings. And treating fellow human beings with love is the practice of ideal Christianity.

The African American militancy that is suggested by the poem must be understood in the context of Christianity. Brooks' answer to the issues of social inequality and injustice is to invoke adherence to both democracy and Christianity. To Brooks the civil rights movement was pushing America to live Christian ideals to become the democracy she claims it to be. So, the promotion of militancy is the promotion of forced adherence to those ideals. Hansell says,

> The positive significance of black militancy as her portrayed [*Riders to the Blood Red Wrath*] cannot be overstressed. Brotherhood, equality, and love are the impelling forces. Despite whatever furious resistance, and without confidence of victory, as the final lines state, the black citizens dedicated to a mission of truly initiating the rule of democracy and

Christianity: "To fail, to flourish, to wither or to win. / We lurch, distribute, we extend, begin" ["Poet-Militant" 76–77].

The poem portrays the Freedom Riders as modern day crusaders who are conquering social injustice, the enemy of Christianity, and spreading the true faith. Indeed, the Freedom Riders are initiating a rebirth of democracy. In the words of Shaw,

> As if to emphasize the spiritual nature of the black's rebirth, Miss Brooks alludes to it often in terms of redemption, the second coming of Christ, or other religious phenomena. The black man like Christ, has borne the cross of persecution largely for being what he is.... The universality of rebirth is implied by the association with the fulfillment of the idea of democracy. Rebirth will be redemptive and corrective of a general evil perpetrated on both blacks and whites. Miss Brooks implies that whites cannot be free themselves until they stop holding blacks in bondage.... Therefore, rebirth does not refer only to the blacks' reclamation of freedom but also to the salvation they will bring to mankind in general [132–133].

Brooks takes yet another position relative to the issue of humankind failing to apply caritas in dealings with others. She addresses the question of Jesus' response to humankind's antagonistic, unchristian dealings with one another. One such poem is "truth." The small "t" in the title implies the smallness and humanness of the subject of the poem. The poem asks how we would greet the sun [son Jesus], whether in "dread" or "fear," "though we have wept for him, / though we have prayed" (2.1–2). The speaker wonders whether we might "flee." The state of humankind is represented as darkness, like it is represented in the Holy Bible. Humankind is presented as having had "so lengthy a / Session with shade" (1.5–6) in "the familiar Propitious haze" (3.4–5) and sleeping in "the coolness of snug unawareness" (4.3–4). In the end she alludes to darkness covering the eyes. People are so unchristian that they are in darkness. Poems that have been previously discussed also come from that vantage point. Brooks creates the situation in which penitent people have to face Mary if she were to come again in one poem, and Jesus when He comes again in another. "A Penitent Considers Another Coming of Mary" asks whether Mary would give birth to a Savior if she had known how the world would negate his teachings; "Emanuel's Nightmare: Another Coming of Christ" expresses the sadness Jesus feels looking at the violent nature of people in the world.

Brooks' poetry symbolizes a society without caritas as the whirlwind — as chaos, which biblically associates with the wrath of God incurred by sin (Is. 66.15, Jer. 23.19, Hos. 8.1, 7). Her "Sermon[s] on the Warpland" illustrate that concept most dramatically. Her poetry expresses a strong belief in the exponents of caritas — peace, love and charity to one's neighbor as evidence of the brotherhood democracy promises.

Although many of the poems show the lack of adherence to those Christian ideals by many people, Brooks' poetry also expresses the need for God in life and a reverence for Him. One such poem, "Infirm," is a prayer; the tone is reverent and imploring. It asks, "Oh. Mend me. Mend me. Lord." The speaker says to others with infirmities,

> [I] say to them, Lord:
> look! I am beautiful, beautiful with
> my wing that is wounded
> my eye that is bonded
> or my ear not funded
> or my walk all a-wobble.
> I'm enough to be beautiful [2.4–10]
>
> You are
> beautiful too [5.1–2].

Not only is the poem a prayer, but it also projects caritas and a reflection of God's love for His children by expressing empathy and unity with all who are infirm. All are beautiful in His sight. Another such poem is numbered XI in Brooks' *The Womanhood* series and opens with the emphatic first line, "One wants a Teller in a time like this." The poem goes on to say that no one can bear the "enormous business" of life "all alone," cannot find "the way back home or even if one has a home" (3.3–4). The uncertainties of life cry out for a teller: "One is not certain if or why or how. / One wants a Teller now" (4.1–2). The final stanza of the poem introduces a parental second speaker who is providing directions, "Put on your rubbers and you won't catch cold. / Here's hell, there's heaven / Go to Sunday School" (5.1–2). The poem looks at the role of faith in one's life and acknowledges the human need for a guiding God and the presence of God. In this poem, like so many others, Brooks demonstrates a belief in Christian theology.

Gwendolyn Brooks' poetry expresses truths of the human experience from the perspective of religious ethics. Madhubuti commented, "Although her work is often analyzed for its literary value, it is also infused with a spiritual force in which one can see the secret to her longevity. That spiritual force has to do with a passion for the truth within the truth" ("Introduction" xi). Historian Lerone Bennett, Jr., also spoke to her ability to capture the essence of truth and become the spirit of the poem. He said, "She not only writes poems but she is a poem ... she is a sermon, she is a rhyme, a rhythm, a Reality.... And what we honor here is not the word alone but the word fed by the blood of the spirit" (13–14). Brooks' work reflected the truth of what she observed and experienced through the lens of Christianity.

The definition of the word "witness" in the New Testament expands the primarily legal one of Old Testament scripture to the religious realm. In the Greek New Testament basically three words are translated as witness. Two are nouns meaning *a person who bears witness,* and *knowledge or a recollection*; one is a verb, meaning *the act of bearing witness or accurately recalling the truth.* As the word evolved with New Testament events, it was applied to the testimony of the Apostles and post–Ascension believers and martyrs, then came to be defined as, "the evangelistic confession of the New Testament" (Reisinger 3). Since the word "witness" focuses on the individual, the meaning also includes the aspect that the person who *can* witness must embody a specific religious state to be spiritually empowered *to* witness. "You must be a witness before you can witness" (Reisinger, 1–5). Indeed, Gwendolyn Brooks was a witness and she used her poems to witness about true Christian morality. Her self-proclaimed religion of kindness *was* Christianity on its purist level. The last line of the poem, beginning with "One wants a Teller in a time like this," serves as the poem's benediction and Gwendolyn Brooks' testimony advocating Christianity and hope. It ends, "Behold, Love's true, and triumphs; and God's actual." One cannot imagine a more powerful, more eloquent, gospel witness than Gwendolyn Elizabeth Brooks.

Coda: A Conversation with Nora Brooks Blakely

MARGOT HARPER BANKS: I'm in Chicago with Ms. Nora Brooks Blakely, ready to talk about her mother, Gwendolyn Brooks, my most esteemed, indeed favorite poet of all time. I feel very fortunate to have had the opportunity to meet Ms. Brooks.

NORA BROOKS BLAKELY: Nora has no idea what she is going to say, but we will see how things go.

MHB: Okay. First thing I want to do is to just show you what I would like to do and what I have been working on. I have gone through a lot of the poetry. You see where it says I will analyze more than 50 short poems? I have already been through more than 50 short poems and three long ones identifying religious references and trying to create a model for how they are used. So I developed a critical framework, which you see listed on this paper. So, what I am going to do today is to ask you some questions; then, we are going to talk about each one of those and also some quotes from interviews of your mother. I've got a bunch of good stuff. I do recognize, of course, that because a writer writes certain things, it does not mean that it is the belief of the poet necessarily, but there certainly is a relationship between the conceptions and perceptions of the poet that play a role in the creative process. So, the first thing I want to ask about Ms. Brooks' religious training as a child in her household. I mean, were they a church-going family? I mean just what was going on there?

NBB: They were a church-going family. I am not sure whether my grandfather, David Brooks, went to church or not, but my mother's mother, Keziah, was definitely a faithful churchgoer. And in fact, even when I was a child, there were times, especially around particular holidays, Mothers' Day, Easter, Palm Sunday and so forth that she would make sure that my mother and I went to church with her. I noticed at the top where you mention that she [GB] stated that she was not specifically religious, and that was the case. So, even then in church, we [GB and NBB] were more likely to listen to the minister's message and sometimes have paper that we would write notes or comments about the minister's sermon back and forth to each other, something that we tried to keep my grandmother from seeing (*laughter*), so I think that she would fall more in the category of being an observer and a seeker, than following a specific religious faith. But my grandmother went to the same Methodist church, Metropolitan Community Church, which is on 41st and King Drive, although I've heard that they are getting ready to move into a new church now, which kind of saddened me because it's a beautiful church.

MHB: But that was her church.

NBB: But that was her church for 30, 40 years or so. So, she'd gone to another church, Carter, which was right down the street from her, on 43rd and Champlain, for a while but then when she moved to...

MHB: This is your grandmother?

NBB: Yes. When she moved to Metropolitan, she was there until the day she died.

MHB: Now, when they were young children, do you know if they went to Sunday school, or whether the children attended church services? Did they participate in activities that kids sometimes do in church-going homes?

NBB: I believe they went to Sunday school because I know for a while my mother struggled to have me follow that pattern of going to Sunday school, but that was not really working for either of us (*Laughter*). So I believe that she did go to Sunday school, you know, as well as church.

MHB: As she was growing up.

NBB: Mmh, hmm.

MHB: You mentioned her father, and according to some of the things that I have read, I know that she was close to both parents, but it seems like she had a really special relationship with her father. The reason I mention that is because one of the first things you said was you don't believe he attended church but that her mother, your grandmother attended church, but yet your grandfather didn't.

NBB: I am not sure; that's very hazy. I know that when we went to church, grandfather didn't go but then he was only in my life up until I was like eight. He died when I was about eight. So, that's why those memories are kind of sketchy, but I don't remember him ever coming to church with us. The times that we did, the three of us went. So that's why I had the impression that he wasn't much of a churchgoer. But he was one of those people that proved that you didn't have to be a churchgoer to be a good person, because he was an incredibly warm and decent human being.

MHB: Oh yes. And there are a lot of people going to church who aren't so warm and decent.

NBB: "Everybody talking about heaven ain't going there," but that's another story.

MHB: I wanted to look at some of these things that I have on this sheet because these are ideas that I really drew from the poetry. And the first one of those has to do with how she portrays God, which appears in a couple of poems, but ministers appear in a few more poems. And often it seems as though often the ministers are not so well presented. I was wondering, whether she had friends who were ministers? I researched her obituaries and news reports about her funeral. I read as many as I could get my hands on, but I didn't find any of them that mentioned a minister officiating.

NBB: A minister did not officiate. Personally, I felt that would have been a little hypocritical because we were not churchgoers, and that always feels a little odd to me when you go to the service of someone that you know rarely or never set foot in a church in their lives, and they have a minister there. You know, their family or somebody decided they should have a minister at the event. Also mama's funeral was such a production. At one point we all, and I mean quantities of people planned it, but we all were talking and working things out. It was at Rockefeller chapel, which is on 57th and Woodlawn, 59th and Woodlawn, one of those two. And it is part of the University of Chicago campus, and it's a huge, well-respected chapel. Occasionally dignitaries have their services there, and so mama's was held there. And at some point it occurred to me that it was becoming more like a production that I would do for my theater company because the mayor was coming and so and so. And this person would cross to this mike and speak, you know, and at some point I said, wait, this is a Chocolate Chips Theatre Company production. This is how I block plays, but in a way it was a very good thing because it allowed me to say, okay this is a service for Gwendolyn Brooks, and I will mourn my mother later. I was able to separate those two. So basically, there was Lerone Bennett Jr., the historian, although we frequently refer to him as the preacher in disguise. He spoke and he was the..., I can't remember the name I started using for him, but the equivalent of a facilitator; he was the person that moved everybody, or tried to move everybody along, as I had asked him to do. I went up and spoke, because the maximum was three minutes. I was one of the first people to speak and told everybody that I wanted to do this so that I could make it clear to them that if I could speak for three minutes, then nobody had to spend more than three minutes. So that did kind of keep people moving, except two people, Margaret Burroughs who would tell people, I am going to talk as long as I feel like talking, and Val Gray Ward, former director of Kuumba Theatre who just talks — the way she said, "I could go on and on and on et cetera." But, coming back from the digression, I think that Lerone Bennett, Jr., was probably the closest to a formal minister, no wait, because I think that Jesse Jackson was there too. So he would definitely be an official minister, but also was a dignitary, too. But somebody speaking from a ministerial position — no.

MHB: Okay. You mentioned Jesse Jackson. Were there ministers who were friends or just associates in the realm of the world apart from being a spiritual leader?

NBB: There were certainly people that she knew, but she knew them as friends, not looking to any one person to be a spiritual leader.

MHB: In some of the poems (and I'll mention a couple of them), you have the preacher ruminating and he is basically off some place else while he's talking, you know, in the sense that he is thinking about these other kinds of things and that's one. And then you have a couple of others where you have the minister who's looking to seduce the sister in the congregation and things like that. So, that's what I meant when I said sometimes not portrayed too well. I don't know if that is for literary purposes only; or if that was kind of reflective because she had seen some troubling things.

NBB: I think it was more observation because I don't believe that she ever, and I know I certainly never have considered a preacher ruminating behind the sermon to be a negative view...

MHB: Oh no?

NBB: That it was just somebody who, you know, as he talked, just thought about these different things and wondered, "Oh, well this would be very interesting. What really goes on in God's mind?" I always considered it to be an extension of the sermon as opposed to separate from it.

And as far as the other, I think that's probably more observation also. And as I was about to say, that Haki Madhubuti, who you are going to interview at some point, I think, made relevant comment in his book about the first 21 years of his life. One of the things in it was about his mother who for some period of his life, did survive basically as a prostitute.

She and at least one friend of hers, basically most of the people that they serviced, were ministers, you know, so...

(*Laughter*)

MHB: It's real, it's real...

NBB: So, yes, so I don't think that — I never had the impression from my mother she ever had a hostile view towards ministers, but I don't think that she had a rose-colored optimistic view either, I think that she just called it as she saw it, the different individuals, you know, people that she knew...

MHB: And the ministers were just people.... Just people first.

NBB: Yes.

MHB: Let's discuss the second thing on my framework; we'd better go through pretty quickly. Look at the spirituality of African peoples, because sometimes there are places where she is just giving us little glimpses, you know, like "Sunday Chicken." That poem satirizes the "carnivorousness" of the tradition of eating a chicken on Sunday, the so-called gospel bird. In others she explores the spirituality in-depth. One poem that examines and expands African American Sunday rituals is the "Sundays of Satin-Legs Smith." I want to talk to you a little bit more about that poem.

NBB: Okay.

MHB: Because to me, although he was obviously irreverent with the things that he was doing on Sunday, still, he put on his best clothes; the poem says that he was "reminded of devotion." Even when he had eaten and then he made love to this woman, at the end, the language is, "She was receptive, soft and absolute," which obviously triggers the thought of absolution. So, as I look at that, I say that this was Sunday ritual. Do you think this poem reflects a suppressed, I'll say, using a psychological word, a suppressed religiousness that has been inverted because of other injustices that he might have faced? How do you interpret the character? It's one of my favorite poems. So I really want to hear what you have to say about it.

NBB: Oh wow, it's been so long since I've read it, so I am hesitant to be too absolute about anything. Oh, and I interpret that line differently too, so, I think that there is (*long pause*), okay, I will say this very carefully because I don't want to say anything that I am going to think later on, that was not what I meant to say.

MHB: I am going to send you back a transcript of what you said, so if you want to change it, like the congressional record, you can change it...

(*laughter*)

NBB: Thank you, thank you. There is (*pause*), okay let me first do this disclaimer, it is very — you are walking a very precarious line when you try to interpret anything of somebody else's...

MHB: Right.

NBB: Because sometimes it's hard to even interpret yourself, you know, so with that disclaimer as an underline to anything I say, my impression of the woman that I grew up with was that she respected religion in others although she did not specifically follow a particular faith of her own. That being said, I have always had the feeling that there is an attention to spirituality in most black people whether they list themselves as born again, Buddhist, Catholic, or agnostic or even atheist, that there is still an attention to spirituality and to a sense of a something and a structure, you know, even if it's not anthropomorphized and I will quote from Sweet Honey in the Rock's "Breaths," you know; are you familiar with that? Okay, There's a line, "Listen more often to things than to beings," that there is a sense of something that is a connection. And that is what I see reflected in mama's, ... in a lot of her poetry. That acknowledgment by characters in her poetry — some extremely devout, others who just pay lip service, and others who seem to leave you with a feeling that there is a subtle thing there and if my memory of Satin-Legs serves me, and it may not, so there is disclaimer 18, but if it does serve me, that attention, that sense there is something there, that attentiveness to that, is one of the things you will find in some of her characters. So as I remember "Sundays of Satin-Legs Smith," that what I do remember of it, is that underlying sense there, but how much of it, he even consciously knows...?

MHB: Oh yeah, yeah. I think that we are actually on one accord. That is just what I am saying, that it's still a part of him, even though, he has, I'll say, inverted it in his day to day life. He has inverted the teaching / learning and kept the routine.

NBB: Because indeed in the "Near-Johannesburg Boy" arguably — at one point when she says, "Oh father," and different people have interpreted it different ways. Some people have thought that it's to a higher father, and other people think he has basically at that point raised up his own.

MHB: Right, because he says "Oh mother" later on. I had thought that, but if it only had said "Oh father," but it says "Oh mother" later, then that's why I thought he was raising up his own father.

NBB: I think he is raising up both of his parents...

MHB: Yeah, yeah, that's what I thought as well, but I can see why people would think that because that place in the poem you could get that.

One of my favorites and I think hers, because I recall her saying so in interviews that one of her favorites is "De Witt Williams on His Way to Lincoln Cemetery." That poem is one of the ones that I have in the imagery and symbolism section. She used "Swing Low Sweet Chariot" as literary texture, something to enhance the poem, to develop the tone in the poem, the music and the message of the poem. It enhances the texture of the poem — the literary texture. Would you agree with that in poems like that?

NBB: Yeah, I would agree with that, there is another layer, that the casket is the chariot, so yes. Oscar Brown, Jr., set the poem to music. He called the song "Elegy." Would you like to hear it?

MHB: I would love to hear it.

(*Music*)

NBB: We use it actually; we did last year; we are bringing it back next year. This might be the show that you would like to have come to Kean University. It is called *A Day in Bronzeville: Black Life Through the Eyes of Gwendolyn Brooks*. We have an older version and we have a younger version, which is for preschool through sixth grade called *We Live in Bronzeville*. The older version is for anybody from sixth grade to adult. The play observes a day in the life of a neighborhood, from 6 am one day to 6 am the next.

MHB: You wrote it?

NBB: Well I put it together. "Elegy" is used in the show. But in that show there is not a single word, not a thing that mama did not write. So it's her poetry, full poems and excerpts, put together to take us through a day in this neighborhood. So I consolidated, selected, considered, you know, but it's all her work. Even the pieces that are already set to music already, "Elegy," or the pieces that we set to music.

MHB: I just did a teacher's in-service seminar two Saturdays ago from 9 till 12 on Gwendolyn Brooks. They were just really impressed. And this is an aside, but your mother is under recognized, you know, in terms of the schools — teachers teaching her work in our area. There are some who know and some who don't. Then as soon as they read her work, they are just mesmerized! Even in my own department, and I am in an English department, there are professors of English who do not know her work well.

NBB: Now that's disturbing.

MHB: The in-service Saturdays are a series of Saturday seminars and each has a different theme. The one I did was "Melody and Improv: The

Poetry of Gwendolyn Brooks." And even the English professor who organized them came to me and he said that there is someone who took your seminar, who now wants to do further research, and I'll send her to you for guidance. So, you can see we need your production of her work at Kean University for faculty and area teachers as well as students. I'll take the information back.

NBB: And some of that I'll have to just mail to you because I am in the process of bringing sanity to my desk and so some things I want to give you, I have no idea where they are.

(*Musical Rendition of Elegy composed and performed by Oscar Brown, Jr.*)

MHB: The next big topic, well I've got two more important parts really. One is the conflict between Christian behavior and racism. It seems to me that a lot of the social commentary poetry in the late '60s and '70s, really made that point. Poems, like "The Chicago Defender Sends a Man to Little Rock" made that point very clear. And it also seems that that perspective correlates with some of your mother's statements in interviews. Are you familiar with this book? I only found it recently although it was published in 2003. *Conversations with Gwendolyn Brooks: The Collection of her interviews?* Published by University of Mississippi Press.

NBB: I've heard of that book, I have not seen it.

MHB: Yeah, these are selected pages from it that I have blocked out, and I want you to just comment on the quotes or add any information you might have to them.

In one of them she says, "during the '40s and '50s I thought the integration was the solution; all we had to do was keep on appealing to the whites to help us and they would." That interview was with Ida Lewis in 1971 who asked her why she held that belief and she says, "Because I relied really heavily on Christianity; people were really good. I thought there was some good even in people who seemed to be evil. It's true I didn't know very much about wicked people, who they were; it was a good world the best of all possible worlds" and so forth. Then she goes on to say that she began to read authors like W.E.B. DuBois and gained a broader perspective.

I want you to comment on the social commentary as it relates to Christianity. I mean, she addresses everything from basically hypocritical people who are professing to be Christians like those in "The Chicago *Defender* Sends a Man to Little Rock," and who are still acting racist. She brings out a second aspect in some of the poems with the idea of religion as anesthesia. For example, some of the black people in "In Montgomery" kind of just attend church service and sing the songs, not really dealing with the reality of their situation and so forth. Could you speak about how she used religion to make her points about the central issues?

NBB: I feel like you basically said all of it. But, however proactive the people in "In Montgomery" may or may not be, they were definitely aware of, and firmly seated in, the reality of their situations.

Are you familiar with the piece in *Children Coming Home?*

MHB: Which one?
NBB: The one where they start off the day by praying...

MHB: "Religion," it's called "Religion."
NBB: You know it is said "In Montgomery" too. The book *Children Coming Home* is reprinted in *In Montgomery and Other Poems.*

MHB: Yeah, in the poem the mother goes off and she meets the girl-friend. And then the family comes home that night and shouts "Hallelu-jah." Ms. Brooks is demonstrating the disconnect between the doctrine and the practice of religion. That kind of hypocrisy permeates a lot of poems through the years actually.

That poem is a vehicle to make a lot of different kinds of points. What do you think?

NBB: So, ask this question again and let me think through it.

MHB: Okay. I am just saying that it seemed to me that she uses the problems with the way people practice religion to make a number of dif-ferent points. The bottom line is I see her [GB] as being too Christian to be a practicing Christian. In other words she really lived her life by the human values that the doctrine sets forth. However the way people practice religion, whether it be Christianity or any other religion, is with behavior that many times is not consonant with their doctrine. My sense as some-body who has read most of her poetry is that there was almost a dissonance that is, disillusionment with organized religion because of that. Everything from the fact that she spoke in the voice of the disenfranchised, that she took her poetry to prisons, took it to schools and shared those kinds of things.... That she worked with children, that she was kind to people. All those things to me are so consistent with Christian doctrine, yet on the other hand, so many observations in her poetry shine an unflattering light on it. So, that's basically what I see. What are your comments?

NBB: I think that mama had the expectation of good. That was her expectation. That if you do right by people they'll do right by you. She lived in the world and so she was very clear that for reasons, for unknowable reasons frequently, that was not the case. And she was a human being so she also had her own occasional inconsistencies, and so forth but fundamentally, and that is how we were raised as well, that you should be good. It wasn't as formal as the Golden Rule, "Do unto others as you will would have others do unto you," which I have always had a few issues with that because maybe they don't want to be "done" as you would like to be done (*Laughter*). So maybe, what you really want to do is treat people as you learn they would like to be treated. But there was that expectation of good, that if you were good to people and treated people with respect that they would in turn be good to you and treat you with respect. An addendum I would add is, at least at that point you know that you've done your best. Whatever else happens, happens.

MHB: Yes, if they do the Emmett Till thing, or they do some other kind of wicked stuff, that it was even more egregious to her.

NBB: So, "Good" was mama's religion. That was what she thought was supposed to happen. And anything else was a disappointment. It might be a sad disappointment, it might be a *what-is-wrong-with-you* disappointment, it might be an almost ready to kick the television in—*crazy-people-over-there* level of disappointment but it was a *that-is-the-thing-that-is-not-right* in the world belief.

MHB: And the racism here and the racism in South Africa I mean all of those kinds of things were not good.

NBB: Right. And therefore "anti" her personal religion.

MHB: I can see that. The other thing I wanted to talk to you about before I have you respond to other interview blurbs is what I call religion as genre. You have just a few poems that are essentially prayers or have a prayer portion in them but what is coming through in the three "Sermons on the Warpland" (which are among my favorites) and "Another Preachment" is a sermonic structure and tone.

NBB: You said that "A Bronzeville Mother Loiters in Mississippi. Meanwhile, a Mississippi Mother Burns Bacon" was one of your favorites. And "Sermon on the Warpland" and "Another Preachment" are certainly favorites of mine. Cute little poems aside (I love "Song in the Front Yard"), but if somebody knocked me down and twisted my arm and made me say these were my favorite poems then I would probably agree that those were as well as "Near-Johannesburg Boy." And probably if you were looking for a religious statement from mama, actually "Paul Robeson" was probably her religious statement. That "we are each other's business, we are each other's harvest, we are each other's magnitude and bond."

MHB: And then, another one that I thought was key, and I want you to talk a little bit more about, the three Sermons. One question is, did she write the third one much later? It was published so long after the first two. Did she write it that long after the first two? The first two were like 1968, thereabouts, and the third one was published around 1980. I mean there was like a ten-year gap in there. There are big differences in the structure of the poem, as well. The first two are more similar structurally and stylistically; the third one has major differences. And I was wondering whether there really was that much time in between or was it, did she work on it and it just didn't get published till later.

NBB: That's a Haki question. Because, I mean there were so many times that she's written things then put it in a drawer until later. So, whether it was very soon after and then just ended up in a drawer or just happened very soon after, I'm not sure.

MHB: "Another Preachment" was a later one too but ...

NBB: That was in "Riot" and the others were "In the Mecca" that is not that far apart. "In the Mecca" was in '68 I believe, right?

MHB: Right, but the third Sermon is what I am asking about.

NBB: Right, but I don't think "Riot" came out that much later.

MHB: I have some other publication questions like that. But to my earlier point, these poems are sermons. They are sermons by title, genre, and also by purpose and intent. They are not based on scripture per se, but each is based on a philosophical concept; one is the Ron Karenga quote, "Being black is our ultimate reality" and the second and third are similarly introduced. They use direct address; they are kind of explaining how black people, I won't say should live, but should approach their lives, so...

NBB: A lot of them are like that, because, for instance, *Black Love*— we use excerpts from *Black Love* as a sermon in the show, when we get to the church section.

MHB: I hadn't thought of that poem that way... It certainly is. Now you are going to send me back through all the poems I have, to examine them from that perspective. That's exactly right ... it has a sermonic tone. That brings me to the next question I will be going back through the Sermons on the Warpland because of the stylistic differences and ponder why she, not she made changes, but they were different. I am putting together a chart as an analytical tool to look at those three poems, e.g., the three movements, they follow etc. Those particular poems follow a sermonic structure, which has three movements. You know, preachers always have three parts to their message. What similarities and differences do you see in the three poems?

NBB: I would say that the first and second are much more preachment and (*pause*) the third is more, internal is not the word am looking for ... but it is...

MHB: Yeah, the third one is ... complicated.

NBB: It is more a commentary of ...

MHB: It's got a lot of different elements, I mean it's also more narrative and it is drama. You have the black philosopher and the white philosopher; you have people speaking back and forth, there's just a lot going on in the third sermon.

NBB: There are pieces of the third sermon in the [*A Day in Bronzeville*] play, too.

MHB: It is almost a play as it is.

NBB: Yeah ... Yes and "whatever is going on is going on" is the transition; that comes up at the end of each section in the piece. That's our transition.

MHB: At the end, you know, the dust has, as they say, settled. "Another Preachment" is a lot more focused in terms of one specific message; that's the one where basically it says, don't be talking black and acting white, (laughter) cutting right to the chase, people going around boasting about being African and so forth and then, you know, lunching off the system and ... it's "Another Preachment."

NBB: I don't remember that one; what is that?

MHB: It is in *Blacks*.

NBB: Oh Yeah! We do it as a gospel song.

MHB: Do you really? She read that one at Kean. When she came to Kean it was March and she passed away that December and she was not well, but I am telling you her spirit, was strong and vibrant.

NBB: She was just skinny in March because she was still going out and touring up through September, you know...

MHB: And she was having trouble with her balance, she said, "Hold on to me so I don't fall down."

NBB: Her balance was off, and that was something as we looked back, you know hindsight is a perfect science, as we looked back we said, mmhhh, okay. But she had just been treating it like it was a balance issue. I am getting old that's what happens. And we suspect that she knew that something was going on before, besides she had a complete hostility to doctors and would not go to any doctor, would not step into a hospital. The last time she had been to a doctor was in the '70s, and the last time she had been to a hospital was when she had me, and I was born in '51. So, she took this very seriously as a commitment. She drank her greens juices, did all of these healthy things, she exercised et cetera and so forth. September she had just come back from another trip. It wasn't until in October when she wasn't feeling well enough to go to the Writer's Conference at Chicago State. That was the first time she had ever missed it. Then it became, "Okay, you have to acknowledge now that there is something wrong," That was late October and by December 3rd, she was gone. So ...

MHB: And when she made those trips she was on a train, she wouldn't fly. She made the long train ride out to New Jersey.

NBB: She would take the train to California. She loved train rides, and she found it was peaceful and since she didn't have a cell phone, nobody could reach her and she liked that. And that was the thing about her signing stuff and everything too. She had the patience of Job; she could sit there, I remember one elementary school, they had 400 kids and she sat there and she signed an autograph for every one of the children in that school, and she could do that.

MHB: If I hadn't seen her in New Jersey I might not have believed you.

NBB: But what people didn't understand was that when she went home, she was home. She almost never answered her phone, you know, and felt no need to answer her phone. She could sit in the house for days or weeks reading, watching TV. She had me, and Cynthia [Cynthia A. Walls] who is not only our [Chocolate Chips] director of operations but she is also my best friend for over 30 years. Cynthia and I would go to the store and get her groceries and stuff. She could not come out for weeks at a time and be perfectly happy.

MHB: The other thing I thought at the time was that it related to the time that she won the Pulitzer Prize. At that time a wonderful black writer did not become a celebrity. When I introduced her that evening at Kean I began by saying that when she won the Pulitzer Prize before anybody ever heard of Martin Luther King, when the armed forces was still segregated, I went through all that stuff so people could really put her genius in context. She actually became "famous" before black writers were celebrated by the media. So it seemed to me that she almost enjoyed the fact that people enjoyed her work. She said to me, "If they are willing to stand here and wait for me to sign, I will just sit here and sign every one of them. I think too, it was more special than for, I'll say, another famous writer, I won't say the person's name. Another famous African American writer who came to Kean, who whisked in, whisked out, and said, 'I am signing no autographs.'"

And you know, for the students, particularly at a college or university like our school — we are a State school too. And we are a school where most of our students work, and they don't get to see writers and people like that, so this is super for them, to have an opportunity to see somebody who's important in American letters. But I am also saying it seemed like to me that to your mother it was more special than it is for today's celebrity writers.

NBB: If we are going to go biblical it was mama's concept of rendering unto Caesar what was Caesar's. When she was outside and she was at a place, she would do everything that she thought that she was supposed to do there. Now she wouldn't let people take advantage of her. Sometimes there are schools where somebody would say, oh we also wanted you to do this panel and stuff, and she wasn't you know, she wasn't crazy. But if people wanted to come up...

MHB: We sold out all the books that we had ordered to sell, that night. And we sold them out because everybody wanted to buy one so she could sign it.

NBB: She would talk to them, she would sign things, and she would be the last person out the door. Whenever I was her chauffeur I would bring, sometimes I would bring a book because I would just go over and sit some place and while she was signing I would read.

MHB: I understand.
NBB: Oh you do, okay.

MHB: And I would say, "Aren't you getting tired Ms. Brooks?" and she says, "Oh, no."

NBB: I would get cramps in my hand before that, but apparently she had built up those muscles from all those signatures. Although it is hard for me to define a particular favorite poem but I can define some of my favorite lines. And from "Sermon on the Warpland" the life message is, "And went about the warpland saying No. My people, black and black, revile the River. Say that the River turns, and turn the River." I just love that so...

MHB: And Haki's book, he took the title for his book.
NBB: Absolutely.

MHB: I don't know; I like the whirlwind in the second one. "Salve salvage in the spin. Endorse the splendor splashes;" and when she gets to the, "but know the whirlwind is our commonwealth." And it is indeed. And it still is. The whirlwind is our commonwealth.

NBB: "Define and medicate the whirlwind."

MHB: Mmmh, hmmm. I'm telling you, look at this "furious flower," oh man.

NBB: I have the vocal to it and am not sure I do, right before you leave if I do this one other that I want you to hear, that we set to music.

MHB: These are miscellaneous sheets but they are, each one is a little something from one of those *Conversations with Gwendolyn Brooks* book. It is a pretty nifty little book because at least it pulls them all together. None of them are very late, you know, none of them are late in her life, I am trying to think; the last one was about '99.

(Conversation about the picture online, Brooks Permissions, Postcards and Posters)

MHB: Anyway I want you to look at these different things. This is the story of Dr. French. I heard her tell this story in interviews as well. When she first got out of school she got a job working for Dr. French. He was a spiritual adviser. And it turned out he wanted her to open up the envelopes and give him the money. He ultimately wanted her to be the assistant pastor at the church and she said she just couldn't do that — to get up there and be a charlatan, and then he fired her because of that. So I didn't know if there was anything that you can add about the context or anything, any information, explanation that she talked about, in this first one?

NBB: No. I mean she's told that story pretty much the same way all the time.

MHB: Now the next one was, this was an interview in 1969 with a man named George Stavros. Many of the things he discussed will not be a part of what we can talk about here, but he also asked about religion in her poetry.

He was talking about the first lines from the *Children of the Poor* poems, including, "Should I tell my children to pray?" And she commented, "Yes. All [first lines] questions I would ask of myself, my mother certainly wouldn't ask that question of herself such as that last one. She feels firmly that you must pray and that only good can come of it." Stavros then asked, "What of religion in your poems? I notice that two or three of your references to men of the church are at least uncomplimentary, for example Prophet Williams in "In the Mecca" — a faith healer "and that is when Ms. Brooks goes on to say yes, he was based on an actual man. He was based on that Dr. French guy, as well. So it seems that Dr. French was really the model for some of the charlatan kind of figures in her poems.

NBB: And that would be a correct interpretation of grandmother too because grandmother also believed in good but she was a little more, I wanted to say severe, but that's not really what grandmother was. Grandmother was. She wasn't one of the comfy, cozy, "we got some hot muffins in the oven, come on here and get yourself some, hon" type; that wasn't grandmother. She was very formal; she was structured. She believed there was a right way to do things and a right thing to do. At the same time she fixed the best oatmeal with brown sugar and she knew if you wanted a dollop of butter on it. So, that's why I took the severe away ... but very formal.

MHB: She was a teacher, right?

NBB: Yes. So, grandmother was a wonderful antique wooden chair and grandfather was a comfy sofa.

MHB: Thank you. That's lovely. Metropolitan Community Church, that was not your grandmother's church.

NBB: Yes, it was.

MHB: That's the church where they saw Langston Hughes and that's the Langston Hughes story I had read about. But that was the church.

NBB: I think it was Carter AME.

MHB: Well now, I have Carter in another place.

NBB: Carter AME was before Metropolitan and I thought that they saw Langston Hughes at Carter. Okay, I can't swear to that.

MHB: This one says that not long after that Langston Hughes came to give a reading at the Metropolitan Community Church and he was altogether different, I mean from James Weldon Johnson and, you know, talked about your mother. This was an interview with Ida Lewis in 1971.

NBB: Then we will go with Metropolitan.

MHB: I was going to say because she does mention Carter in another place.

NBB: Then maybe she met James Weldon Johnson at Carter.

MHB: That could have been.

NBB: That's maybe what happened.

MHB: Because he was MISTER important. He was important. He was too important to be encouraging to a youngster. She also talked about Robert Hayden in this particular interview, and this was Gloria T. Hall and Posy Gallagher in 1977. The interviewers stated that people had said that she and Robert Hayden were the most structurally sound African American poets of that time. Your mother responded that she thought he was more formal than she; although I am not sure I would agree with her, but she did. But then went on to say that he is a Baha'i too. She said, "Which is another difference; I don't have any special religion." I never even heard of that religion. Have you?

NBB: Yeah. In fact, outside Chicago, the first suburb is Evanston and just north of Evanston is Wilmette and there is an absolutely beautiful Bahaii temple there, absolutely gorgeous.

MHB: Well, what she went on to say is "my religion is I guess I'll say something corny," this is your mom speaking, "is PEOPLE. LIV-ING. I go to church on Mother's Day and Easter Sunday. I will say, however, that when I am up in a plane and lately when I am in a car or any other conveyance, I say, 'dear, please protect us all,' and then sit back and enjoy the ride." I thought that was great. I loved that. Another comment that she had made in another interview with Gloria Tate in 1983, when she was talking about the many aspects about life that need to be written about more and among them she said the black church. She said that "the whole church area needs more attention. I am not just talking about sisters in their white hats shouting, there's a whole lot more going on in church and somebody ought to tackle it." I think that in her own way she did a little bit of it, though, I'll say, she used it as a vehicle but she never really just focused on the church head on.

NBB: She probably felt somebody who was really of that experience should really be the one to do it. And I have a friend I have been trying to get to do a piece, she sometimes says that she's going to, but I've really tried to actively get her to say "yes, yes, that's what I am going to do. I am going to write this piece about church..."

MHB: There's a lot going on in church, I know because I am in the church.

NBB: You could do a play or movie on a choir just all by itself. I know it just from my friends who do choir rehearsal.

MHB: Howe and Fox asked her in their interview whether she was "aware of the religious and human values that you [she] put into your poetry?" Ms. Brooks answered, "I like the phrase 'human values.' Not everyone in this world of humanity is religious.... I can't speak for the mass-murderers, of course, or the rapists and so forth, but I think that most people have some decency, some values...." Of course it just takes one to make things wretched for the rest of us. That is my optimistic view."

That corroborates what you were saying, the belief in good. And then they asked her the source of her values and she said her parents. So, we are right back to your grandparents.

NBB: Are you familiar with "Beulah" from *Bronzeville Boys and Girls?* It takes place in church.

MHB: No, I do not know that poem! I'll have to look at including it.

Your grandmother lived to be 90, right? Here's where your mother talked about it. She said your grandparents moved right down the street so there would never be an excuse not to go to church. So, if it rained or it snowed the family could still get there. She talks about questioning and how it bothers some people that in some poems she is kind of questioning what it feels like to be God although she feels that that's life.

NBB: Because I have some very seriously devout churchgoing friends I wondered if some things are acceptable to a Christian audience. I take some material past them to see — is this going to be an issue? And I might still do it if it's an issue but I like to get into it. And I didn't know how people were going to react to "The Preacher Ruminates Behind the Sermon." I didn't know how they were going to react to that. But ...

MHB: I read that poem in church during Black History Month. People loved it; people absolutely love it because it's so real. And you know what, the conception of God is so much like that. If you've ever spent any time reading about perceptions of God, you might look at an old book called *The Negro God* that talks about how African Americans conceptualize God completely differently from white folks. The white folks' God is like way up there sitting way back up there on some big white cloud and to black folks God is like, you know, your big brother in the sky. There's much more warmth and relationship and closeness and things like that.

NBB: And I think that everything could be taken too far. I am a staunch supporter of the concept of separation of church and state. At the same time, we were doing at one point, a show that we do called *How The Snake Got Its Rattles,* based on the Julius Lester story. And so we get people from Naperville, a suburb northwest of Chicago, where we were going to do it. Then they came, they saw it before we did it there and they said, "Oh, we can't do this here because we can't talk about God and everything." And I said, "We are not preaching." So they wanted to know if we could remove God from the story. And I said no. I said because there's an entire genre of black folklore where snakes are talking to God, people are talking to God, God's making butterflies and figuring out they didn't work out well, you know, then having to redo them and everything. He's kind of your handy dandy master repairman. In this folktale the snake comes up [to God] and is ticked off, and the rain dropping on the leaves makes him jumpy, you know, "What is going on" and "I know you better fix this." And that is the kind of relationship in this folklore. So I explained it's up to you and your school. We do the folklore or we don't do the folklore. But I would not be true to the folklore if I said we were going to take that out and try to have some of the characters as something else because that's not what the folklore is, so if you are looking for black folklore, this is it. If you want something else, you know there are other shows that we do and hopefully you'll come back for some of those shows but I can't change this. It's not my work.

MHB: Ms. Brooks drew from that tradition in "The Preacher Ruminates Behind the Sermon"—that's the kind of God, He is. He's walking around like the people.

Your mother drew creatively from our African cultural and spiritual essence and left us a wonderful legacy to read and study and enjoy.

Thank you so much for talking to me. It has been a real pleasure.

November 18, 2005, Kennedy-King College, Chicago

Appendix 1:
Books by Brooks

1945 *A Street in Bronzeville*. New York: Harper & Brothers
1949 *Annie Allen*. New York: Harper & Brothers
1953 *Maud Martha*. New York: Harper & Brothers
1956 *Bronzeville Boys and Girls*. New York: Harper & Brothers
1960 *The Bean Eaters*. New York: Harper & Brothers
1963 *Selected Works*. New York: Harper & Row
1966 *We Real Cool*. Detroit: Broadside Press
1967 *The Wall: For Edward Christmas*. Detroit: Broadside Press
1968 *In the Mecca*. New York: Harper & Row
1969 "Riot." Detroit: Broadside Press
1970 *Family Pictures*. Detroit: Broadside Press
1971 *The World of Gwendolyn Brooks*. New York: Harper & Row
1971 *Aloneness*. Detroit: Broadside Press
1971 *Black Steel: Joe Frazier and Muhammad Ali*. Special Broadside.
        Detroit: Broadside Press
1971 (ed.) *A Broadside Treasury*. Detroit: Broadside Press
1971 (ed.) *Jump Bad: A New Chicago Anthology*. Detroit: Broadside
        Press
1971 (ed.) *The Black Position*. [Annual]
1972 *Report from Part One*. Detroit: Broadside Press
1972 *The Tiger Who Wore White Gloves, or What You Are You Are*.
        Chicago: Third World Press
1975 *Beckonings*. Detroit: Broadside Press
1975 *A Capsule Course in Black Poetry Writing*. With Keorapetse
        Kgositsile, Haki R. Madhubuti, and Dudley Randall.
        Detroit: Broadside Press
1980 *Primer for Blacks*. Chicago: Black Position Press

1980   *Young Poet's Primer*. Chicago: Brooks Press
1981   *To Disembark*. Chicago: Third World Press
1983   *Mayor Harold Washington; and, Chicago, the I Will City.* Chicago: Brooks Press
1983   "Twenty-Four Poems from Four Decades." *Time Capsule,* Summer / Fall.
1983   *Very Young Poets*. Chicago: Brooks Press
1986   *The Near-Johannesburg Boy, and Other Poems*. Chicago: David Company
1987   *Blacks*. Chicago: David Company
1988   *Gottschalk and the Grande Tarentelle*. Chicago: David Company
1988   *Winnie*. Chicago David Company
1991   *Children Coming Home*. Chicago, David Company
1996   *Report from Part Two*. Chicago: Third World Press
2003   *In Montgomery, and Other Poems*. Chicago: Third World Press

Appendix 2:
Selected Honors and Awards

1946	*American Academy of Arts and Letters Grant*
1946 and 1947	*Guggenheim Fellowship*
1950	*Pulitzer Prize for Literature*
1964	*Thormod Monsen Award*
1964	*Ferguson Memorial Award*
1968	*Anisfield-Wolf Award*
1969–2000	*Poet Laureate of Illinois*
1970	*Gwendolyn Brooks Cultural Center established, Macomb, Illinois*
1971	*Black Academy Award*
1976	*Shelley Memorial Award*
1985–1986	*29th Consultant in Poetry to the Library of Congress* [now renamed *Poet Laureate*]
1988	*Frost Medal (Poetry Society of America)*
1988	*National Women's Hall of Fame Award*
1989	*Senior Fellowship in Literature by the National Endowment for the Arts*
1992	*Aiken Taylor Award*
1994	*Medal for Distinguished Contributions to American Letters by the National Book Foundation*

1994	*Jefferson Lecturer from the National Endowment for the Humanities Lifetime Achievement Award*
1994	*National Book Foundation Medal*
1995	*Shelley Memorial Award*
1995	*National Endowment for the Arts Lifetime Honors Medal of Art*
1995	*Gwendolyn Brooks Elementary School Dedication, Aurora, Illinois*
1997	*Lincoln Laureate Award*
1998	*International Literary Hall of Fame for Writers of African Descent*
2000	*65th Academy Fellowship (Academy of American Poets)*
2000	*Living Legend Library of Congress Medal*
2000	*Gwendolyn Brooks College Preparatory Academy Dedication, Chicago, Illinois*
2000	*Gwendolyn Brooks Middle School Dedication, Harvey, Illinois*
2002	*Gwendolyn Brooks Middle School Dedication, Oak Park, Illinois*
2002	*Named one of 100 Greatest African Americans*
2003	*Gwendolyn Brooks Illinois State Library Dedication, Springfield, Illinois*
2005	*Gwendolyn Brooks Middle School Dedication, Bolingbrook, Illinois*
2010	*Induction into Chicago Writers Association Literary Hall of Fame More than 75 honorary degrees*

Works Consulted

"Agape." *New World Encyclopedia*. n.d. Web. 5 May 2011.

Angle, Paul. "An Interview with Gwendolyn Brooks." *Conversations with Gwendolyn Brooks*. Ed. Gloria Gayles. Jackson: University Press of Mississippi, 2003. 13–25. Print.

Avey, James. "The History of the Christian Fish Symbol." *Avey Incubator*. n.d. Web. 30 April 2009.

Barker, Kenneth, ed. *The NIV Study Bible*. Grand Rapids, MI: Zondervan, 2002. Print.

Berkhof, Louis. *Summary of Christian Doctrine*. Grand Rapids, MI: William B. Eerdmans, 1938. Print.

"Better to Light One Candle Than to Curse the Darkness." *Answers.com*. n.d. Web. 20 May 2009.

"Bible Gateway." *biblegateway.com*. n.d. Web.

Blakely, Henry. *Windy Place*. Detroit: Broadside, 1974. Print.

Blakely, Nora Brooks. Telephone interview. 7 Feb. 2011.

Bloom, Harold. *Gwendolyn Brooks*. Philadelphia: Chelsea House, 2004. Print.

Bluestone, Daniel. "Chicago's Mecca Flat Blues." *Journal of the Society of Architectural Historians* 57.4 (Dec. 1998): 382–403. Print.

Bolden, B. J. *Urban Rage in Bronzeville: Social Commentary in the Poetry of Gwendolyn Brooks, 1945–1960*. Chicago: Third World Press, 1999. Print.

Boykin, Randson C. "Red Beans and Rice Lady." *Say the River Turns: The Impact of Gwendolyn Brooks*. Ed. Haki R. Madhubuti. Chicago: Third World Press, 1990. 21. Print.

Bradshaw, Robert I. "Hezekiah." *biblicalstudies.org.uk*. 1999. Web. 24 June 2008.

Bratcher, Dennis. "Psalm 30." *The Voice*. 26 September 2010. Web. 29 Dec. 2010.

"A Brief Guide to Negritude." *Poets.org*. n.d. Web. 5 May 2009.

Brinkley, Douglas. "Unmasking Writers of the W.P.A." *nytimes.com*. 2 Aug 2003. Web. 24 May 2011.

Brooks, Gwendolyn. *Beckonings*. Detroit: Broadside Press, 1975. Print.

_____. *Blacks*. Chicago: Third World Press, 2000. Print.

_____. *Bronzeville Boys and Girls*. New York: HarperCollins, 1956. Print.

_____. *In Montgomery and Other Poems*. Chicago: Third World Press, 2003. Print.

_____. *The Near-Johannesburg Boy and Other Poems*. Chicago: Third World Press, 1986. Print.

_____. *Report from Part One*. Detroit: Broadside Press, 1972. Print.

_____. *Report from Part Two*. Chicago: Third World Press, 1996. Print.

_____. *Selected Poems*. New York: Harper and Row, 1963. Print.

_____. *To Disembark*. Chicago: Third World Press, 1981. Print.

_____. "What Prayer Did for Me." *Chicago American*. February 26, 1958: XX–XX. Print.

Brooks, Keziah C. *The Voice and Other Stories*. Detroit: Harlo, 1975. Print.

Browner, Stephanie P., ed. "Lynching Statistics." *The Charles Chestnutt Digital Archive*. 29 Jan 1999. Web. 16 Mar. 2011.

Campbell, Donna M. "Sermon Structure: A Brief Outline Guide." *Literary Movements*. 21 Mar 2010. Web. 5 June 2010.

Carlberg, Heather. "Political Discourse-Theories of Colonialism and Postcolonialism: Negritude." *Postcolonial and Postimperial Literature: An Overview*. 1989. Web. 5 May 2009.

"Charles Baudelaire." *poets.org*. n.d. Web. 18 July 2009.

Collins English Dictionary Complete and Unabridged. 10th ed. *Dictionary.com*. 1998–2009. Web.

Coogan, Michael David, et al. *The New Oxford Annotated Bible*. Oxford: Oxford University Press, 2007. Print.

Davis, Arthur P. "Gwendolyn Brooks." *On Gwendolyn Brooks: Reliant Contemplation*. Ed. Stephen Caldwell Wright. Ann Arbor: University of Michigan Press, 2001. 97–105. Print.

"E. D. Nixon, Leader in Civil Rights, Dies." *New York Times*. 27 Feb. 1987. Web. 11 Oct. 2008.

Fitzgerald, Sally. "Chicago Gangs Aid in City Violence Control Effort." *Daily Defender*. 9 April 1968. Print.

Fuller, Hoyt, Eugenia Collier, George Kent, and Dudley Randall. "Interview with Gwendolyn Brooks." *Conversations with Gwendolyn Brooks*. Ed. Gloria Wade Gayles. Jackson: University Press of Mississippi, 2003. 67–73. Print.

Gayles, Gloria Wade, ed. *Conversations with Gwendolyn Brooks*. Jackson: University Press of Mississippi, 2003. Print.

"George Darley." *poemhunter.com*. n.d. Web. 17 July 2009.

Gibson, Robert A. "The Negro Holocaust: Lynching and Race Riots in the United States, 1880–1950." *Yale-New Haven Teachers Institute*. Feb. 1979. Web. 16 Mar. 2011.

Gross, Terry. "Get on the Bus: The Freedom Riders of 1961." *npr.org*. 12 Jan 2006. Web. 7 June 2011.

"Gwendolyn Brooks." *Great-Quotes.com*. 2011. Web. 11 December 2011.

Hansell, William H. "Essences, Unifyings, and Black Militancy: Major Themes in Gwendolyn Brooks' Family Pictures and Beckonings." *On Gwendolyn Brooks: Reliant Contemplation*. Ed. Stephen Caldwell Wright. Ann Arbor: University of Michigan Press, 2001. 106–115. Print.

_____. "The Poet-Militant and Foreshadowings of a Black Mystique: Poems in the Second Period of Gwendolyn Brooks." *A Life Distilled: Gwendolyn Brooks, Her Poetry and Fiction*. Eds. Maria K. Mootry and Gary Smith. Urbana: University of Illinois Press, 1987. 71–80. Print.

Hedrick, Charles. "What Are Major Christian Beliefs?" *rutgers.edu*. n.d. Web. 10 Aug 2010.

Henning, Bishop Garnett Cornal Sr., comp. "The Apostles' Creed." *The Doctrine and Discipline of the African Methodist Episcopal Church*. 46th Ed. Nashville: AMEC, 2001. 503–504. Print.

Holbourn, Diane, site mgr. "What Do Christians Believe?" *broadcaster.org.uk*. n.d. Web. 10 Aug 2010.

Howe, Susan Elizabeth, and Jay Fox. "A Conversation with Gwendolyn Brooks." *Con-

versations with Gwendolyn Brooks. Ed. Gloria Wade Gayles. Jackson: University Press of Mississippi, 2003. 140–148. Print.

Hughes, Sheila Hassell. "A Prophet Overheard: A Juxtapositional Reading of Gwendolyn Brooks' "In the Mecca." *African American Review* 38.2 (2004): 257–280. Print.

Hull, Gloria T., and Posey Gallagher. "Update on Part One: An Interview with Gwendolyn Brooks." *Conversations with Gwendolyn Brooks*. Ed. Gloria Wade Gayles. Jackson: University Press of Mississippi, 2003. 85–103. Print.

"Hyacinth." *greek-gods.info*. n.d. Web. 6 June 2009.

Jones, Gayl. "Community and Voice: Gwendolyn Brooks' In the Mecca." *A Life Distilled: Gwendolyn Brooks, Her Poetry and Fiction*. Eds. Maria K. Mootry and Gary Smith. Urbana: University of Illinois Press, 1987. 193–204. Print.

Jones, William Augustus, Jr. "Introduction." *Outstanding Black Sermons*. Ed. J. Alfred Smith, Sr. Valley Forge, PA: Judson Press, 1976. 6–7. Print.

Kent, George E. *A Life of Gwendolyn Brooks*. Lexington: University Press of Kentucky, 1990. Print.

Kirby, Peter, ed. "Infancy Gospel of James, a Protevangelion of James." Trans. Roberts-Donaldson. *earlychristianwritings.com*. 2006. Web. 25 May 2008.

Kohlenberger, John R. III, ed. *The Contemporary Parallel New Testament*. New York: Oxford University Press, 1997. Print.

Konig, George. "People in the Bible: Hezekiah or Ezekias, King of Judah." *About-BibleProphecy.com*. 2001–2008. Web. 24 Jan 2008.

Lewis, Ida. "My People Are Black People." *Conversations with Gwendolyn Brooks*. Ed. Gloria Wade Gayles. Jackson: University Press of Mississippi, 2003. 54–66. Print.

Lewis, Jack P. "Introduction: Hosea." *The NIV Study Bible*. Ed. Kenneth Barker. Grand Rapids, MI: Zondervan, 2002. Print.

"Lord Alfred Douglas." *poemhunter.com*. n.d. Web. 18 April 2009.

Madhubuti, Haki R. "Gwendolyn Brooks: Beyond the Wordmaker — the Making of an African Poet." *On Gwendolyn Brooks: Reliant Contemplation*. Ed. Stephen Caldwell Wright. Ann Arbor: University of Michigan Press, 2001. 81–96. Print.

_____. "Introduction: Gwendolyn Brooks at 70." *Say That the River Turns; the Impact of Gwendolyn Brooks*. Ed. Haki R. Madhubuti. Chicago: Third World Press, 1990. xi–xii. Print.

_____. ed. *Say That the River Turns: The Impact of Gwendolyn Brooks*. Chicago: Third World Press, 1990. Print.

Malewitz, Raymond. "My Newish Voice: Rethinking Black Power in Gwendolyn Brooks' Whirlwind." *Callaloo* 29.2 (2006): 531–544. Print.

Matthews, Kevin. "Ludwig Mies van der Rohe." *greatbuildings.com*. n.d. Web. 22 June 2009.

"Meaning of Pepita." *meaning-of-names.com*. n.d. Web. 11 Dec 2010.

Melhem, D. H. "Afterword." *Report from Part Two*. Gwendolyn Brooks. Chicago: Third World Press, 1996. 146–160. Print.

_____. *Gwendolyn Brooks: Poetry and the Heroic Voice*. Lexington: University Press of Kentucky, 1987. Print.

_____. "In the Mecca." *On Gwendolyn Brooks: Reliant Contemplation*. Ed. Stephen Caldwell Wright. Ann Arbor: University of Michigan Press, 2001. 161–181. Print.

Millard, Alan R., and John H. Stek. "Introduction: Amos." *The NIV Study Bible*. Ed. Kenneth Barker. Grand Rapids, MI: Zondervan, 2002. Print.

Miller, R. Baxter. "Define ... The Whirlwind": Gwendolyn Brooks' Epic Sign for a Generation." *On Gwendolyn Brooks: Reliant Contemplation*. Ed. Stephen Caldwell Wright. Ann Arbor: University of Michigan Press, 2001. 146–160. Print.

_____. "Does Man Love Art? The Humanistic Aesthetic." *A Life Distilled: Gwendolyn Brooks, Her Poetry and Fiction.* Ed. Maria K. Mootry and Gary Smith. Urbana: University of Illinois Press, 1987. 100–118. Print.

Mootry, Maria K. "Down the Whirlwind of Good Rage: An Introduction to Gwendolyn Brooks." *A Life Distilled: Gwendolyn Brooks, Her Poetry and Fiction.* Ed. Maria K. Mootry and Gary Smith. Urbana: University of Illinois Press, 1987. 1–20. Print.

Mootry, Maria K., and Gary Smith, eds. *A Life Distilled: Gwendolyn Brooks, Her Poetry and Fiction.* Urbana: University of Illinois Press, 1987. Print.

Morrison, Michael. "The Apostles' Creed." *christianodyssey.com.* 1999. Web. 15 Jul 2010.

"La Negritude: Introduction to the Francophone Literary Movement Known as La Negritude." *About.com: French Language.* n.d. Web 5 May 2009.

Nelson, Thomas, et al. *The King James Study Bible.* Nashville: Thomas Nelson, 1999. Print.

_____. *3,458 Bible People and Places.* New York: Inspirational Press, 2001. Print.

Newquist, Roy. "Gwendolyn Brooks." *Conversations with Gwendolyn Brooks.* Ed. Gloria Wade Gayles. Jackson: University Press of Mississippi, 2003. 26–36. Print.

"Pablo Neruda." *nobelprize.org.* n.d. Web. 22 July 2009.

"People and Events: The Black Star Line." *PBS American Experience Teachers Guide.* 1999–2000. Web. 10 August 2010.

"Percy Bysshe Shelley." *poemhunter.com.* n.d. Web. 18 July 2009.

Perkins, Mark. "Israel in Hosea's Time." *Grace Notes.* Ed. Warren Doud. n.d. Web. 7 July 2009.

Reisinger, Ernest. "The New Testament Meaning of Witness." *Founders Ministries Journal.* n.d. Web. 5 July 2011.

Richards, Lawrence O. *The Teacher's Commentary.* Wheaton, IL: Victor Books/Division of Scripture Press Publications, 1987. Print.

"Robert Browning — Biography and Works." *onlineliterature.com.* 5 Nov 2007 Web. 18 July 2009.

Ryken, Leland. *How to Read the Bible as Literature.* Grand Rapids, MI: Zondervan, 1984. Print.

Salaam, Kalamu Ya. "Black Arts Movement." *Oxford Companion to African-American Literature.* New York: Oxford University Press, 1997. *aalbc.com.* Web. 7 Aug 2008.

Shaw, Harry B. *Gwendolyn Brooks.* Boston: Twayne Publishers, 1980. Print.

Sickels, Amy. "Biography of Gwendolyn Brooks." *Bloom's BioCritiques — Gwendolyn Brooks.* New York: Chelsea House, 2004. 5–62. Print.

Sielaff, David. "The Tomb of David and Psalm 30." *Newsletter: Associates for Scriptural Knowledge.* Feb. 2008. Web. 6 July 2009.

"Sir Philip Sidney." *poemhunter.com.* 18 April 2009. Web. 17 July 2009.

Smith, Gary. "Gwendolyn Brooks' 'Children of the Poor' Metaphysical Poetry and the Inconditions of Love." *A Life Distilled: Gwendolyn Brooks, Her Poetry and Fiction.* Eds. Maria K. Mootry and Gary Smith. Urbana: University of Illinois Press, 1987. 165–186. Print.

_____. "Paradise Regained: The Children of Gwendolyn Brooks' Bronzeville." *A Life Distilled: Gwendolyn Brooks, Her Poetry and Fiction.* Eds. Maria K. Mootry and Gary Smith. Urbana: University of Illinois Press, 1987. 128–139. Print.

Smith, J. Alfred, ed. *Outstanding Black Sermons.* Valley Forge, PA: Judson Press, 1976. Print.

Sorensen, Mark W. "The Illinois State Library: Extension, Reorganization and Experimentation, 1921–1955." *lib.niu.edu.* n.d. 24 May 2011.

Stavros, George. "An Interview with Gwendolyn Brooks." *Conversations with Gwen-*

dolyn Brooks. Ed. Gloria Wade Gayles. Jackson: University Press of Mississippi, 2003. 37–53. Print.

Strickland, Arvarh E. *History of the Chicago Urban League.* Columbia: University of Missouri Press, 2001. Print.

Sullivan, James D. "Killing John Cabot and Publishing Black: Gwendolyn Brooks' Riot." *African American Review* 36.4 (2002): 557–569. Print.

Taylor, Henry. "Gwendolyn Brooks: An Essential Sanity." *On Gwendolyn Brooks: Reliant Contemplation.* Ed. Stephen Caldwell Wright. Ann Arbor: University of Michigan Press, 2001. 254–275. Print.

Walters, Ronald Dr. "Rosa Parks and E. D. Nixon." *The Black World Today.* 15 June 1999. Web. 11 Oct 2008.

"Western Wall." *bibleplaces.com.* n.d. Web. 22 June 2010.

Wheeler, Lesley. "Heralding the Clear Obscure: Gwendolyn Brooks and Apostrophe." *Callaloo* 24.1 (2001): 227–235. Print.

Williams, Kenny J. "The World of Satin-Legs, Mrs. Sallie, and the Blackstone Rangers: The Restricted Chicago of Gwendolyn Brooks." *A Life Distilled: Gwendolyn Brooks, Her Poetry and Fiction.* Ed. Maria K. Mootry and Gary Smith. Urbana: University of Illinois Press, 1987. 47–70. Print.

Wright, Stephen Caldwell, ed. *On Gwendolyn Brooks: Reliant Contemplation.* Ann Arbor: University of Michigan Press, 1996. Print.

Index